PENGUIN BOOKS

A DRY SHIP TO THE MOUNTAINS

Daniel Farson is the son of US Foreign Correspondent Negley Farson. He travelled extensively as a child and was evacuated to Canada and America in the Second World War. At the age of seventeen he joined the Central Press, becoming the youngest Parliamentary and Lobby Correspondent. The following year he enlisted in the US Air Corps. He worked as a staff photographer for *Picture Post* and later as a freelance journalist, until he joined the Merchant Navy and sailed around the world. In 1956 he joined ITV and became a leading television interviewer with series of his own such as *Farson's Guide to the British*.

After running his own entertainment pub, the famous Waterman's Arms in London's East End, he moved to North Devon in 1964 to work as a full-time writer. He writes regularly for national newspapers and magazines and is the author of over twenty books including the bestseller *Jack the Ripper*; *The Man Who Wrote Dracula*, a biography of his great-uncle Bram Stoker; *Soho in the Fifties*; and, more recently, *The Gilded Gutter Life of Francis Bacon*.

DANIEL FARSON

A DRY SHIP TO THE MOUNTAINS

DOWN THE VOLGA
AND ACROSS THE CAUCASUS –
IN MY FATHER'S FOOTSTEPS

PENGUIN BOOKS

For James Birch, the most good-natured of travelling
companions; Ali, our powerful Karachaite guide; and Yuri,
our loyal interpreter and friend. With a special gratitude
for Hadji, our faithful companion and protector –
the noblest Russian of them all.

PENGUIN BOOKS

Published by the Penguin Group
Penguin Books Ltd, 27 Wrights Lane, London W8 5TZ, England
Penguin Books USA Inc., 375 Hudson Street, New York, New York 10014, USA
Penguin Books Australia Ltd, Ringwood, Victoria, Australia
Penguin Books Canada Ltd, 10 Alcorn Avenue, Toronto, Ontario, Canada M4V 3B2
Penguin Books (NZ) Ltd, 182–190 Wairau Road, Auckland 10, New Zealand

Penguin Books Ltd, Registered Offices: Harmondsworth, Middlesex, England

First published by Michael Joseph 1994
Published in Penguin Books 1995
1 3 5 7 9 10 8 6 4 2

Copyright © Daniel Farson, 1994
Map by Peter McClure
All rights reserved

ACKNOWLEDGEMENTS

The author and publisher are grateful for permission to reproduce quotations from *What Am I
Doing Here* to the Estate of Bruce Chatwin and Jonathan Cape in the UK, and in the US
copyright © 1989 by the Estate of Bruce Chatwin, used by permission of Viking Penguin, a
division of Penguin Books USA Inc. The extract from *Tolstoy* by A. N. Wilson, published by
Hamish Hamilton, is reprinted by permission of the Peters Fraser & Dunlop Group Ltd;
and those from *Sabres of Paradise* by Lesley Blanch, published by John Murray Ltd,
are reprinted by permission of the Peters Fraser & Dunlop Group Ltd.

Photographs 7, 8, 9, 10, 15, 19, 22, 32, 33, 35 were taken by James Birch; 18 copyright © the Hulton
Deutsch collection. All other photographs were taken by the author.

Printed in England by Clays Ltd, St Ives plc

The trouble with us Russians is that the Tartar is close behind us. We are a semi-barbarous people still. We put Parisian-gloves on our hands instead of washing them. At one moment we bow and utter polite phrases, and the next, flog our servants.

TURGENEV

Contents

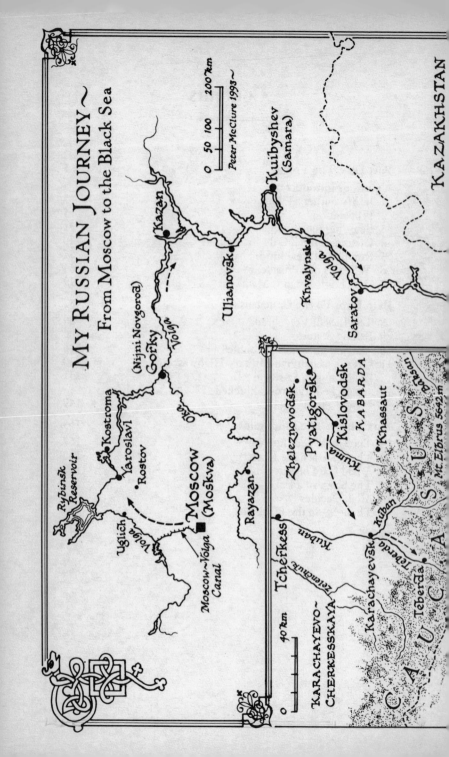

My Russian Journey ~
From Moscow to the Black Sea

Peter McClure 1993

0 50 100 200 km

KAZAKHSTAN

Rybinsk Reservoir
Uglich
Kostroma
Yaroslavl
Rostov
Moscow-Volga Canal
Moscow (Moskva)
Rayazan
Volga
Oka
(Nijni Novgorod) Gorky
Volga
Kazan
Ulianovsk
Kuibyshev (Samara)
Khvalynsk
Saratov
Volga

40 km

KARACHAYEVO-CHERKESSKAYA
Zheleznovodsk
Pyatigorsk
Kislovodsk
KABARDA
Khassaut
Kuma
Tchefkess
Kuban
Rubah
Zelentchuk
Karachayevsk
Teberda
Kuban
Baksan
Mt. Elbrus 5642 m
CAUCASUS

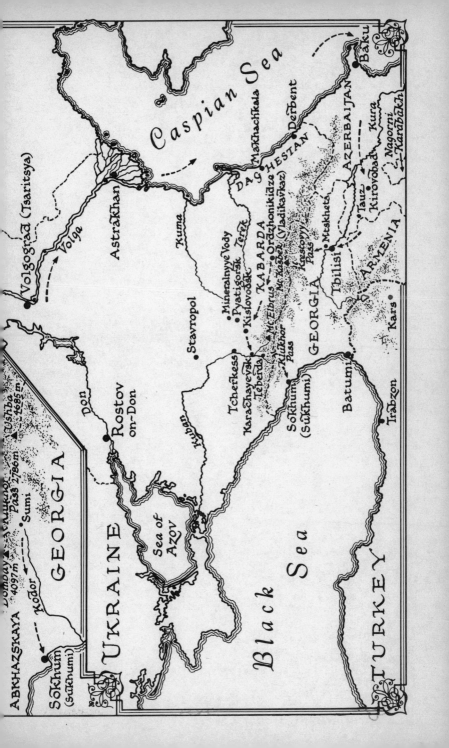

PART ONE

The Volga

A Curious Introduction

'I think I'm going mad,' I said to James, my travelling companion.

'How do you mean?' he murmured, trying to translate the menu.

'We're in the ship's saloon but there is no food and nothing to drink.'

He looked up. 'And have you noticed something very odd?' James pointed to the phlegmatic passengers sitting in silence at the surrounding tables. 'They've given their orders to the two waitresses, but nothing is being served. Not a sausage.'

I had noticed this, though my brain could hardly take it in. Now the passengers started to leave the saloon in grim silence after their foodless meal.

'This *is* madness,' I continued. 'They gave their orders, though there's no choice, and now they're leaving.'

'Don't you understand,' said James patiently, 'this is Russia. Nothing makes sense.'

I sighed. 'What in God's name are we doing here, sailing on a dry ship down the Volga?' This was a silly remark for I knew exactly why we were there – though I had not expected it to be like this. In my naivety, I had expected the voyage to be idyllic.

I yearned to follow in my father's footsteps.

The story began over sixty years ago when he sailed down

the River Volga on the way to the Caucasus, as he explained in this tremendous opening to *Caucasian Journey*.

> In the spring of 1929 I set out to ride horseback over the western Caucasus with Alexander Wicksteed, an old English eccentric who, for six years, had been trying to live like a Russian in Red Moscow. Our intentions were to get the first pair of horses at Kislovodsk, then to proceed by easy stages, camping out on the northern spurs of the Caucasus wherever we liked a place, or I found some good trout fishing; finally, to try and take our horses over the snow-clad Klukhor Pass (9,200 feet) and ride down beside the foaming River Kodor to the melon beds of Sukhum on the shores of the Black Sea.

These images thrilled me. Though not so famous as *The Way of a Transgressor*, his best-selling autobiography of the 1930s, *Caucasian Journey* has a freshness and a modesty which makes me proud to be his son. Using the notes he made in 1929, he wrote the book twenty-two years later with the benefit of contemplation. Re-reading it frequently, I became determined to fulfil his journey, should such an opportunity arise. My father was forced to turn back after a hazardous night on a narrow ledge above Lake Klukhor while the mountains cracked around him as they cooled. He was defeated by yards the next morning. His guide, Yusuf, told him in a low voice, 'It is better to live.' My father was not so sure: 'I have often wondered since that day if Yusuf was right; though we had no doubts on that sunny morning.'

At the time he felt the 'disgust and humiliation of having to turn back'. Ironically, the turning back is the high point of *Caucasian Journey*, but he was left with such a sense of impenetrable loss that I wanted to complete the journey for him. What motives lay behind my yearning? Vanity? Yes, undeniably a bit of that. Filial duty? That smacks of vanity too, but a bit of that as well. A wish to prove myself as good as my father? No! I can be absolved of that, for he was a great man. Above all, I was curious to learn why he had failed when he was younger and more experienced than myself. Also, I envied him his *adventure*, one of the joys of life which are becoming increasingly hard to find.

I envisaged a restful though jolly cruise down the Volga, much as my father enjoyed on a little paddle steamer when he left Moscow in 1929. After ten days I would reach Astrakhan and take a train along the Caspian Sea to Baku, then a bus to Tbilisi and from there by car across the Georgian Military Highway, described tantalizingly by my father as 'one of the most sensationally beautiful mountain highways in the world'. From Kislovodsk I would set out with horses towards the great range of the Caucasus mountains, sleeping in tents beside a surging river after an evening meal of trout cooked on an open fire. The descent after I climbed the Klukhor Pass would be the climax.

How wrong I was.

CHAPTER ONE

In my Father's Footsteps

WHEN I wrote that my father was a great man, I did so deliberately. This is more than the natural respect of a son for his father, for Negley Farson was an exceptional man who did the things that most men dream about. Readers of his autobiography, *The Way of a Transgressor*, are likely to agree with Sinclair Lewis, who wrote of its publication in 1936:

> I know of no international journalist who has written a personal chronicle so exciting, so authentically romantic, yet so revelatory of what forces have been surging through the world ... A grand picture of a grand man who found every hour exciting.

Colin Wilson wrote of him:

> Farson was the only man I have ever met who seemed cast in a bigger mould than other men. Unlike Hemingway, who tried hard to play the archetypal hero, and who, as a consequence, often struck false notes, Farson's impressiveness was completely natural and unselfconscious.

It seemed that he was born with a sense of wanderlust. Born in 1890 in Plainfield, New Jersey in America, he was self-reliant, largely brought up by his grandfather, a broken-down but marvellously eccentric relic of the American Civil War, General Negley, whose name he adopted. At the outset of the First World War he came to England and from there he moved to Russia, trying to sell munitions to the corrupt Tsarist war department. My mother, who shared his wanderlust, worked as a VAD nurse in St Petersburg at the same time. They were certain that they must have passed each other along the Nevskoye Prospekt, but were actually introduced later in London by mutual friends when my father lay in hospital, having crashed his plane in Egypt after enlisting with the Royal Canadian Flying Corps.

They lived for two years on a houseboat on a remote lake near Vancouver where my father fished and wrote the short stories which kept them alive, until life became so idyllic that he feared he would be lulled into staying there for ever, and stagnate. Instead, he veered to the other extreme, selling Mack trucks in Chicago so successfully that he was offered their head position in New York. High wages were no compensation for the freedom they knew on the lake in British Columbia, and one stifling Sunday when there was no wind in the windy city, they took a map and planned a journey over a lunch of his favourite lobster salad: 'We only live once!' he declared with mock profundity. 'Hear, hear!' agreed my mother. 'What's the use of waiting until we are seventy?' It needs strength to walk away from success, but he was strong and chucked up his lucrative job in New York. On 15 July 1925 he left Rotterdam in a small boat, *The Flame*, with my mother as 'the crew', and sailed up the Rhine and the Danube until they emerged in the Black Sea. The stories he sent to the *Chicago Daily News* appealed to the emigrants from the countries he sailed through, and when he returned to America he joined the *News* as a foreign correspondent.

Foreign correspondent – what glamour that name evokes, of a legendary species now extinct, frequently making news in the course of reporting it. Reviewing *A Mirror for Narcissus*, the hangover to the binge of the *Transgressor*, in which my father wrote honestly of his alcoholism, *The New Yorker* described him as

a phenomenon of our time – the star-billing American foreign correspondent, an interesting creature who flourished most luxuriantly in the 1930s. The men of Farson's breed – if such a congerie of eccentrics and prima donnas can be called a breed – were not so much serious as cynical; 'I know,' he says, speaking of his job, 'of no profession more calculated to kill one's enthusiasm for the human race.' They were personalities (the titles of their books are indicative of the objectivity they brought to the world scene – *Personal History, The Way of a Transgressor, I saw ...*) and they were egoists and snobs – achievement snobs, that is, the reverse of money or position snobs. And many of them ultimately became bored, and many became drunks.

My father's drinking was undeniable but he was rarely bored; nor did he lose his enthusiasm. He was the least cynical man I have known. On the day of his death at the age of seventy, he was tying labels on his luggage for yet another journey abroad.

The glamorous image of the foreign correspondents was due to their extrovert personalities, which were larger than those around them, including the politicians, for whom they had a healthy disrespect. These foreign correspondents were men like Walter Duranty and H.R. Knickerbocker, my father's closest friend and at one time the highest-paid journalist in the world (for Hearst). But 'Red Knick' was idealistic and saw Russia through rose-tinted glasses, while Duranty furthered an active sex life in Moscow with his eulogies of the Stalinist regime. My father could not be bought, nor was he starry-eyed. He despised the type of correspondent who travelled by train through Russia 'with the blinds pulled down' and wrote a definitive study with a meaningless title such as *The Absolute Truth of Soviet Russia*. He knew from experience that there is no single truth about Russia but a mass of contradictions.

My parents' knowledge of Russia, and their admiration for certain Russians, gave me the incentive to follow in their footsteps, though they travelled at a time when the going was good, probably better than it has been before or since, with the means to explore and the zest of the unexpected, before the uniformity of the package tour made so many places accessible.

My yearning to follow in his footsteps through Russia remained a wistful dream, like a vicarious jaunt through a travel brochure, until I had the luck in the spring of 1990 to go to Moscow with the artists Gilbert and George to cover their historic exhibition at the New Tretyakov Gallery for the *Sunday Telegraph*.

This gave me my opportunity: while the others flew back to London on 2 May, I took the Aeroflot to Tbilisi and from there, one radiant morning three days later, I flew over the shimmering peaks of the Caucasus to Mineralnyye Vody on the other side. Mountain ranges have distinct personalities, and that of the Caucasus is both immense and reassuring. They stretch from the Black Sea to the Caspian Sea with twelve peaks higher than Mont Blanc. Between Mount Kazbek and Mount Elbrus (18,784 ft) there are 125 miles of glaciers, ice and snow. From above it was possible to believe that some of the former tribes who lived there were so snow-bound that their remote valleys could be reached only at certain times of the year. It was this isolation which made the Caucasus a refuge for the outlawed and repressed since history began. In my excitement I moved from my seat on the aisle to try to have a clearer view of the valleys below, but the Aeroflot was full as usual and the passengers stared ahead of them, unmovable and unmoved by the glory surrounding us. What I did glimpse was exhilarating. The snow peaks looked not only astonishingly near, but also clean and comforting. That is the magic of the Caucasus.

After forty-five minutes we landed at the air terminal named after the mineral water for which the Caucasian spas are famous, where I found Yuri, a young schoolteacher, waiting for me on the tarmac as arranged, smiling nervously in case he missed me, for we had not met before. His father, a retired army officer with the privilege of a smart car, drove us to Pyatigorsk. He had never spoken to a foreigner before but Yuri spoke very good English and acted as my interpreter.

The Intourist Hotel proved a pleasant surprise, situated at the start of a park and flights of steps with Lenin, his arm outstretched, at the top. Young men played fruit machines in the lobby and the central heating was so fierce that I staggered gasping on to my balcony, to be recompensed by a view of Mount Elbrus rising sixty miles away, now seen from the other side. Pyatigorsk below me looked like any alpine town, hardly the frontier outpost of my imagination. Even here, an obstacle typical of Russia occurred at lunch when I suggested we discuss our plans with one of the six hundred varieties of Caucasian wine. No, that was impossible, but we could have Georgian Cognac instead. I settled for this, but was further dismayed when we were refused a bottle of mineral water.

'Not even your famous Narzan water?'

'Niet!' The first of so many.

'But Yuri,' I asked, 'I landed at a place called Mineral Water and we are surrounded by springs. Why can't we have any to wash the Cognac down?'

'Because no one has asked for it before.'

The next morning I walked down to the flower market – there may be no food in Russia but there are always flowers – and stood in a crowded tram to the station, named Voxall in Russian after our own Vauxhall in London. From there I took an equally crowded train to Kislovodsk, as my father had done sixty years earlier, and experienced an irrational burst of exhilaration, as if I were a young soldier returning home. We crossed a countryside of lilac woods in heavy blossom, with head-scarved women tending small, immaculate plots, while others sunbathed on the green banks in the first warmth of spring. When my father rode through the Caucasus he knew the same elation: 'It is seldom, as we get on, that one feels the sudden unaccountable, bubbling happiness of youth. But I had a burst of it.' Even in this rattling, overcrowded train, I had a burst of it too. It is a feeling you are lucky to get a few times in your life and it lasts for just a matter of seconds, like *déjà vu*, and there is nothing like it. In that train, for that moment, I was aware that I was blissfully happy; and I remembered the moment in Tolstoy's *The Cossacks*, which many Russians admire more than *War and Peace*, when the world-weary young officer Olenin, whose life has disintegrated due to gambling debts and debauchery in Moscow, sees the mountains for the first time:

> seeming to run along the horizon, their rosy tips gleaming in the rays of the rising sun. All his Moscow recollections, his shame and his regrets, all his trivial dreams of the Caucasus, departed and never returned again. 'Now it has begun!' a sort of triumphant voice said to him.

My own approach to the Caucasus could hardly have been more mundane by comparison, yet I understood his emotion. This, again, is the magic of the Caucasus. They welcome you home.

The journey took an hour by train. Yuri and his girlfriend waited for me at the station in Kislovodsk and we walked to the centre, past attractive shops into a square free from traffic, with grand old buildings and a tea-garden beyond. Unexpectedly, Kislovodsk was elegant. Yet, even here, we faced the usual bureaucracy. I was heading into the mountains to the village of Khassaut which my father had reached by cart, since he had been unable to hire his horses in Kislovodsk. The 'bus lady' in the garden outside the Narzan Gallery, built in 1894 to provide the Narzan water from the natural springs, was unable to help us. While I waited among the flowers and fountains, with children playing while their families posed for photographs, Yuri tried to find us transport but returned with his face creased with anxiety.

'Big problem!', a phrase becoming increasingly familiar; 'There is no bus, Daniel, no car, and foreigners cannot go further without permit from the militia.'

So we went to the tourist office in the Kavkaz (Caucasus) Hotel, which was empty except for three plump ladies who polished their nails behind a desk, adding quantities of mauve to their already exorbitant eye-shadow.

Yuri explained that we wished to go to Khassaut and they gave a negative smile – '*Niet!*' When he persisted, even the smile snapped off: everything was closed, and anyhow the people we needed to talk to were back in Intourist in Pyatigorsk. Would they telephone them for us? An outraged shrug. Did they have the number? Another smiling '*Niet!*'

As we left, Yuri said dejectedly, 'Of course they do know, but they don't want to tell us.'

'They remind me of the three monkeys,' I told him. 'Hear nothing, say nothing, do nothing.'

'Three baboons,' he scowled, remembering their mauve eye-shadow.

Yuri and I set out two days later with a guide called Ali, driven by a cheerful man called Sasha in his taxi. I paid 100 roubles, which was negligible compared to his goodwill. 'He is really surprised to find an Englishman,' Yuri explained. 'He is being very hospitable.'

The moment we left Kislovodsk the landscape changed. We entered a green valley where black sheep fed beside a river, tended by a solitary shepherd, as he would tend them day after day, probably year after year, against attack from wolves and bears. A few wild horses romped across the hills; smaller than most, they are among the finest in the world and the Circassians are the most skilful of riders, able to bend down and pick a wild flower as they pass.

We reached Khassaut at noon. I had brought a copy of *Caucasian Journey* with me, which I had shown to our guide Ali, who was a Karachaite, for this was a Muslim village and Russian was hardly spoken, replaced by Karachay. He was fascinated by the photograph taken by my father in 1929 for it showed a fine village with a mosque and minaret, houses with cupolas, and clusters of the villagers. Altogether, wrote my father, there were then 600 households. Yet as we entered Khassaut we found a village in ruins with less than twenty people. The mosque had gone and so had the elegant houses. The place was desolate. We fell silent until a few head-scarved women came running to greet our arrival and cried out with excitement when Ali showed them the photograph in the book which they studied with evident amazement. Ali explained why I was there, following in my father's footsteps, and they smiled and nodded. Unlike those of the three baboons, their smiles were spontaneous and warm as they studied the photograph and spoke excitedly.

'Bless the gentleman from England,' Yuri translated, and I asked him why. 'Because for the first time they know what their village looked like.'

As we drove back we passed the same shepherd and it seemed he had not moved. The day was fading and we stopped at the top of a mountain pass for a final look at the range behind us of smouldering, tumbling shapes with details lit by shafts of the last sunlight. Echoes reached us of dogs barking in an invisible valley far below, and as I raised my eyes I experienced that heart-stopping moment in the Caucasus when you see the mountain peaks *above* the clouds.

Yuri broke the silence. 'Every day in life should be like this one!'

My own emotions were as deeply stirred; I knew the day had been exceptional. But I was left beset with curiosity: who were the Karachaites, of whom I knew so little? Why had Stalin punished them, if that was the reason for the desolation of Khassaut? How had the few survived? I longed to learn the truth about Khassaut. This resolved my determination to return and find a way to undertake the whole of my father's travels across the Caucasus, and complete them by crossing the Klukhor Pass.

CHAPTER TWO

Preparations

I SHOULD admit from the outset that most people could have taken this journey in their stride, but at sixty-four I was nearly twice the age of my father when he attempted it in 1929, and I was in a horrible condition.

Shortly after I made my decision to return to Khassaut, I took the London train from Devon and coincided with my doctor. Over a British Rail breakfast I told him of my intention to climb the Caucasus.

'S.O.B.,' he remarked in mid-kipper.

I knew that Dr Hunt was a 'character', but I thought this unwarranted.

'Son of a bitch?' I echoed.

'No. Short of breath.'

Afterwards, he wrote me a personal letter in which he confirmed:

Yes, you are overweight and your blood pressure could be a problem. You are certainly not in serious danger, but it is a very difficult thing to itemize exactly as in my experience people with your abominably unhealthy lifestyle tend to go on for years longer in defiance of all the laws of nature.

This was encouraging. He concluded with the wise though unheeded advice, 'It would be an advantage if you could get into some gentle training, preferably by cutting down the bottle to a certain extent.' He doubted if it would help to take pills to reduce the blood pressure 'as these have complications of their own and can produce dizziness and fainting, and if you are going up to considerable heights you will get more trouble from treatment than you would from your blood pressure.'

The height of the Klukhor Pass was not really the problem. As mountains go, this was low – a mere 9,200 feet, which is below the level where breathing starts to be difficult, but even a hill can be hard work if vertical. I had no idea how tough it was going to prove, apart from knowing that it defeated my father, so I ordered *The Exploration of the Caucasus* from the London Library. Dated 1896, this is a splendid two-volume account with the ring of authority by Douglas Freshfield, a mountaineer in the best English tradition. He was the first to climb the twin peaks of Mount Elbrus in 1868, only nine years after the Tsar subdued the rebellious Circassians led by their great warrior Shamil. Later, Freshfield also attempted the Klukhor Pass. He described his ascent up the Teberda valley which divided after 4,683 feet, continuing beside a stream with cliffs of gneiss rock and forest above him until he reached walls of black rock with steep sides and a Dru-like needle among the summits – 'a group of wild precipitous peaks, such as is seldom met with even in the Caucasus'.

This was daunting – a view shared by his Teberdine guides who refused to take him further over the Klukhor Pass. Freshfield's black-and-white photograph of the 'Ice-Lake Near the Klukhor Pass' confirmed the grimness.

What I needed was a recent description, and this came unexpectedly when a friend in my Devon village of Appledore brought me a copy of *Trout and Salmon*, a magazine which would not have landed on my doorstep in the usual way. Noticing an article with the title 'In Farson's Footsteps', he assumed this referred to myself, but it proved to be a welcome tribute to my father by Gavin Dollard:

There are those who have read Negley Farson's *Going Fishing*, and those who are happy with home waters and intimate knowledge on small yardage. This article concerns the former: explorers and fishermen who believe there is always a virgin river just around the corner, bursting with trout and enclosed by sublime scenery and wildlife. Having fished some Farson waters, I thought it would obviously be fun to try to gain access to the river and place where he caught the most fish in any one day – thirty-five trout in the Caucasus in 1929.

Reaching Teberda, Dollard fished in the 'aquamarine' river:

Bliss. A perfect day. I had fished the Kuban and Teberda, and caught on Farson's fly in surroundings that nearly surpassed those of glorious Devon.

Finally, to my astonishment, he revealed:

I nipped over the Klukhor Pass, joining a group of English climbers. Now, in earliest August, it was breathtaking and I could have done it on Farson's description alone; almost stone for stone the same. This spectacular world of watercolours was inspiring material; fresh pines, buttercups, peaches, apples, haystacks and butterflies, all competing ... Negley Farson's descriptions are word-perfect.

Yes, but 'nipped across the Klukhor Pass'! That sounded suburban. Buttercups and butterflies? A far cry from Freshfield's 'wild precipitous peaks' which made his guides turn back.

I discovered that Gavin Dollard lived on a farm in south Devon and we met in Plymouth. He is a cheerful personality inclined to the boastful exaggeration of fishermen who tell you expansively that the one which got away was '*that big!*' He had the honesty to confess that his 'nipping' was a fisherman's licence too. Like my father and Freshfield, he had to turn back when his guides refused to go further – 'I feel they did not want to, or know how to continue.' As this was never his main objective, it hardly mattered. Given the right weather conditions, he saw no difficulty in my reaching the Pass: 'It is a steep climb, all uphill but I am sure you could take a mule – otherwise you would need to be fit.'

I chose September as the best month for the climb, when the last winter's snow would have melted and next winter's was still to fall. This was motivated by father's extraordinary misjudgement in starting his ascent on 27 June when the snow was melting. Inexplicably, he wrote, 'the Klukhor is only supposed to be open for two and a half months of the year. It is not free from snow until August.' So why did he choose the end of June? Presumably because he expected it to be firm enough to carry the weight of his horses and their packs. But his mistiming was all the more baffling because his companion, Alexander Wicksteed, knew the Caucasus, having once stayed with a Karachaite family at Teberda (who regarded him as the greatest man they had ever met, which was probably true). In those days Teberda, where Wicksteed intended to part company with my father, had considerable charm, extolled as the Davos of Caucasia with a climate finer than that of the Swiss Alps, and sanatoriums for those who suffered from tuberculosis and found they could breathe more freely in the mountain air.

My father knew he was going to lose Wicksteed to the Karachaite family when they went on a picnic to collect wild strawberries, with the Russian sculptor Ginsberg, a Soviet writer, a People's Commissar, and several young girls.

> Some of the most desperately ill cases, and as one looked at their flushed cheeks, and glittering eyes, and the joy they were getting out of hunting for strawberries or shyly making up little bouquets of wild flowers, one felt that the spirit of the good god Pan was in these wild woods. This little picnic, so bubbling with the hopes of all the wonderful life that lay ahead, now seems, because of the way these hopes have been travestied, like something from another world.

Rarely was my father so sentimental. Possibly the idyllic setting distracted him when he should have been checking up on the climb ahead. After a few days staring at the mountains beyond the valley, he regained his lust to be away and climb them. Wicksteed told him: 'I am too old. Yusuf [the best of the Teberdine guides] says that the Klukhor Pass is filled with snow, anyhow. So is the valley leading up to it. We have just had the spring of our lives – you and I! – and now I think I will just find a tree here and laze throughout the summer.' My father was younger with no wish for such a lazy contentment. When they parted, Wicksteed came out in red and orange pyjamas to wish him luck: 'Hope I don't see you again, for that'll mean you've been turned back.'

But he did, for June proved the wrong time of year, which is why I chose September. I admit, with some bashfulness, that I had another reason: though I have my doubts about astrology, there is one man whose horoscopes are often accurate, Patric Walker, who predicted, 'When Jupiter changes signs on 12 September it will be at the best possible angle to your natal sun in Capricorn and astrological tradition has it that you can now turn almost any situation to your own advantage.' Like many people, I believe in my horoscope when it offers good news, but a friend roared his incredulity – 'I can't believe I'm hearing this!' I was relieved when Gavin Dollard assured me that the Klukhor was impassable from October to June due to snow, 'so early September should be perfect.'

He believed there was a village on the other side, which I confirmed when I bought a CIA map from Stanfords, the famous cartographers in Long Acre, London. I noticed that the track from Teberda ended near the pass and did not resume until it neared the village. In between there was a gap – nothing. It occurred to me for the first time that it might prove more difficult going down the other side than climbing to the top. Gavin Dollard had a final word of advice: 'Your problem is getting permission and therefore a guide.'

This was wise advice, but I was not prepared to take it. From the beginning, I was determined not to ask for permission because I knew it would be refused. In Russia there is only one response – *'Niet!'* – and by then I would have drawn attention to myself and jeopardized my freedom. Neither had I any wish to be obligated to Intourist, after my encounter with the 'three baboons'.

I did, however, have a guide in Ali, the Karachaite who had

come with me to Khassaut the year before. He knew the territory, spoke the language and was a trained mountaineer. I was happy to place my life in his hands. This is not the sort of claim to make lightly and I doubt if I could make it of anyone else, but in the short time I knew him Ali impressed me as someone exceptional. He was a born horseman, half-animal, able to see in the dark with an alertness far beyond my own. At the age of thirty-five he was still respected for his strength, and seemed to be popular with everyone we met − a man's man adored by women. If I collapsed, as well I might, I was sure he could carry me over the pass. My claim that I could trust him with my life was not mawkish; in the circumstances I could think of no one better. But there was one major problem: would he agree and would he be free to guide us? Obviously, Yuri should join us as interpreter, and the problem applied to him too; as a teacher, he could be in mid-term.

Phoning Kislovodsk from England is a marathon of raised hopes. The simplest way would be to give the operator the number you want and wait to be rung back when they get through; but that is too simple for our telephone service, as well as for the Russians'. Instead, the operator checked that I was waiting beside my phone, and then tried to get through, which meant that I had to leap to answer it every few minutes, to confirm my readiness, only to be told a moment later, 'Sorry, the lines to Moscow are busy.' After thirty attempts I gave up, but had swifter luck on my next attempt, connected at once by Moscow to Kislovodsk where Yuri's voice was reassuringly clear.

His instant response was better than I dared to hope. He was keen to join me and would contact Ali, who was not on the phone. He believed that Ali had crossed the pass and knew the terrain on either side, but he would need to be paid, as I intended, and would also need equipment, such as boots, which were difficult to buy in Russia. Otherwise, Ali would arrange everything, including mules or horses to carry our packs. Then Yuri gave the unexpected news that he was coming to England to stay with his former teacher in Scarborough, and was not due back in Kislovodsk until the beginning of September. This was disconcerting, for I hoped to be there by then myself, ready to start the ascent, and I worried that there could be some delay to upset our plans. It startled me also that Yuri spoke of his visit quite airily in spite of all the official and financial problems involved. However, I realized it would be helpful to meet beforehand in London where he could be fitted out with his equipment; he could also take Ali's back to Russia, which would ease the weight of my own prodigious luggage, with summer clothing for the Volga and heavy gear for the mountains. I said goodbye cheerfully, for everything was proceeding smoothly.

Like Toad of Toad Hall, a character I resemble increasingly, I relished my new role as 'explorer' and started pestering people who might help me, particularly Robin Hanbury-Tenison, a genuine explorer, who had been the other speaker at a travel dinner held in the Groucho Club, in London, a few weeks earlier. He advised me

> to take as little kit as possible (tempting though it is to buy everything on sight when you enter one of those stores) and concentrate instead on raising as much money as you can from literary promises and advances – your field, and much more likely to produce results than sponsorship – while depending on the spot on the local knowledge of your contact. A few dollars in the Caucasus are likely to produce ten times the food and clothing you could acquire in a smart shop.

This was wiser advice than I appreciated. Unfortunately, I was playing the role of explorer too dramatically, determined to set out as well equipped as my father.

I had gone back to my father's book to find out why he had been inspired in the first place. The journey began one night in Wicksteed's room in Moscow where he lived – and eventually died – in a dingy, Dostoevsky-like tenement in the old quarter, a block containing 200 rooms and 1,000 people. The greasy communal kitchen was revolting enough and my father did not dare to use the communal toilet – 'the Russians were not yet house-broken, even when I went back there in 1941: they are, so far as disposing of their excrement goes, the dirtiest of all the animals.'

Wicksteed's room, of which he was so proud, was a cell so jam-packed with furniture that no one could have crossed it in a straight line in any one direction. It was there one evening, joined by a grim, pale-faced engineer who knew his days were numbered, as indeed they were for he was liquidated in the spring, that my father listened to Wicksteed rhapsodizing about the Caucasus – 'a land of water wet, grass green and mountains steep'. When he produced a map to show the places he had been to, the engineer's face became animated as he traced a line from Kislovodsk. 'If you go in there you will find that "they" [the Communists] have not yet got much above 500 feet. There you will find the Caucasus as they used to be – the home of absolutely free men! And men of a fierce freedom such as you will find nowhere else in the world. This part of Russia is like the North-West Frontier of India.' The engineer had gone there on a survey and described valleys which were deserted.

Wicksteed, who was thinking of going back to Teberda, listened impatiently. 'Deserted valleys, eh! Where would I get my *food*?'

'We could take horses,' said my father.

'*We?*' gasped Wicksteed. 'Do you mean it?'

My father assured him with his usual enthusiasm that he had never meant anything more. 'The minute the engineer began to talk about that part of the high Caucasus where arrogant Communism had not yet been able to establish its irritating sway, I knew that I was going there.' The next morning he wired the *Chicago Daily News* suggesting a horseback ride into the remote Caucasus: '"Strange people in strange places" – something like that.' He got the immediate reply, 'EXCELLENT YOUR SUGGESTION HAS GREAT SYNDICATION VALUE PROCEED.' They don't make editors like that any more – nor wives: my mother gave her blessing too. So my father flew back to London with all expenses paid by his generous paper to see the first night of a play on which he had collaborated with a woman who changed his words while he was away. When Raymond Massey had to utter the line '*White* men don't run!' my father left the theatre; but before he flew back to Moscow he bought 'the finest camp kit' that Fortnum & Mason could supply, and the food to match it. This was before the Wall Street crash when the expense accounts of foreign correspondents were passed without a moment's scrutiny.

> Prize purchases were two bedrolls with two rubberized ground-sheets ... and then, as we had decided that our main diet would be from mountain sheep we could buy from the shepherds, I had two waxed-cloth bags made, large enough to hold a leg of lamb each. This to prevent the flies from blowing the meat. Other waxed bags were made for rice, etc; a complete folding cooking outfit of aluminium utensils. Then with a duffle bag full of tea, coffee, tins of jam, etc – most of them unobtainable in Russia – 1,000 Gold Flake cigarettes in tins, and my favourite trout rod.

I remember that duffle bag when we travelled across Europe, and the cooking outfit too. What an impression he must have made on Fortnum's as the dashing young American about to ride horseback through the Caucasus. The horses, I should explain, were needed to carry the packs and relieve my father whose leg was festering from his flying accident in Egypt.

I was neither so young, nor so dashing, and could not afford Fortnum's. Yet I tried to emulate his romantic image, ignoring Hanbury-Tenison's advice to take as little kit as possible, even though this was confirmed by Susan Richards whose *Epics of Everyday Life* in Russia provides the sanest insight into the tortuous Soviet mentality that I know. She wrote to me:

> At all costs, travel light, or you will spend too much of your time thinking about your pieces of luggage, counting them, finding somewhere safe to leave them, and too little concentrating on the encounter in hand. For three months I

lived mostly in two skirts. Just keep washing things night after night. Don't take things that need ironing, as that's another dependency. Like you, I love my comforts. But once you have decided to set off, the worst thing is to *half* let go.

But I had to cope with the heat as I sailed down the Volga, and then the freezing cold of the mountains, while appearing smartly dressed in Moscow as well as at the Pera Palas Hotel in Istanbul, which was to be my final destination. My luggage swelled until the point was reached where I might as well add everything, for there was no hope of carrying it all myself. As for the Caucasus, mountain boots were crucial. A friend recommended Blacks in Rathbone Place, London, where I arrived with a formidable list sent by Yuri including such mysterious items as 'snow-gaiters, jockey caps and breeches'. In addition to the obligatory sleeping-bags, there were 'sun-glasses and supplies of medicine, especially for the heart'. I assumed that meant *my* heart, which was viewed as especially suspect. As for the money-belt recommended for any visitor to Russia, I decided against this because of the discomfort and because of the danger that if a thief thought I was wearing one it would be easier to kill me than untie the thing and tear it off. Ironically, Russians today wear money belts on the *outside* as status symbols; presumably they are empty.

I am always an impatient shopper, but this was not tolerated by the assistant, a dedicated young man called Kes who sized me up instantly and told me to return when I had more time. I did so, chastened, for the lengthy fitting of the mountain boots with cutaway heels to help in the descent. After half an hour, Kes instructed me to walk up and down and asked if I could feel my toes touching the cap. I was forced to admit that I could not.

'Excellent!' enthused Kes. 'You're not supposed to.' I had passed a test. Though he was baffled that anyone so unsuitable should contemplate climbing up mountains, Kes loved his work and seemed touched by my stupidity. When I apologized for putting him to so much trouble, he wrote back emphatically, 'Let's get one thing straight – it's no trouble! Only too glad to help. It's a lot more interesting to deal with a "guest" than it is a bunch of naive idiots off to pillage the great outdoors.' I was uncertain what he meant by 'guest', but I was gratified.

The cost, including the equipment for Ali and Yuri, and the 'snow-gaiters' which proved to be 'waterproof leggings', came to £383.31, with my anorak and other items still to come. Too much. The snow-gaiters were never used.

A vital addition remained, the hardest choice of all – the right companion. Though tempted to travel on my own with the promise of the unexpected that comes when you are forced to rely on yourself, I was aware that the journey would be enhanced with someone to talk to and, especially, someone to laugh with. I needed a Wicksteed, but that was an impossibility. I knew no one remotely like him.

How would I find someone who could stand my company, for I am the worst of travellers, as anyone unfortunate enough to accompany me will testify. To go on holiday can strain the closest friendship; to travel through Russia could break it.

Several possibilities were rejected with surprising speed: *she* would not have the stamina; *he* would sink to the occasion; *he* would sulk when things went wrong, as they were bound to. Also, and importantly, none of them could pay for themselves. All along, I knew there was only one person who could cope – James Birch.

James is not the person he seems; that is one of his advantages. Too many people prove to be a cul-de-sac but James surprises me the more I know him. A deceptively flopsy façade conceals a ruthless impatience with those who irritate him. A typical public schoolboy, though he did not go to Eton as everyone assumes, he is barely literate and unable to spell, though highly knowledgeable with instinctive good taste. He looks ten years younger than his age, mid-thirties; it came as a shock when I learnt that he has a teenage daughter. With his falling lock of hair he has a deceptive innocence.

And he could afford to pay his way. Above all, he knew and loved Russia, having gone there on a dozen occasions to arrange the first Western exhibition of Francis Bacon in Moscow in 1988, followed by the Gilbert and George exhibition in 1990, when I had first-hand experience of James's rapport with the Russians, who trusted him. I trusted his judgement too; and there were no emotional traumas to trap us. He did not have my personal incentive of following in my father's tracks, but his affection for the Russians would make his journey worthwhile.

There was no reason to hesitate, and we met for a glorious lunch when we discussed our plans, brimming over with foolish optimism as we infected each other with our enthusiasm. The anticipation of travel is the best part. Now I had to make the arrangements.

A discreet approach to Intourist had received the unhelpful reply, 'Boat trips down the Volga River are only available to groups. It is not possible for individual tourists to cross the Klukhor Pass.' Instead I went to the Barry Martin agency which specializes in Russian travel. After rejecting a sailing which left Moscow on 20 July, arriving at Astrakhan on 16 August – which was too long and seemed surprisingly expensive at 600 roubles – I learnt that other boats left in August on uneven dates taking seventeen days with a de luxe cabin at 591 roubles; 'Foreigners can only travel by agreement with the chief, i.e. a bottle.' By then, I realized that 600 roubles was only twenty pounds, so the chief could have several bottles if necessary. I reserved a de luxe cabin for James and myself, sailing on 17 August.

Throughout, I had the advantage of my friendship with James Butterwick, a cheerful young Etonian who learnt Russian at the Language School in Pyatigorsk, which is how he had met Yuri and was able to introduce us the previous year. Now fluent in Russian, James had married a Russian girl in Kiev in 1990 and was helping to run the Harrington Galleries in Berkeley Square, London, which specialized in Russian art. Helping me with my plans, he secured us visas for every town we stopped at, through a friend in the Soviet Trade Delegation. This was a favour I was scarcely aware of at the time; it was to prove our salvation.

Encouraging from the start, James Butterwick wrote to me:

> I do envy you both. I cannot imagine a more fascinating trip, right through the very heartlands of Russia. I remember a passage in your father's book when they sail past old monasteries, disused for ten years. I do hope they're still there. I find the thought of them being either in ruins or simply torn down too terrible to contemplate. The Bolsheviks really do have a lot to answer for.

It occurred to me that if he had been free James Butterwick would have been the ideal companion, especially as James Birch, who was vague at the best of times, had now vanished. Unable to contact him, I became increasingly anxious and after a few weeks' silence I assumed he had decided against the idea and phoned Barry Martin to confirm that I should be travelling alone. When the phone rang that evening I knew instinctively that it was James, and the reason for his silence was sad and simple: his mother had died after a brief illness at their country home in East Anglia. She was an exceptional woman with a zest for life and good food and drink. A voracious traveller herself, she had urged James to make this journey – and now it was on again.

However, James was alarmed by the reports of civil war in Azerbaijan which we would be crossing. His fears were exacerbated by the warning of a close friend that it might be 'dangerous' and it would be wise to take revolvers.

'That's madness,' I exclaimed. 'If we take revolvers we might use them, and that could be fatal, for that is the nature of revolvers. Anyhow, I wouldn't know how to use one.'

James pointed out the recent cases of tourists who had been mugged in Moscow or taken for more of a ride than they intended by pirate taxi-drivers. His 'friend' convinced him that this could happen in Astrakhan. 'How will we get from the ship to the railway station?' James asked, for it was my intention to take the train from Astrakhan to Makhachkala and Derbent on our way to Baku.

'By taxi,' I replied.

'How will we know if it's safe? Perhaps we should have someone with us?'

'Come on! By the time we reach Astrakhan we're bound to have made friends with someone on board who'll be able to help us.'

'I suppose so,' but he sounded doubtful and suggested that Ali might join us by car in Astrakhan, as Yuri would still be in England then. I explained that this would be too complicated, for Ali was not on the phone, nor could he speak English, and I doubted if he had a car. For me, one of the joys of this journey was the risks which we would have to overcome when travelling on our own. That is why an Intourist cruise ship filled with Germans on their pilgrimage to Stalingrad was so unappealing. There had been the possibility that an independent television company would film my Caucasian journey for a travel series on Channel 4, but this fell through when the commissioning editor saw me on television chairing a discussion at a village hall on Exmoor and decided that I was too 'formal' (a verdict which astounded my friends). Now I was thankful not to be trailed by a camera crew, with all the artifice involved, and wondered how I could have contemplated it in the first place.

Suddenly, with everything settled, there was an anticlimax. I over-insured myself for 50,000 pounds in the case of my death, and started to buy the gifts which are indispensable in Russia, not just to open doors but to reciprocate the hospitality which is compulsive, even with so little to be hospitable with. The hard currency of Marlboro cigarettes (more viable than roubles), whisky, Mars Bars (for extra energy for myself on the final ascent), chocolates for children, could all be bought at the Duty Free shop at Heathrow. Susan Richards advised me on gifts for Russian mothers and girlfriends:

Scent is perfect. Make sure it's French or a make they will

have heard of. Forget soap as Mornay will be lost on them and it's too heavy. Also forget socks. In the Caucasus they are rich beyond imagining after Russia/Ukraine/Belorussiya. And even in the north they can be quite easily insulted by being given underclothes. It is only what is on *top* that matters to them. These are hard times, and they feel they need treats. Silk scarves are good and light. They're fairly sophisticated down there. I bought twenty calculators the size of Barclaycards. Also never forget to take little things like calendars, mugs, which are very visibly from Devon/London, very English for less grand people on the way. You can't have too many presents. They are generous and you'll be really embarrassed without things to pull out of your pocket which are decent.

So much for travelling light.

Advising dollars as a stronger currency than pounds on the black market, she confirmed the need for a money-belt: 'Wear it even at night. The nicest people in the Caucasus might find the temptation too great.' Instead, I decided to distribute my dollars rather than keep them in a lump which could be lost or stolen. Cunningly, I chose such hiding places as empty tubes of vitamins, inside envelopes concealed in books, and so many unlikely caches that I had to make a list in case I threw them away by mistake.

Finally, the absolute necessity – food. James Butterwick phoned a doctor friend in Leningrad who had taken a similar boat trip down the Volga and assured him that the cuisine in the dining-room was first-class, advising us that it was cheaper to pay roubles in the bar and not to offer dollars. Butterwick reported, 'Dr Mikhail is very fussy about his comforts so the food should be pretty good.' As the Caucasus was so 'rich' that anything could be obtained if bargained for, there would be no problem there. Our needs would be simple and we could live off the land as we made our way: eggs for omelettes, and lamb to be bought from the shepherds as my father had done, marinated in oil, herbs and wild garlic, for succulent stew or *shaslik* to be cooked over an open fire. As for fruit, this would be plentiful in the season of melons and apples and pears. I need only take a few tins of sardines and tuna fish for treats on lonely nights.

Had I been more experienced I should have realized that my hopes were being fulfilled too easily. At the last moment Barry Martin's assistant phoned to tell me the bad news that the journey was no longer possible: Astrakhan was closed to foreigners due to an outbreak of cholera, and anyhow this was irrelevant, for it was necessary to book a cabin eighteen months in advance. The chief's 'bottle' must have gone astray. Remembering James Butterwick's insistence that you can do anything in Russia provided you persevere and pay in dollars, I told her not to accept this set-back but to keep on trying. I considered postponing the journey until the following year, but the long delay might prevent us from going at all, and spring presented problems in the Caucasus.

Then, with equal suddenness, everything was on again, after the agency's representative in Moscow had bribed the captain, if we agreed to pay a further 400 dollars. I spoke to James and confirmed that indeed we would at this late stage, and our de luxe cabin was re-confirmed for the seventeenth as intended all along, which suggested that the venal game of Russian roulette had been played throughout. James would collect our tickets, leaving for Moscow a few days earlier with Sebastian Boyle to discuss an exhibition by the Boyle family the following year. Ostensibly the tickets would take us to Astrakhan, though we would have to leave the ship at Volgograd due to the alleged cholera.

Armour-plated in my naivety, I arrived in Moscow on the Friday, slept the night on the floor of James's Russian friend, photographed James and Sebastian sitting on Kim Philby's tombstone on Saturday, 17 August 1991, and drove to the ferry port in the afternoon. Never had Moscow seemed so tranquil.

CHAPTER THREE

Boarding the *Pipkin*

AFTER my father's spending spree in Fortnum's, he laid out his kit before Wicksteed who watched, flabbergasted, until he was able to point at one item he would not need, jabbing his pipe at the bed-roll and Jaeger flea-bag.

'No? Got a better one?' asked my father, surprised.

'No. Just a special one. Made it myself.'

While he was in London, my father was inoculated against every affliction he could think of, for he was still recovering from the bone operation on his leg. With the wound still open, he was forced to wear a surgical boot, which is why he needed a horse to rest it, while Wicker (as he called him affectionately) was determined to walk the whole distance: 'I will go at just such-and-such a pace, no faster, no slower. Gravity notwithstanding. Up hill, down hill – on the flat. You will see!' He refused the supply of flowers of sulphur which my father had found a blessing on a mule-ride through Spain, coating himself with the yellow insecticide.

'Then eat it!' laughed my father. 'You will sweat it through your pores and no bug will touch you.'

Wicker replied that he was not beginning their trip by eating sulphur. His contribution was a kilo of tea, collected during the winter by trading his own tea leaves with the other inmates of his human warren, on the basis that for four parts of his tea – once used – he received one of fresh tea leaves from them. As my father pointed out, they had to take his word for it that his had been used only once, but Alexander Wicksteed was an English gentleman and somehow, in all that gruesome slum, the other people knew it.

When they sailed on a sunny afternoon in May on a tiny paddle-steamer called the *Thanks*, Wicksteed arrived at the second bridge below the Kremlin dressed as an English gentleman for once, still grey-bearded and with a shaven head, disdainful of necktie with sandals on his feet, but wearing a well-cut Scottish tweed and a not-too-badly-pressed pair of flannel bags. With a friend carrying his heavy rucksacks, he walked straight through the fighting crowd of Russians and on to the boat.

'Why on earth did you wear that get-up?' asked my father as they stuffed their gear in the cabin. 'On this day of all days!'

'There are occasions,' Wicker rejoined, 'when one must be what one is. This day is one of them. You saw how it worked.'

At six o'clock the *Thanks* gave a shriek and cast off.

Our ship was due to sail at six o'clock also, but of course she did nothing of the sort. Surprisingly, she was named after Lenin's mistress before he married the formidable Krupskaya. Her name was *Clara Tsepkin*, which is difficult to pronounce in Russian so I referred to her as the *Clara Pipkin*, a simpler name that stuck.

The port of Moscow is attractive, with a terminal in Stalinist baroque, and impressive flights of steps, decorated with roundels of past Soviet achievements to commemorate the construction of the Moscow–Volga Canal which was dug between 1933 and 1937. It looks less cheerful when you learn of the political prisoners who lost their lives in the digging in conditions which were so wretched that they may have been glad to terminate such an existence.

Several ferries were tied to the quayside with others moored beyond, waiting to replace them. They came in two sizes: extremely long, reminiscent of a Mississippi paddle-boat, or three-decked and squat. Both were low and without funnels in order to pass under the numerous bridges ahead. My fantasy of an old steamer with comfortable cabins and delicious meals ended abruptly. The *Pipkin* had a no-nonsense, sturdy air, and she lacked romance. Even so, she looked practical. I was unaware that looks are deceptive in Russia, where the façade has more importance than the reality behind; that 'practicality' usually entails inefficiency, carelessness and no imagination. We had been ordered to report at five o'clock or forfeit our tickets, but it was six thirty before we were allowed on board, joining a surge of jostling, screaming passengers. While I guarded our luggage, James struggled ahead with our tickets and returned a quarter of an hour later, ashen: 'You're in for a shock. The cabin's tiny.'

'Seriously tiny?'

'Deadly serious.'

I had travelled by train from Istanbul to Lake Van, a journey of several days, and though my cabin then was cramped it was comfortable enough and the experience enjoyable. This could hardly be smaller, I thought; but when James opened the door it proved to be half the size and this time there were two of us. Even with James relegated to the upper bunk, for he was half my age, there was still no room to swing a mouse, let alone a cat. The prospect of being confined in this cell until we reached Volgograd, formerly Stalingrad, in a week's time was unbearable, so we locked our luggage inside and set off with the ubiquitous packets of Marlboro to see whom we could bribe. Told by his Russian friend to seek the help of a sailor, James accosted a burly man in a denim uniform, who proved to be an indignant passenger, while I traced the first mate, who was not in uniform, and demanded our luxury cabin for which we had paid our 400-dollar bribe.

'*Niet!*' he exclaimed angrily, once he understood. Shamelessly, I produced some more of our precious dollars but he crossed his hands in a negative gesture and hurried away with a fainter '*Niet!*'

Our packets of Marlboro were accepted ungratefully by the two women in charge of the tickets, who studied their lists and shook their heads. De luxe cabins did not exist. And all

the while we were pushed by the passengers forcing their way
up the staircase placed inconveniently next to the ticket table,
and were harassed by a small boy in a peaked cap who
practised his English 'please' and 'sorry' learnt at school, with
sudden disconcerting gestures as he raised his arms to his head
and then flung them apart in a form of military exercise. At
least he liked us, though he was highly irritating.

'Oh God,' I said to James, the first of a million moans, 'let's
go to dinner and then try again. Perhaps we can get a second
cabin, once things have settled down.'

The restaurant looked promising, prow-shaped with curtains
around the windows and on every table a solitary carnation
made of plastic. After finding a table at the far end which
overlooked the foredeck, I began to perk up.

'Vodka,' I beamed at the waitress who approached us with
the hostility and looks of a pugilist.

She shook her boxer's head.

I tried again. 'Cognac?'

'*Niet*,' with the usual satisfaction.

'Not even *mineral-vodiye?*' I asked, for this is sold in bottles,
as you might expect.

'*Niet*.' Even more emphatic.

'*Voda?*' I was reduced to asking for water simply to quench
my thirst which was now considerable. I feared that even this
would be refused, as it was.

'*Nichevo?*' I asked, knowing the word for 'absolutely nothing
whatsoever'.

'*Nichevo!*' she declared with the pride of all the Russians
when they slam the last door in your face. This was the
surreal situation which I recounted at the beginning.

'Now everyone has left,' I said to James.

'But they can't have eaten, for there is no food.' He looked
stunned.

'Yet they were studying the menu. It doesn't make sense . . .
Unless . . .' An appalling thought had struck me.

'Unless what?'

'Unless there is no food.' We laughed at such absurdity; but when the waitress with the beaten-up face returned and we mimed as if we wanted to eat, she shook her head, smiling at such ignorance, though she shoved the menu in front of us and produced a pencil and piece of paper to take our order. As there was nothing to order, this seemed a cruel charade.

'What sort of madness is this?' I turned to James. 'A restaurant with neither food nor drink, not even water?'

'This is Russia. I told you. You simply don't understand. You expect everything to work.' We sat there in anguished silence while I wondered what we should do. The *Pipkin* was moving, passing under the first bridge across the Moscow–Volga Canal. Should we get off at the next stop and try to take a train? Or could we board an Intourist ship which I had resisted and now regretted. Even if it was filled with Germans, at least there would be a bar and food and water. Curiously, the lack of water was the worst deprivation of all. If it came to a choice between water or champagne for seven days, I would choose water every time. It is only when you are without it that you realize how precious it is. As for the food, we had brought no provisions, though I had left London the day before and could have stocked up with cold meats, fresh fruit, cheese and wine. I cursed James Butterwick's doctor friend who had told him that there was no need to bring anything with us. Dr Mikhail was either on a diet or shrewd enough, as proved to be the case, to have sailed on one of those élite briefer cruises from Leningrad, intended for an expensive holiday. The *Pipkin* was strictly functional, a ferry boat whose sole purpose was to take the passengers from one port to another with no thought for their comfort.

I discussed the alternatives with James and produced the map, as I was to do so often, but we knew in our hearts that there was no jumping off. Quoting Kafka, I told him, 'There is a point beyond which there is no turning back. This is the point that must be reached.'

'I think we've reached it,' I said. We sat in the empty dining-room rigid with gloom; and then, as always in Russia when a grisly situation seems irreversible, the wheels begin to grind again, especially when they are oiled with bribery.

We noticed that the dining-room was filling up again as if for a second sitting, which was carrying the charade too far. Passengers studied their menus intently yet not a sausage was served, and they left unfed.

'I think I've got it,' said James. 'They're making orders for tomorrow. I've seen the waitress scribbling in a notebook.'

'So that's it! And the fact that there doesn't seem to be any choice makes no difference. That really is Russian!'

'I told you. Don't expect logic.' We were able to laugh, which was so surprising in that sombre atmosphere that the other passengers looked across at us as if we had transgressed, except for one youngish man who dared to come over and introduce himself because he heard us talking in English and had a smattering himself. Our relief at finding someone who could understand us was infinite. I flourished the Marlboro but he told us he did not smoke. His name was Vladimir; he was nearly handsome and I could imagine that some women would find him so. His hair was crinkly and light brown, his build was slight, and he wore good casual clothes of a kind unusual in Russia. He could have been a student from any Western European country – Germany, Holland, Denmark or Finland – but he explained that he was not a student and was twice married. There was something peculiar about him, especially his declaration that he was 'a philosopher'. When I asked if he was on holiday, he replied, 'Every day is a holiday for me, and every day leetle work. Unofficial. Everything in Russia today has to be unofficial.' He was travelling all the way to Astrakhan in spite of the cholera epidemic, and then he was sailing back again. Though far from fluent, his slight knowledge of English was a godsend, and when we spoke slowly with constant repetition, he was quick in understanding us.

It was dark outside and though we were sailing down a canal there was that sense of cocooned limbo which envelops every ship at night. By now the other passengers for the imaginary second sitting had given their orders and left, but we stayed on, as we were to do every night. The two waitresses relaxed with a sigh of relief: the older, pugilistic Lou, and the younger Nina who took a fancy to James and Vladimir and to my packets of Marlboro. Suddenly they produced a plate of coarse, sliced salami never to be seen on board the *Pipkin* again, with a sliced tomato and some sticky marmalade sweets. This was a treat beyond all expectation, surpassed by a small bottle of fiery Cognac at a cost which was derisory with the rate of exchange so monstrously unfair in our favour, especially as I would have paid a king's ransom for such a treat. Plainly, the *Pipkin* was a dry ship. There was no bar, nor did the other passengers ever touch a drop, so this was a personal concession from Lou who had taken pity on us. Presumably, like so many things in Russia, it came from an illicit cache, and I noticed it was produced after the passengers had gone to their cabins. It had to be drunk neat, for we remained waterless. It was later that Vladimir discovered a tap two decks below where boiled water – I feared from the filthy canal – dripped into the stained decanter that I brought from my wretched cabin.

By then, I had the first cabin on my own. With Vladimir as interpreter and Marlboro as our treasurer, we made another attempt to find a larger cabin, fortified by the Cognac after that first strange meal. This time James returned with the good news that there was no de luxe cabin but he had found one for us which was slightly bigger.

'Us?'

'Yes, we've still got to share it.'

'Oh no we haven't,' I stated firmly. Disconcerting the stewardess, I started to unpack while Vladimir translated her instructions that I should move at once. I continued to unpack while James lugged his massive bag away. He thought he was travelling light with only one case, though he was scarcely able to lift it. At this point the stewardess had a mild attack of hysterics. She was calmed down by more cigarettes, though she informed Vladimir that James and I must pay for the second cabin: 'It could be as much as 120 roubles,' he said, shaking his head. This is where I should have been tactful, for although it was the equivalent of four pounds for me it could

have represented two weeks' salary for the average Russian –
though I doubted if Vladimir was average or even worked in a
salaried job. 'No problem!' I exclaimed hastily, using the
universal phrase. 'We shall pay it.'

Life on board the *Pipkin* was becoming more bearable. I was
still in the dreary cabin but at least I was on my own, a rule
which James and I adhered to from then on. There was boiled
canal water below, the Cognac and a sort of sausage. Above
all, we had Vladimir as our ally and interpreter, though he
remained an enigma. He asked nothing from us and never
smoked or drank. Perhaps all he wanted was to practise his
English and learn some more. Unlike the other passengers,
who were middle-aged and unsmiling, he symbolized the
young, the sly and the brave who dared to hope for change. He
retained a zest for life and, miraculously, shared our taste for
the ridiculous. When I referred to the boat as the *Clara Pipkin*
he was convulsed, echoing the name with a ringing delight –
'the *Pipkin*!' – collapsing with laughter while the other passengers watched him disapprovingly for consorting with the
enemy, for this was how they regarded us. In his turn he did
not conceal his contempt for them and showed considerable
courage in taking our side throughout. After he went to his
cabin, which proved more spacious than either of ours, James
and I wondered if he was a KGB agent planted by the
authorities when we paid our 400-dollar bribe in London for
the deluxe cabin that never was. Such an idea sounds fantastic
until you find yourself in such unfamiliar circumstances, and
then it seems possible. Vladimir's detestation of Communism
seemed too open, too unafraid, as if he had protection or
astonishing audacity. Nor was he an innocent unaware of the
consequences. Yet we trusted him instinctively.

Before I retired to my narrow bunk, I went to the prow of
the *Pipkin* as she slid silently through the canal whose sides
were just discernible as we approached the locks. I experienced
the sense of relief which overtakes one on the start of any
journey once it has begun, when you know you are out of
reach of 'urgent' phone calls which are never to your advan-

tage, and letters in demanding brown envelopes. I remembered a similar moment after I joined the Merchant Navy and came up on the deck of the *Orcades* after we passed Gravesend and headed through the marshes towards the open sea. We were sailing round the world, I had put the past behind me and everything lay ahead, largely the unknown. I felt a surge of joy as we left the land behind and it started to rain. I was beholden to no one but myself and the strict laws which govern an ocean liner. I was younger then and I cannot say I felt the same elation on the *Pipkin*, which was a parody of a ship by comparison, but we were moving and that in itself was a relief. The day that travel becomes predictable I shall stop travelling. At least the *Pipkin* was unpredictable.

CHAPTER FOUR

Crisis and the KGB

AUTUMN had come early to Moscow and travelled with us down the Volga. In the grey light of morning, life on board the *Pipkin* had not improved. Most of the Russians had retired early the night before, so they woke early too. I was distracted by a noisy chattering outside my cabin window as a Russian family sat down on one of the benches that lined the deck, but I would have been woken anyhow by the mind-breaking martial music played over the loudspeakers at full blast, followed by interminable announcements exhorting the passengers not to do this or that. Driven on deck by the din, I met James and we waited until the announcement for the last sitting for breakfast, which we guessed rather than understood. Even then it was awkward to squeeze our way through the tables because the Russians refused to give way.

'They're so rude,' muttered James, usually the most patient of men.

There is a type of television travel presenter who speaks with gushing breathlessness – 'As darkness falls there is not a soul in sight' – ignoring the gaggle of the camera crew, and the pert personal assistant dressed as if she is *en route* to an ethnic party. Blazing with insincerity, the presenter confides to the camera crew that he or she is 'immensely proud and privileged to be travelling alone in the same train across Mongolia as these pure and simple people'.

On board the *Pipkin*, I studied my fellow-travellers and felt far from proud or privileged. Simplicity is a virtue, but these Russians looked devious and self-satisfied with eyes that did not shine. Here was the *petite bourgeoisie* personified, with the widows and wives of army officers covetous of their status and their perks. Their resentment of us was tangible, which was understandable, for a suspicion of everyone and everything had been ingrained for years until it was a natural instinct.

Yet, to be fair, we were foreigners and therefore unwelcome as intruders. I doubt if they feared or envied us, but they suffered from the passivity which resents any departure from the norm. Remembering the passion expressed by the Russian novelists, I asked James if they had lost their love of the Motherland.

'It's extraordinary,' he said, 'that however tough life is today, people are drawn back to the Motherland.'

'Do you mean that this is why they are sailing down the Volga?'

'No doubt of it.'

I may have misjudged them too hastily, though they showed no emotion, as if their journey was a penance rather than a joy. I had not appreciated the symbolic importance of the Volga, the largest river in Europe over 2,000 miles long, the 'Mother Volga' of folklore and the last frontier and lifeline of Russian colonization in the East. To be sailing down it to the Caspian Sea was the fulfilment of a lifetime, which was why they reserved their cabins for months in advance.

A few had different reasons for being on board, like the honeymoon couple at the next table who limped in, eyes half-closed from satiation as they stared at each other, blissfully unaware of the ghastly food. After a few mouthfuls, they escorted each other out and returned to their cabin for the more serious and happier business of sex. They were never seen on deck, relishing their rare chance for privacy away from their families in an overcrowded room in a Moscow tenement, with prying ears on the other side of a curtain. Other passengers used the *Pipkin* as a ferry to some port on the way to Astrakhan.

Yet for those travelling through the Motherland there was no passion. This was a contrast to the novelists who rejoiced in their love of Russia, exemplified by Maxim Gorky with his hopes for the future, when he returned from exile in 1928 to receive the highest honours (his birthplace Nijni Novgorod was renamed after him four years later, as Gorky). He recalled a woman called Velikova who stood on a hill overlooking the River Kazan and the Arsk Plain with the blue line of the Volga beyond,

> until, suddenly turning pale, she had, with tears of joy sparkling in her fine eyes, cried under her breath, but sufficiently loudly for all present to hear her: 'Ah, friends, how gracious and how fair is this land of ours! Come let us salute that land for having deemed us worthy of residence therein!'

Or Dostoevsky in *The Brothers Karamazov* when the Russian monk remembers meeting a 'good-looking peasant lad' on the riverbank:

> We talked of the beauty of this world of God's and of the great mystery of it. Every blade of grass, every insect, ant and golden bee, all so marvellously know their path, though they have not intelligence, they bear witness to the mystery of God and continually accomplish it themselves. I saw the dear lad's heart was moved. He told me that he loved the forest and the forest birds. He was a bird-catcher, knew the note of each of them, could call each bird. 'I know nothing better than to be in the forest,' said he, 'though all things are good.'

Not even Dickens, among English writers, would have dared to be so sentimental. This was the deep-rooted urge to return to nature which I hoped to discover for myself.

It was this urge which inspired my father to quote from Tolstoy's *Resurrection* as the foreword to *Caucasian Journey*, celebrating the return of spring:

> Plants, birds, insects, and children rejoiced. But men, adult men, never ceased to cheat and harass their fellows and

themselves. What men considered sacred and important was not the spring morning, not the beauty which inclines the heart to peace and love and concord. What men considered sacred and important were their own devices for wielding power over their fellow men.

This was written in 1899. The last sentence is prophetic, as if it is the nature of the Russian people to be tyrannized by an élite, as perhaps it was, and even is.

Yet as late as 1929 the human spirit had not been entirely subdued. The Moscow–Volga Canal had not been constructed, so my father sailed the first 700 miles on the same rivers that took Ivan the Terrible to his conquest of Kazan. First, 115 miles down the little Moskva to Ryazan; then 550 miles down the River Oka to Gorky, or Nijni Novgorod as it was renamed yet again. The *Thanks* had been prettier than the *Pipkin*, the rivers lovelier than the canal:

Complete peace. The ship seemed to paddle on for ever under its great bowl of blue sky. The ice had gone, and the steppes, which had lain locked in snow for the six winter months, were now sweeps of green to the far horizon. They were flowered. Islands of that yellow bloom that the Russians call 'chicken blind' seemed to float on the sunny grass.
Cliff swallows skimmed ahead of the bows, ducks beat up from hidden reaches and whistled down the sky ... a yellow ribbon of road leads to a peasant village.

The *Thanks* seemed to stop everywhere – 'even to put a gangplank on to a sandbar, to trade vodka for pigs'. It was a lazier journey, with a *Huckleberry Finn* quality. One morning he saw the dawn come up across the steppes:

Instantly, thousands of birds leapt into the sky to greet it. We swung a bend, a sandy cliff, a wall of pine forest. Down below on the foredeck, I saw a girl. We had the boat to ourselves, except for the man at the wheel. She was leaning, chin on her folded arms; and I saw her rise and hold up her hands to the sun as if in adoration. I went down to talk to her. 'I love it – love it!' she cried, pointing to the steppe. 'I love all Russia.'

When they approached Nijni Novgorod, my father was caught by her enthusiasm.

'Is it the Volga?'
    'No – not yet.'
We passed through a fleet of black fishing skiffs. I looked for the wooden bridge across the mouth of the Oka that is rebuilt every spring, saw that it was not yet up – and then found myself staring across a swirling silver flood.
    'Volga! Volga!' cried the Russians, emotional as they are. But I felt the thing too . . . it was just the sight of this mighty volume of water flowing past. Volga on its journey to the sea. The superb indifference of the thing!

It was understandable that my companions were less ec-static, for our passage to the Volga was prosaic. Unless on the immense scale of Panama, or the modesty of the lower Thames, a series of locks is not inspiring, and far from sailing into a sunnier clime we started by heading north to Yaroslav, to join the Volga there. This was a shorter journey than my father's, without the stops which were inconsequential yet redolent of Russia, like the dirty little Chekhovian town of Ryazan, 115 miles from Moscow. Staring at the dusty streets, my father declared it was 'boredom personified', and Wicks-teed gave his verdict that 'Nothing but unmitigated and incessant vice could make life in that town bearable.'
In 1929 the rivers were spared the pollution which is so dense today that scientists reckon it now takes a drop of water as many years as it used to take months to reach the Caspian. Most of the fish have been killed off, though I was to see optimistic fishermen on the banks, and some in small boats with nets – even one courageous swimmer. My father had swum regularly from the small sandy beaches near the stops.
As James chewed morosely on a disgraceful sausage over lunch, I tried to whet his appetite by reading my father's

account of the sterlets, the delicate little fish that looked like miniature sturgeon, though they were seldom more than a foot long, and which were kept in a tank with holes bored into the ship's side to give a constant flow of fresh water.

'Their flesh is unbelievably delicate,' I enthused, 'and they are served with steaming boiled potatoes and hollandaise sauce.' My father said that when the chef gave him caviare for breakfast, he wanted to stay on the ship for ever.

James gagged on his piece of gristle and looked at me with dislike.

I began to realize that his attitude towards Russia was ambivalent. When James shook his head at my naivety, muttering 'You have no idea, there is no logic in Russia,' he was defending the people, not condemning them. He loved the Russians. In Moscow his closest friends were determined that he should marry their daughter, who was woken every time he called on them, even if it was after midnight. Embarrassed at seeing her clutching her teddy bear, he was dismayed when she was produced a few minutes later in jeans and dreadful make-up with the inducement, 'James, please stay, dance a little and take your pleasure.'

Before he changed his mind, James assured the frightened girl, 'Don't worry,' and took an interminable taxi back to his hotel after inventing some excuse.

I realized that his love for the Russians was being tested on the *Pipkin* when he quoted the Marquis de Custine, who wrote in 1839 that the Russians were 'a half savage people who have been regimented without being civilized'.

'Good God,' I exclaimed, 'nothing changes.'

'They are incapable of change.'

Only the children smiled at us, especially the plump little boy in the peaked cap with his exaggerated gestures. The military exercise had been replaced by agitated thrusts of a pointed finger and vast, imaginary puffs of smoke. 'Even the child wants a Marlboro,' surmised James until we realized that he wanted James to smoke-out the mosquitoes which descended as we continued, confusingly, to sail north.

We were saved by Vladimir, who grew in mystery. It came as a surprise to learn that he was thirty-five, much older than he looked, and married his first wife, a Syrian, when she was only thirteen. His second wife was a Tartar, a former prostitute, and he married her when she was twenty-four. He had just divorced her, which was why he was travelling alone. His daughter was left in the care of his mother in a Moscow room. 'She is very beautiful,' he shrugged, referring to his wife. 'Now she is prostitute again.'

He brightened our meals like a cheque in the post on a hungover morning. The only other Russians who dared to join our table were a fat, jolly woman and her son who toyed at the meat or fish — it was hard to tell which it was — with such suspicion that the son shoved it away untouched. With maternal solicitude, his mother attempted to encourage him by swallowing a morsel, after which she abandoned the attempt and nodded to him sympathetically. After this, they appeared intermittently, cooking their food in their cabin, like most of the passengers, which accounted for the reek of boiled cabbage in the passageways.

In spite of their delicious sterlet served on the *Thanks*, my father and Wicksteed had done the same, though with them it was more of a dormitory feast, until my father was unable to bear Wicker's eating habits any longer.

'Look under your bunk,' he told him, pointing to the egg shells he had used for making omelettes. Having gone this far, he then pulled Wicker's handkerchief off their block of butter. 'Do you see this?'

Wicker coughed. 'That handkerchief,' he explained hoarsely. 'I suppose you know the principle of evaporation? The air passing over that wet handkerchief cools the butter. And . . .'

'But you'd *used* it!' cried my father angrily.

As Wicker got down on his knees and started to rake the egg shells and even some fish heads together, my father went on deck and said he had seldom felt so ashamed. Returning to his bunk, he saw Wicker with his face to the wall and started to read *The Cossacks* until he was interrupted by a triumphant cry: 'A-ha, so *that's* the lesson is it? That you should substitute your cigarette ash — *look* at that table, *look* at that floor — for my *Shakespeare!*' My father reached out and took his hand — 'In such ways are undying friendships made.'

I had an echo of that when we went ashore at Uglich that night to admire a church with walls lined by golden illustrated panels. I noticed that Vladimir had disappeared and wondered where he could have gone, for Uglich was strictly a one-church town. Earlier, when Lou brought us our small bottle of Cognac, which gave us the illusion of a proper meal, I bemoaned the absence of anything else to drink except for the over-sweetened tea and sickly indeterminate fruit juice which I found undrinkable, and was all that the passengers drank on the dry ship *Pipkin*.

'How do the children manage?' I asked James, thinking of the foul tap water.

'None of it makes any sense,' he sighed.

Back in my cabin that night, I started when I heard a knock on the door. When I opened it, Vladimir proudly thrust five bottles of mineral water into my arms, as welcome as a long-lost dog. With a beaming smile of satisfaction, he wished me good night, and my answering smile was his scant reward. In such ways is friendship made.

At breakfast the next morning, Lou was called away and reappeared with that curious, wide-eyed smile which people assume when they have witnessed a street accident.

'*Odin*', she announced, holding up a finger, which made no sense until Vladimir explained that the Kapitan had commanded us to appear on the bridge in an hour's time. I have an aversion to being carpeted, be it in the headmaster's study, the bank manager's office or the captain's bridge. I had experienced all three, and hoped that such experiences were now behind me. James and I were guiltless but I realized that this made little difference in Russia and feared that we might be dumped at the next port and detained.

When we reported on the bridge, the first mate glared at us

with unconcealed hatred, while I smiled graciously and James looked docile. Then the Kapitan started to harangue us through Vladimir, who acted as interpreter. One sure sign of age is when the captains of ships look young, like this man. He appeared reasonably pleasant on a first impression, thick-set, slightly balding, reminding me of the English actor and comedian, Bill Maynard, whom I have met and greatly liked. This favourable image went out of focus and was swiftly shattered. Far from being pleasant, the man was plainly neurotic as he ranted and rambled hysterically at Vladimir for several minutes. The mate interrupted the tirade with unintelligible yells of support of his own. When the violence abated, I tried to respond with the impartial authority of a district officer calming a native uprising, and produced a travel feature with pretty photographs which I had taken for the *Daily Telegraph* the previous year, and other bits and pieces, as if they were official documents. These provoked the Kapitan to further fury. He examined our passports, turning them upside-down in case they revealed a forgery or code. Plainly he could not understand a word, nor had any passenger produced such a passport before. Vladimir pointed out that we had visas for the ports along the Volga, which seemed to confirm our presence as a threat to the *Pipkin*.

'He asks why two Englishmen are on board his ship,' Vladimir translated. Why indeed? Hardly for the delicious food or a jolly little bar.

'We are on the *Pipkin* . . .' I began, but he stopped me with a roar and turned to Vladimir who translated impassively, 'He says what is this *Pipkin*? I say you mean *Tsepkin*.'

'We are on board your beautiful *Pipkin*,' I continued, 'because we wish to see the Volga, the greatest waterway in Europe, which my father saw in 1929 when he, too, sailed from Moscow. We wish to see the true Russia in all her glory and nobility.'

Vladimir had a tough time with this rigmarole and it was obvious that the Kapitan found it inconceivable that we should be travelling on his ship for pleasure.

'He repeats, "What are you doing here?"'

Finally, the Kapitan was reduced to demanding 200 more roubles for the second cabin, which James handed over on the spot.

'No problem!' I beamed.

With evident disappointment, the Kapitan waved us away and as we left the bridge he shouted a final volley at Vladimir, who made no reply. He had acted impeccably throughout, remaining cool as the Kapitan became hotter.

'That is crazy man,' he said when we were out of range. 'He says he will report you to the KGB. Crazy man. Communist.' He shook his head and I found, to my surprise, that I was trembling with anger, unless it was mortification or fear. Yet again, though fleetingly, I wondered if Vladimir had been instructed to report on our movements, for he seemed too good to be true. I dismissed such a thought as unworthy though inevitable in Russia, where every stranger is suspect including, and in this case especially, ourselves.

Later that morning we went ashore at Yaroslav, where the canal joined the Volga, to find the city strangely deserted and sombre, though a few grinning soldiers waved from an upstairs window and lowered a mug on a string which we filled with cigarettes and they hoisted up again with grateful laughter.

The longer stop in the afternoon, a full four-and-a-half hours in Kostroma, proved more rewarding. While most of the passengers stayed on board or went in a group, guided glumly to the local monuments, we walked with Vladimir and took a public bus. Reaching the large monastery on the far bank of the river, with a wooden thirteenth-century church inside the walls, I was rewarded with an echo from the past, for this was a voyage of recollection, in memory of my mother as well as my father. The buildings today form a labyrinthine museum and we chanced on an exhibition devoted to the Tsar which could not have been held a few years earlier, with photographs of the royal family with the glass shattered, as if by bullets. I was particularly moved by the pictures of nurses with crosses on their white uniforms, as worn by my mother when she joined the Anglo–Russian Hospital in Petrograd in January 1916 as a VAD nurse at the age of eighteen.

They struck such a chord that I half-expected to see a photograph of the opening of the hospital with my mother at the feet of the Empress Marie Feodorovna. This was not too fanciful, for there was a photo of the young Tsarevitch among the wounded, which fitted precisely my mother's account of the 'unforgettable day when the little Tsarevitch came, one of the most beautiful children I ever saw' and how the Russian soldiers were overcome with pleasure. The photo in the monastery's exhibition mirrored this exactly.

My mother had volunteered for the mission after a sheltered childhood, confirming a wanderlust which was later to complement my father's. Her letters home to my grandmother are the antidote to official reports, full of freshness and irreverence as she described the people, from grand duchesses to hospital orderlies, as well as the corruption and incompetence, the brutality and cold-bloodedness which seemed to be embedded in the Russian mentality.

> We have the nicest ward in the hospital, a big, long one with fifty-four beds in it, running along the Nevsky to the Fontanka canal and with a huge row of windows and a splendid view. Our Russian orderlies are too killing – twelve of them, all very Russian and military in Russian coats with belts and high boots. Very childish and simple and most cheerful and willing, rather like the Irish – a great deal of talk about everything and much admiration of any little bit of work they may have done! In fact the whole country reminds me awfully of Ireland, in nature – so happy-go-lucky and pleasant and untruthful and charming about everything. Their one great word is '*Cechass*' which means literally 'this hour' but being interpreted is more like 'any time in the next fortnight if we don't forget about it'. They are the most hopeless people to work with. The hopeless lack of organization in everything simply knocks you down. Everyone seems to think that everything is very much on a volcano here, and an internal bust-up is only a matter of time. Matron was warned that we should always avoid a crowd as

the police have orders to fire on any collection of people who do not disperse at once. There were some food riots near here the other night and two people were killed. Apparently certain people are hoarding food to run the prices up, and there is a dreadful shortage.

As always in Russia, *plus ça change*! After she had spent days greasing and cleaning hundreds of medical instruments, while the orderlies polished the floors, the hospital was ready for the grand opening by the Tsarina, reputedly Queen Victoria's favourite grand-daughter:

By two thirty we were all standing there dressed up to the nines in starched everythings, and the priests began to arrive, and dress in their wonderful gold and silver and purple clothes. Then we heard a crowd moving slowly up the stairs, and a small dowdy woman in black, like a plain edition of our Alexandra, but with a very sweet expression, came in, and behind her such a crowd of gold and medals and ribbons and orders as you never saw – or certainly as *I* never did! The two little princesses, Olga and Tatiana, came and looked quite charming and so pretty in little ermine hats with white ospreys in them and little low-necked rose-coloured frocks and ermine furs and muffs. Olga is the prettiest and is really lovely I thought, and so jolly-looking and natural ... All our embassy were there in full fig, and all the attachés and secretaries we used to dance with made us roar – all covered in gold lace and things.

Sir George Buchanan [the British Ambassador] looked very well, but she is fat and rather common-looking though good at her job. The Empress smiled so sweetly and Marie Pavolva [her sister-in-law] came up to me and talked and a strange and very beautiful Russian seized me by the hand though I can't remember who he is and said '*Zdrazwoite* Sister'. When she had been all round we went into the big hall to be photographed and dear old Colonel Fenton, who had on nearly all the medals in the world, seized me by the arm and said, '*Là – au pied de l'Impératrice*' and pushed me down, so I have come out larger than life, leaning against her knee. Then she and the two princesses departed and the rest of us went back and had the dickens of a tea off the hired gold plate!

Colonel Fenton rushed forward at the last minute and pinned the Order of the White Elephant of Siam on my chest, only Matron said much as she would like it in the group photograph she feared the Siamese Embassy would make trouble.

Other of my mother's images stuck in my mind: a visit from the Princess Anastasia who was rumoured to have escaped the subsequent massacre of the royal family – 'a little girl with her hair down her back and an Alice in Wonderland comb' – and a distressing incident when my mother was caring for a young soldier from Siberia whose legs had been amputated. His father travelled 1,000 miles to see him but when he saw Vassili lying outside his bed with his stumps on a pillow, the old man started to shout, the tears coursing down his cheeks. The interpreter explained that he was cursing the boy – why hadn't he died? Then they would have been given a small pension. Now, just look at him, another mouth to feed and they were nearly starving.

My mother remembered the historic night when the Crown Prince Dimitri burst into the hospital, his former palace, with Prince Feliks Yusipov, an effete aristocrat married to the Tsar's niece. They were in such a hysterical state that the doctors thought they were drunk, until they noticed the blood. They had just murdered Rasputin.

The drunken, dissolute Gregory Yefimovich Rasputin, revered by some as a mystic holy man, and reviled by others as a holy devil, dominated the Tsarina because of the powers which healed her son, the Tsarevich, who was a haemophiliac. Rasputin outraged the court by kissing the hands of the Tsar and Tsarina, an intolerable intimacy. The nobility were shocked even more when the Tsar and Tsarina kissed Rasputin's hand in return, and he called them Mama and Papa. Regarding him as a danger to the future of Russia, influencing government policies through his hold over the Tsarina, a group of noblemen determined to rid Russia of this dangerous monk.

I had dinner with Baroness Budberg (the mistress of Gorky,

Bruce Lockhart and H.G. Wells), who was one of the guests at Yusipov's palace on the night of 29 December 1916. To my bitter disappointment she was slightly drunk and recounted the events flatly: Rasputin was offered poisoned cakes and ate them without apparent effect, possibly because he had immunized himself with small amounts of arsenic taken over the previous months. Then one of the conspirators shot him, but to their horror Rasputin stumbled out of the house still miraculously alive. Catching him, he was shot a second time and finally pushed down a hole in the ice of the River Neva. When my father was taken there the next morning, he saw the scratches where Rasputin struggled to get out before he drowned.

Meanwhile, Dimitri had left for his estate in the Caucasus while Yusipov disappeared.

The Empress, known contemptuously as 'that German woman', ordered that Rasputin should be buried in the grounds of her palace at Tsarsko Selo, while the Tsar, who was said to have expressed his relief privately, placed Dimitri under arrest, even though he was his favourite nephew – 'I am ashamed before Russia that the hands of my relations should be smeared with the blood of this peasant.'

Years later in Cairo, my father tried to cajole Dimitri into revealing who had fired the first shot, but the Grand Duke was adamant in his refusal, having made a pledge with Yusipov that neither would tell the truth.

After being exiled to one of his country estates, Yusipov made his way to the West, while Dimitri joined the British Army as an officer in the cavalry. 'Being exiled to the Caucasus was the one thing that saved my life,' he told my father. 'If I had been in Petrograd, I would have been murdered. When the Revolution came I managed to escape – and here I am!' He settled in England, married an American heiress, and led a carefree, guilt-free life.

Back in Russia, Rasputin's forecast to the Tsarina, that if he was killed by members of her family, her own family would die within two years, was fulfilled.

As we left the monastery and caught a crowded bus back into town, the growling thunder fulfilled its threat and the rain belted down. Luckily, when we had to get out, we were able to splash across the muddy pavement into an elegant shop which sold crafts – the only one that I saw in Russia. To my annoyance James bought a small tin head of Gagarin, and a hooded Hero of the Soviet Union, which proved to be the last. I assumed, wrongly, that such things would be abundant in towns like Volgograd but this was too logical. Vladimir discovered that there was a tea-shop opposite called the Fantastica and though it came as no surprise that the tea was 'off' we had a reasonable cup of coffee and an excellent vanilla ice-cream with a hint of honey on the top. 'The best meal I've had in Russia,' said James. 'It reminds me of school.' Vladimir and I echoed 'Fantastica', which became a new byword. After the alleged food on the *Pipkin*, it was understandable that our 'tea' seemed the height of luxury, but I yearned for apples and melons, and now that the rain had stopped I persuaded the others to cross the main square where I noticed several ample *babushkas* selling gladioli.

'Where there are flowers, fruit must be close behind!'

James reminded me that I was in Russia, but I was right, for one *babushka* did sell several tiny, sour, pock-marked apples. Then through some wooden gates behind her I discovered a large market, which sold the remnants of more apples, wild mushrooms, even a few tomatoes and some rough-looking pears which proved delicious. From this point, every market became richer in choice the further south we sailed.

Vladimir forbade me to buy a round, green melon of the type I enjoy at home, rejecting a perfect small water-melon for one which was so huge he could hardly carry it, after beating the man down from 25 roubles to 17.

The official rate was approximately 54 roubles to the pound. At this stage I had no Russian currency with me, for James was contributing the 3,000 roubles he had received in Moscow for arranging the art exhibition, which sounded a fortune until

I calculated that it was less than 100 dollars. Yet that *was* a fortune here. Even a top official earned 300 dollars a month. When James handed over 80 roubles on the *Pipkin*, to cover the day's breakfast, lunch and dinner for us and Vladimir, plus our small but precious bottle of Cognac, it was less than two pounds, yet a week's salary for many of those on board. This was a salutary lesson, warning me not to be ostentatious with our occasional tin of sardines and our Cognac when there was no such extravagance on the part of the other passengers. Even in Moscow, vodka was rationed to one bottle a month with two packets of cigarettes, though this was largely ignored.

I realized gradually that for many of the passengers on the *Pipkin*, this was a luxury cruise simply because they were getting away from the monotony they were used to. This accounted for the constant change of clothes, with the older men sporting rows of medals. I was startled at first by the quantity of one-armed men until I realized that the same man was reappearing in different outfits. He was married to the malevolent woman who wore a false, bright red hair-piece bordered by her own grey hair, as bizarre a top-knot as I had ever seen.

The *Pipkin* sailed from Kostroma at seven and we raced back with the panic of passengers who fear they might be left behind. Once we were on board, Vladimir retired to his cabin to listen to his radio while I lay down on my bunk and struggled with the interminable suffering of Sholokhov's *And Quiet Flows the Don*, a book I began to hate.

The day had been invigorating, but Vladimir was no longer bright-eyed when we sat down for dinner.

'Is anything the matter?' I asked.

'I heard announcement on radio,' he confided grimly. 'They say Gorbachev is ill, but I do not think so. It is all confusing but I think he has been overthrown by the Politburo. It is finished.' Even he pushed his plate away, his food scarcely touched and he gave a great sigh. 'From now on, dictatorship again.'

The Kapitan might have been bluffing when he threatened to report us to the KGB, but he now had the incentive to do so.

CHAPTER FIVE

Rumbles of Revolution

OVER breakfast, Vladimir relayed the latest news from Moscow, gleaned on his radio though not repeated on the ship's loud-speaker. We could only guess at the truth: was Gorbachev dead? It seemed likely. Vladimir told us quietly that tanks were on the streets, presumably as a warning against any demonstration in support of Gorbachev, though there was no way of knowing.

News continued to filter through, thanks to Vladimir – otherwise we would have been sailing in limbo. As it was, I had a pronounced and eerie sense of *déjà vu*. My father witnessed the Kerensky Revolution in 1917 and I had been present in Red Square when the first crack appeared in Gorbachev's authority in 1990, the previous year.

My father revelled in the life of St Petersburg when he came there as a young man to sell munitions at the start of the war.

I am not so sure it did not provide the perfect life all around. Englishmen who were born in Russia declared it was the finest life in all the world. There must be many whose life has been spoiled by having known Romanov Russia, yet I think that a certain comradeship was established ... we have passed through one of the greatest experiences that life could offer a man.

At first it was all gaiety: nights at the Maryinsky Theatre, heated discussions with his friend John Reed, love affairs with Russian beauties, picnics with champagne, caviare blinis, and balalaikas – then a

> summer of dejection [from his failure to sell his munitions], with deliberate dissipation as an antidote. In the summer of 1915 I don't think I ever went to bed before six o'clock in the morning. I know I saw every sunrise ...

At the same time, he heard the first rumbles of revolution, stirred by Alexander Kerensky, a moderate Socialist who became the provisional premier in February 1917. This was effectively the first Russian Revolution, though his subsequent vacillation led to his overthrow by Lenin in November and his total eclipse. Over lunch at the London Carlton Grill in 1933, Kerensky assured my father, Bruce Lockhart and Alexander Woollcott that he would return, infuriated by the New Yorker's sceptical witticisms regarding Communist Russia which he thought of as a tragedy. He died a forgotten man in America.

The Kerensky Revolution gathered momentum on 4 November 1916 when he addressed the Duma, the representative parliament established after the earlier, abortive revolution of 1905. Kerensky declared that the main enemy was not at the front but here 'in our midst. There is no salvation for our country until, with a unanimous and concerted effort, we force the removal of those who ruin, humiliate and insult it.'

Though reproached by the chairman for this open rebellion, Kerensky concluded with the first intimation of a coup: 'You must annihilate the authority of those who do not acknowledge their duty.' His warnings were strengthened by economic hardship and the queues for food which grew in 1916, in a striking parallel to the events in the early 1990s: 'the streets of Petrograd and Moscow presented not only pitiable but frightening signs of privation and starvation. There were queues around each provision shop that sometimes encircled the whole block in which it stood.'

In October 1916 the Ministry of the Interior warned of the

strong threat of the relentless approach of great turbulence explainable exclusively by economic factors: hunger, the unequal distribution of food and articles of prime necessity, and the monstrous rise in prices. This movement needs only to take a concrete form to find expression in some specific act (a pogrom, a large-scale strike, a major clash between the lower strata of the population and the police) to assume at once, absolutely, a purely political aspect.

Exasperated by the Tsar's reactionary policies and the reverses suffered by the Russian army in the war against Germany, the workers seized Petrograd early in 1917 and the Duma defied the Tsar's order to dissolve. In February 1917 my father had his usual luck in being there at the right moment, when the movement erupted. He had gone to see the American Consul, North Winship, and looked down at the crowds collecting in the streets. They were used to this, and to the Don Cossacks who usually charged the demonstrators.

'But look,' said Winship, 'the Cossacks are *laughing!*'

They were actually leaning down and talking peacefully to the people, waving to each other with their *naigaikas*, the little whips tipped with steel that could cut a man's face open like a knife.

'This is the Revolution,' said my father, 'this is it.' At first the crowd did not know what to do: 'It was like watching some savage beast that has broken out of its cage and did not yet know where to go; it might head for anybody – it might make for you.' Later he saw a detachment of the élite Uhlans galloping down the Nevskoye,

their lances pointed like a row of bayonets. Their momentum carried them through the crowd, and their wake was a scatter of black shapes rolling about in snow. Whether anyone died as the result of this charge I do not know. At the last instant I had seen the Uhlans throw up their lances ... but the mere impact of a horse at that speed would be enough itself to kill

... I saw people rising to their feet screaming and shaking their fists at the Uhlans, who were reforming to charge them again. And at that moment a tram conductor tried to drive his tram through the mob. I believe he was the first person killed in the Kerensky Revolution; for an instant that tram was buried under a mass of shrieking people, then the tram conductor was dragged out and beaten to death with his own brake-bar.

That night the officers and policemen, the chief victims of the Revolution, were hunted out and murdered: 'The first hysterical reaction to the sudden freedom from this terror of the Romanovs was this eight-day frenzy of revengeful murder in Petrograd. The police, as symbols of Tsarist oppression, were naturally the first victims. Then, as each regiment mutinied, it usually killed its officers.'

As he met some British sailors off a submarine, they told him they had seen an old colonel walking down the street, his hands pressed in prayer – 'and walking behind him was a sailor with a cutlass. While we were looking and before we could stop him, the sailor took a swing and cut the poor old blighter's skull wide open.'

My father became embroiled in an argument between a crowd of workers and a massive guardsman who was abusing them. 'You want ten roubles a day for eight hours' work, do you? And our soldiers are to work twenty-four hours a day in the trenches for seventy-five kopeks a month. Boorjoie! Capitalists! Go back to your factories.'

The young men, who actually carried a flag with the skull and crossbones and the words 'WELCOME ANARCHY', snarled in response, while my father cried '*Horosho!*' (Good!) in support. He found himself looking straight into the muzzles of about forty rifles.

Cr-u-ump. The big soldier fell away from my hand. I was still holding it up where his back had been – and then he lay sprawled at my feet. The big guardsman, for whom I now felt a strange sense of personal responsibility, was quite dead. A bruised hole under his hair was enough to show that, without having the evidence of those pinkish brains, like sweetbreads, oozing out of the back of his skull. I lost no time in getting out of that street and found to my astonishment that the Nevsky was empty. I could see the 'gunmen' retreating in confusion, obviously appalled by what they had done.

After the Tsar's abdication, Kerensky held power for seven months between the two revolutions, increasingly torn between the right, represented by the army, and the left, led by Lenin. My father saw Lenin on a raised platform across the River Neva and described him as a short, dumpy figure, with an enormous dome of a head, high cheekbones giving a sinister contemptuousness to his Tartar eyes.

The great Lenin! But he was not 'great' to any but a very few people then. He was just this undersized new agitator in an old double-breasted suit, his hands in his pockets, speaking with an entire absence of that hysterical arm-waving that so characterized all his fellow countrymen.

'Yes,' he was saying, 'it is the Capitalists and our diplomats who make wars. Not the people. They get rich, we get killed. You left the soil and the factories to go to war, and when war is over – what? You will go back to the soil and the factories to work under the capitalist system again – those of you who are left alive. What do you get from war? Wounds, suffering and death.'

John Reed hurried to my father after seeing Lenin for the first time. 'His eyes were still half-blinded, as if he had seen a vision, as if he had seen God!' He told my father, 'The next time you hear the machine guns, old boy, you put on a red necktie. It's going to be the only safe colour in Petrograd. And this time it will be a real Revolution.'

There used to be two May Days in Moscow. The famous military parade took place on the 9th; but this was preceded on the 1st by an innocent celebration with gymnastic girls in skimpy skirts twirling hoops.

This was not the case on my first visit on 1 May 1990, the year before my journey to the Caucasus as James – who was with me then too – and I learnt when we joined the crowds surging towards Red Square. After being stopped constantly by the militia, I saw a procession with jolly flags and a priest carrying a banner with the crucified Christ, heading up the hill. Running ahead to take photographs, we were caught up and swept into the square, where the procession halted opposite Lenin's tomb with Gorbachev among the leaders on the poduim, unmistakable in a grey hat. This was everything I hoped for – except that it was not a procession: we were in the middle of a demonstration. Keeping us isolated were lines of plain-clothes police who stared at us with unconcealed hatred as the demonstration exploded. A man with a loudspeaker, his face contorted, shouted obvious abuse at the Soviet leader, while another led the rest in a chant of support, louder and fiercer every time. For several alarming though thrilling moments, it seemed there must be violence and I turned to James with a shrug as if to say, 'If anyone throws a firework, there is nothing we can do.'

A woman beside me clutched her ears against the noise. The nervous young policeman facing me developed a tic, his cheeks fluttering like the wings of a small bird. All the time Red Square reverberated with the din of martial music intended to enhance the occasion. A man near by, plainly not one of the demonstrators, was shaking his head, and I asked if he spoke English. Haltingly, he explained, 'They are shouting for freedom – they are telling "Gorbachev resign." There has been nothing in our history like it.' He wiped his face with his glove. Throughout, the most powerful men in Russia watched us from the podium only yards away. Suddenly Gorbachev's patience snapped and he drummed his fingers on the ledge as a signal to leave. The leaders descended the steps and disappeared. I learnt later that Gorbachev had given orders that there should be no violence, but this had been a shocking insult to his authority. The outside world recognized this at once, amazed by the newsreel film of the few who had dared attack the President. The first crack had appeared.

*

And now a year later we had the coup.

'Yeltsin has demanded permanent strike,' Vladimir told us at lunch, after sifting through our dictionary with startling speed.

'If the army arrest Yeltsin,' I asked, 'and Red Square is filled with his supporters, will they be fired on or will the soldiers desert?'

Vladimir shrugged; he could hardly do otherwise. James and I argued, though we did so calmly. This was not the moment to fall out. James claimed there would not be a civil war in Moscow until the people started to eat their cats and dogs. I reminded him, romantically, of Poland, Hungary and Czechoslovakia where the first giddy taste of freedom could not be denied.

'Once the impossible becomes a hope, there is no stopping it,' I said pontifically.

'The Russians are not like the Eastern Europeans,' he corrected me. 'They are masochists.'

'For someone in love with Russia, you're very critical!' I observed, remembering the massacre in Tbilisi in 1989. 'The Republics are obsessed by nationalism. They have the madness of martyrs and will die for independence.'

James sighed. 'You never understand.'

All the while, the passengers on the *Pipkin* munched their food without a change in their expression.

'Don't they *know*?' I whispered to Vladimir.

'Oh yes,' he replied sarcastically. 'They *know*. This is what they wanted. To go back.'

CHAPTER SIX

'Where is our President?'

THE *Pipkin* sailed on, cocooned in her complacency, impervious to the turbulence outside. The discrepancy had the unreality of a dream, especially as the *Pipkin* began to assume a homely air in her neutrality. Walking around the deck I noticed that several of the cabins had flowers, and James put the metal head of Gagarin on his bedside table. Probably due to the food, he had developed a stye in one eye, in spite of taking a multi-purpose vitamin after a nasty experience on a previous visit when he returned to the Hotel Ukraine and discovered he had haemorrhaged, his underpants thick with blood. I was armed with the inevitable vitamin B 12 used by heavy drinkers, though hardly needed on the dry ship *Pipkin* where the only problem with alcohol was finding it, apart from our nightly Cognac which amounted to only a couple of glassfuls each. In addition, I had brought cod-liver oil capsules, garlic perles, and fizzy Redoxin Vitamin C with a blackcurrant flavour. And due to my enforced diet at mealtimes and the absence of a bar, I felt surprisingly fit.

Seagulls joined us as the Volga widened. We had glimpses of small beaches like those my father swam from when the water was clean. The smaller Oka River, down which he had sailed, joined us at Nijni Novgorod, though the Kapitan referred to the town as Gorky on the loudspeaker. It was here that the passengers on the *Thanks* cried out 'Volga, Volga' as the rivers swirled together, but there was no such emotion on board the *Pipkin*. At times, looking at those stern faces, I felt that no one disliked Russia more than the Russians.

Today Nijni is a large industrial town, deserted on the eastern side where the steppes stretch infinitely towards Siberia, for this is the traditional borderline between Europe and Asia. From a high point in the town, I looked out to the other side on to – *nothing*.

That night, I saw the lights of a long, lit-up cruise ship and asked Vladimir if it was 'touristic'.

'For excursions, bar, music, disco,' he agreed.

I looked across enviously as we passed and then felt a pang of betrayal towards the poorer *Pipkin*. Familiarity was making me possessive: the plastic carnation posing as a flower; the lifeless condom in the communal shower – these were hardly a few of my favourite things but I was becoming used to them. I looked forward to that shower, in spite of the human detritus, whenever I had the luck to discover the lady with the key, undressing quickly only to find that the hot water had run out.

Back in London I learnt that James Butterwick's friend, Dr Mikhail, had indeed travelled de luxe on the *Kirov*, recently built in Germany and run by the Swiss, which sailed from St Petersburg to Moscow. Every cabin was endowed with a private shower and air-conditioning and even a refrigerator; the 'public facilities' included bars in the plural, lounges, a sauna, clinic, shop and restaurant. No wonder that Dr Mikhail found nothing to complain about. A 'clinic' seemed superfluous in such comfort, though it would have been invaluable on the *Pipkin*.

Surprisingly, we had yet to sail south, but, as I had hoped, the Volga became more interesting. There was a sweep of chocolate water lined by green hillocks and trees on the European side, with low land opposite. At times it was possible to imagine that we were cruising down the coast of Turkey, for any distant shoreline is deceptive. There was a refreshing lack of building, with the occasional glimpse of a tent hiding among the trees above a yellow sandbar, or a small settlement of *dachas* on stilts painted in mustard, dark blue and darker green, with pointed Dutch-style roofs, backed by firs. Huntsmen lived outside the Soviet system in these woods, trapping and fishing for survival, and were known as 'trolls'. As the sun set, I was elated by the sight of the faded splendour of a long, low-lying white monastery which stretched to the water's edge, recognizing it as the 'Dead Monastery' photographed by my father in 1929. That it was still there was reassuring.

At dinner, Vladimir was alarmingly silent as he looked at the impassive passengers at the end of the second sitting. After they left, he told us, 'The news is now very bad. There is state of emergency and curfew in Moscow. Now all Russia is quiet, waiting.' He paused: 'The West has been accused of making trouble. This could be bad with the Kapitan and you.'

It meant, also, that Vladimir was courageous in remaining loyal.

'He is putting his head on the block by being with us,' said James, and we feared for his safety on the journey back, although he had a street-wise sense of survival. Vladimir added that President Bush and Prime Minister Major urged the new regime to continue with reform, though this seemed unlikely if the military had taken over.

The news of the coup was shocking. I had not appreciated that it was inevitable after the leaders opposed Gorbachev's Union Treaty which they believed would spell the end of the Soviet Union. It had been due to be signed with the Republics on 20 August. I had lost all sense of time, but this was the 20th, so they had acted promptly as soon as they knew of Gorbachev's intentions, having bugged his meeting with Yeltsin and the President of Kazakhstan, using his own chief of the KGB to do so. With fatal optimism, Gorbachev had emerged from that meeting declaring, 'It's a great feeling, like climbing Everest.' Now, it seemed that he had fallen off. James and I reconsidered our plans, unaware that the British Government had advised all Westerners to leave at once if they were able to do so. Roy Miles, who blazed the way in the art world by bringing contemporary Russian art to his gallery in London, flew into Moscow on the Monday of the coup and flew out again that evening. Perversely, I ached to be in the thick of it with my camera, though in retrospect it was a unique moment to be sailing down the Volga.

Thinking aloud is a dangerous practice. I made the mistake of producing my map and telling James that we might be able to fly direct from Volgograd to Tbilisi without continuing to Baku. The moment I said this I regretted it, for our earlier plan to sail to Astrakhan and take the train along the Caspian had been dashed by the alleged outbreak of cholera, and I had no wish to compromise our journey again, but James seized on the idea, repeating, 'I have no wish to put my own head on the block,' a phrase he was warming to. I backtracked ineffectually, assuring him that the civil war in Baku was unlikely to be aggravated by the events in Moscow, for the Azerbaijans were preoccupied with the Armenians and their rival claims to Nagorni Karabakh.

'If there are tanks on the streets of Tbilisi, there is just as likely to be trouble there,' which was hardly reassuring as we were due to go to Tbilisi anyhow.

As a fatalist, I told James the parable of the wealthy merchant who went into the market square and recognized the figure of Death staring at him intently. Appalled, he hurried home to tell his servant that he was leaving for Samara. Later in the day, the servant went down to the market himself and, seeing the figure of Death, he asked him why he had frightened his master. 'I was surprised to see him here,' Death replied, 'for I have an appointment with him in Samara.'

'In other words,' said James, unimpressed by my showing off, 'if our card is marked there's nothing we can do about it.'

'Exactly.'

James remained unconvinced, suspecting that I was determined to lead us into the firing line, which was true. Partly to irritate, I continued with Sandy Powell's story of the old man who goes to his doctor and announces that he is about to marry a beautiful girl of twenty. The doctor looks alarmed: 'You realise this could be fatal?' 'Oh well,' says the old man airily, 'if she dies, she dies.'

James, who is half my age, had no intention of dying yet but regretted he had not made his will. I suggested we write official letters home and exchange them: 'After all, it is most unlikely that *both* of us will be shot.' It must have been the food: he was looking paler and the stye was worse.

Finally, after further discussion, James and I agreed to chance our luck and stay on course for Baku as planned.

I woke early on the Wednesday morning of 21 August. Kazan was our next port of call. Routine is all-important on a river boat, starting with 'ablutions', which is not a word that springs to my mind in England. It was difficult to sleep after five, due to the banging of cabin doors and the loudspeaker announcements – more concentration than holiday camp – though I managed to lower the volume by twisting a screw with the point of my indispensable serrated knife from Boots, as valued a companion as my all-fitting bath plug, towel, and small soap-box purloined from the Mamounia in Marrakesh where I had stayed overnight as a journalistic 'guest' earlier in the year. I wished I had brought toilet water to make me feel fresher and was tempted to open Miss Dior's Eau de Cologne which I brought as a present for Yuri's girlfriend.

After my vitamin pills and a sachet of Resolve, I felt strong enough to brave the communal lavatory and emerged on deck, where I found three burly Russian men in skimpy briefs performing exercises on the portion of the bow which passed itself off as a sun deck. They could have been averting the daily deterioration caused by the diet but I suspected from their glum expressions that they were fitness fanatics. The wind was fierce, whipping streaks of white foam on the brown Volga; it was invigorating as I took my morning promenade, pausing when I heard the sweet sound of someone playing a lute in their cabin. After collecting my excellent plastic mug, one of the few instances where plastic is practical, I descended to the lower depths for boiling water from the tap and returned to my cabin to spread out my map to see exactly where we were. Finding the latitudes, I understood why the weather was so autumnal in late August, for we had sailed east and were still on a level with Warsaw. We would turn south at Kazan and after that the days should become hotter, unless they too defied all logic.

I was looking forward to landing at Kazan with the treat of three and a half hours on shore. Apart from offering the possibility of learning more about the coup, Kazan marked the westernmost fringe of the Tartar conquest, the main destination of the Golden Hordes led by Genghis Khan from Mongolia. Though an industrial city today, it was noted once for the university founded in 1804 attended by Tolstoy at the age of sixteen in 1844 when Kazan was a lively town with a population of 30,000. After studying oriental languages for a year, he turned to law. The white university building was beautiful, with a green roof and golden cupola, but A.N. Wilson reveals in his brilliant biography of Tolstoy – and how I wish it had been my travelling companion instead of the wearisome *And Quiet Flows the Don* – that educationally the university was closer to Dotheboys Hall, run on the principles of Mr Squeers. Lenin studied there too, until he was sent down for taking part in a demonstration against the University Inspector in 1887.

We docked at ten thirty. Unaware that Kazan was still the Tartar capital, with two separate languages, I was startled to see the names of Kazan in huge lettering in both Russian and Tartar above the landing stage. The 'Tartar capital' promised romance but the modern city proved depressing, with the usual dereliction and disinterest, unwashed buses bumping over pot-holes, buildings abandoned and left to die – though a few showed traces of former splendour. The massive main road was lined with modern buildings of no virtue and dust flew in the faces of people who looked exhausted enough without this further aggravation. They were dressed wretchedly, often bearing the scars of beatings-up, and when Vladimir asked the way they continued without answering. Unlovable, probably unloved. It is wrong to judge a city by its outskirts but though London's suburbs make me deeply despondent, it occurred to me that a Russian would welcome the garish conformity of a suburban high street and regard our supermarkets with their infinite variety as nirvana. Even so, Kazan's outskirts were exceptionally unalluring.

The city perked up the further we went. After a dutiful visit to a Tartar mosque, the first mosque Vladimir had seen, in an attractive street with low, wooden houses, we continued to a church of unexpected charm, Dutch or German in style, decorated on the outside with garlands of fruit and flowers in cheerful contrast to the oppressive ornamentation of the Orthodox churches laden with gilt. After this proof of past splendour we returned to the present with queues stretching everywhere – though at least there were objects to queue for. The covered market was richer than those at any of the previous river ports, with marble counters and shops along the side where smiling *babushkas* sold such luxuries as jars of honey and even a glass of fresh goat's milk which I downed on the spot to avert impending malnutrition on the *Pipkin*. Peasant women walked through the aisles with a shopping basket suspended at either end of a wooden yoke which they bore on their shoulders like oxen, the best way to balance the weight more evenly.

In the busy street outside we entered a dark bar where a man lay prone on the floor due to a surfeit of vodka, ignored by the silent queue around him. Then Vladimir led us eagerly to a record shop crowded with teenagers, a faded poster of the Beatles above the counter, flanked by one of Pink Floyd.

How different those Volga ports were: at Uglich we saw the gilded Church of St Demetrius but there seemed to be little more; Yaroslav might have been abandoned due to plague; but as we neared the centre of Kazan it was seething with people as if we were in the wake of a big parade. An atmosphere of tense excitement was almost tangible and the reason soon became clear – the coup. People were asking each other what was happening in the hope that someone might have inside information.

Soon we had to squeeze our way through the crowds outside the office of a newspaper where they tried to get close enough to read the latest news on handwritten placards pinned up beside blown-up portraits of Gorbachev and Yeltsin. It was encouraging to find such a sign of support. Vladimir dived into the scrum and returned a few minutes later: 'Everyone is asking, "Where is our President?", "Is he alive?", "What is happening to us?"' adding that one of the news sheets revealed that Yeltsin had branded the new regime as 'criminal'. Caught up in the crisis, I had the advantage of a different viewpoint denied to the press corps in Moscow. This was a bizarre moment to be sailing down the Volga.

Unsure if the *Pipkin* would be leaving early, having arrived early, we hurried back, through the park, which looked even more dejected than the buildings. I averted my eyes as a silly little dog trotted through the traffic, expecting it to be hit at any moment, but it managed to join a sad, youngish man with lank receding hair and brick-red complexion who squatted miserably on the weary grass, and patted it. He called out to ask the time but Vladimir had neither a watch nor time to spare. Anxious that the man should befriend the dog which he was leading into a copse – surely not to eat it? – I resisted the impulse to run back and give him a packet of Marlboro for the dog's sake if not his own, in the hope that he would feed it. Yet, if I pointed to the dog he might have given it to me in exchange. Beware of pity; it causes so much harm.

The *Pipkin* was waiting, due to sail at the appointed time, and I changed from my sticky clothes. I was interrupted by a sharp knock on my cabin door. When I opened it, I was confronted by a smartly suited young man and three impassive colleagues behind him. He studied me intently as I struggled into a clean shirt and he shoved an identification card in my face. This was it! The KGB. At least he had the courtesy to say '*Strasvitye*' (the Russian greeting) followed by a demand for 'documents'. Even in the chaos of my tiny cabin, I found my passport at once and blessed James Butterwick for his foresight in obtaining visas for every port we stopped at, including Kazan. The KGB man seemed to recognize the visa, though he turned the pages of the passport with the usual incomprehension. I hoped my frequent visits to Turkey would not strike him as suspicious, though I doubted if he could read the visas.

While he examined my documents, even turning them upside down, I examined my position: presumably the crazed Kapitan had radioed ahead asking that the two British passengers should be interrogated to discover what they were doing on his ship. By now it was becoming obvious that he regarded us as spies.

Smiling graciously throughout, I produced my jar of honey from a carrier bag and placed it conspicuously on the table in order to show the innocence of my time on shore. The KGB man hesitated. Then with an emphatic gesture he handed the passport back, barked some instructions, and left with the other unsmiling men. For a moment I wondered if everyone on board had had their papers checked, but I doubted it and this was confirmed by James. He suggested that the Kapitan had reported us in order to protect himself. He had just seen the first mate, who had glared at him – 'If looks could kill!' – and Vladimir said my suspicion was correct: 'The passengers ask me if you are Western spies.' As we had behaved impeccably, I did not feel the usual guilt of the innocent when involved with the police, but James shattered this illusion.

'Innocence has nothing to do with anything in Russia. I've had other brushes with the KGB,' he added surprisingly, 'but never in such terrifying circumstances as this. Now they are bound to deport us from Volgograd.'

When I referred to my harmless jar of honey, he shook his head pityingly. 'That will really make them think you're up to something, like showing your wretched articles to the captain. Nothing is that straightforward in Russia. Have you asked yourself how they knew we would be in our cabins at that moment? And did you notice that the fourth man was the *Pipkin*'s "sailor" who flirts with our waitress? That's rather nasty.'

'You mean he's a spy?'

That way lay paranoia, and I pointed out that the KGB

could have looked for us earlier and waited for our return. Also, it would be natural for a member of the crew to show them to our cabins.

'I think James is nervous, yes?' smiled Vladimir.

'Decidedly,' I agreed.

'Absolutely,' said James.

As a distraction, I produced my last bag of Maltesers and offered one to Nina, the more attractive waitress, and mimed to James aghast when she withdrew her hand.

'I noticed,' he whispered, after she had gone. 'Her hands are covered with sores. She wouldn't be allowed to wait on table in England.'

'Not *that*,' I exclaimed impatiently. 'She's taken the lot!'

To our considerable relief, the *Pipkin* sailed from Kazan after a ten-minute delay which set me wondering if the KGB were deciding if they should take us into custody. After that, the lunch was almost bearable: little bowls of grated carrot sprinkled with sugar, and over-ripe tomatoes with tinned sour cream, followed by a sort of soup and a piece of meat that posed unsuccessfully as steak, defying my serrated knife. We finished with white grapes and apples which Vladimir had bought for us in Kazan. Possibly in return for the last of the Maltesers, the waitress whispered to Vladimir that twenty bottles of beer had been smuggled on board. At once we bought twelve and I dared to ask if she could keep them in the fridge which I noticed in the galley. Incredibly, she had done so already, so the meal ended in triumph as we toasted the KGB. We were still ignored by the passengers after several days. Now the *Pipkin* thrust her way south through the rain and the Volga widened so dramatically that we might have been at sea with just a glimmer of land on either side, and we had the luxury of chilled beer.

The Volga might have widened but my cabin seemed to have narrowed. For a moment I thought I was hallucinating, that the entire journey was a figment of my fuddled imagination, until I realized that a very large lady who had boarded the *Pipkin* at Kazan had moved into the adjacent cabin and every time she leant against the dividing partition, which she did with all her bulk, the wall buckled and my ledge narrowed.

On an impulse I took my Mars Bar tin and looked for the jovial woman and her son who joined our table at the beginning until they were driven away by the food and now cooked for themselves in their cabin. There was only one Mars Bar left (except for another I had kept to give me energy for the Klukhor Pass) but the box itself had a combination like a small safe which I thought might amuse the boy. I was disappointed that the simple slogan – 'A Mars a day helps you work, rest and play' – had been changed to 'Working together, helping others to work, rest and play', which sounded positively Communistic. They seemed delighted when I handed the box over and a few minutes later there was another knock on the cabin door, but this time it was the lady with the beaming boy who had brought me a present of a decorative wooden trowel which she had bought on shore. I could not imagine its purpose but accepted it gratefully. There were now three passengers who liked us.

My state of well-being was short-lived. We reached the next port of Ulianovsk at eleven that evening and as there was only a thirty-minute stop we did not bother to go ashore. Instead, the KGB came on board to look for us and demand our papers. This time there was no courtesy: an unpleasant, slant-eyed official blustered and bullied us. While he interrogated James in the dining saloon the middle-aged lady who was acting as inter-preter whispered to me urgently, 'Things are bad in Moscow', and made the alarming gesture of slitting her throat. Then she turned away hastily before the squat man could see us. So this was not a mere formality: the coup did implicate us. Presum-ably all Westerners were suspect, especially on board the *Pipkin* where the Kapitan had declared our presence 'illegal'. It was fortunate that we had not gone ashore, for our visas did not include the small town of Ulianovsk. Otherwise they were in order and the KGB had to either arrest us on some pretext or let us continue, which they did reluctantly.

We sailed on, but this time I found the harassment unnerving. Was the Kapitan going to play this vindictive game at every stop? Did he realize that we were leaving the *Pipkin* in two days' time and would not be continuing to Astrakhan like Vladimir? A new dread was the possibility that he would place us under ship arrest, take us to Astrakhan and back again until we docked in Moscow where he would hand us over to the new authorities. I expressed my anger loudly in the dining-room for the benefit of any ship's spy who might be listening, in the belief that it was best to match Soviet bullying with steely English arrogance, but James was wiser in thinking that the less attention we drew to ourselves the better. Even so, the Russians were so used to submission that a vigorous retort on our part might have been unexpected, and fun.

'Life isn't like that,' he reminded me.

After my parable to James about the appointment in Samara, it was eerie to dock at Samara the following morning. It used to be known as Kuibyshev, which my father hated in the Second World War when he covered the Russian front for the London *Daily Mail*, though the foreign correspondents were kept as far away as possible. He described Kuibyshev as 'that stink-hole where the Russians, still not house-broken, stood on the seats of the toilets and where the floor of our one washplace (there was no running water in our rooms) was covered with human excrement.'

Managing to return to Moscow, he was ordered back to Kuibyshev on what he regarded as an official whim and refused to go, cabling his paper for his recall, which he duly achieved via Murmansk and the Arctic convoys, thoroughly disillusioned with Russia as well as Communism.

Having fallen in love with Russia in the days of the Tsar, and the Caucasus in 1929, my father had his last vestige of sentimentality destroyed when he was taken off the train halfway to Murmansk and found the small station crowded with NKVD – the secret police – with their own office where he heard the commandant mention his name, and that of his companion, an Australian journalist called Mac, on the telephone:

I have experienced various degrees of fright in my life, but this was something I had never known before and have never known since. It made our battering on the convoy, which was continuous from the afternoon after we left Murmansk until we got air-cover off the coast of Iceland, a mere joke by comparison. This was Terror.

It worsened in the afternoon when he saw a prison train for Russian political prisoners:

It made me sick with fear, for I thought that, by some incredible act at Moscow, I might soon be on one. Better people than I had been put away. There were about forty long red-painted box cars. And now I at once understood the reason why so many NKVD were about. They at once posted themselves at intervals the entire length of that train as it slowly came to a halt at the station. It remained there all day.

Projecting from between the two sliding doors at the centre of each car were what I at first thought were the tails of salmon or some other fish. They were not, of course. Approaching as close as the hostile backs of the NKVD would permit, I saw that each of these strange contraptions was a long V-trough made of two boards nailed together. They were the latrines for the poor wretches confined inside the dark cars. The only light that could possibly enter that long red box on wheels was through two little apertures high up at either end – eighteen-inch-square windows.

There were faces at these windows. Some of them opened their mouths and poked their fingers in them. This was the way they begged for food. From one or two of these ghastly squares with a sub-human face in it, a little canvas bag tied on a piece of string was hopefully lowered. No one came near them. No one looked at them. All day the faces remained at the windows: eyes that looked at passing life with a misery beyond description.

Why didn't the Russians look at that terrible prison train? In the old Tsarist days the Russian political prisoner, sent to Siberia, was regarded by almost everybody as a hero. He was marched through the streets to the long green train in broad daylight. His relations and friends could, in that way, see him off. There was a moment of glory in all that, brief as it was.

But today what happens? The prisoner is never seen. He vanishes from sight as quickly, and in most cases as finally, as a stone thrown overboard in mid-ocean. 'Forget him. Forget that he ever lived.' That is the Russian official advice to his relatives. They recommend you to exercise the psychology of forgetfulness.

A few nights later the commandant ran up shouting that they could leave on the train, 'Murmansk! Murmansk!' They needed no urging.

This disillusionment lay ahead in the evil days of Stalin's tyranny, worse even than Hitler's. In 1929 my father was still optimistic, though his initial buoyancy subsided slightly after the *Thanks* joined the Volga and they were transferred to a larger boat. 'We made no friends on this Volga boat. We, in the first-class, had passed out of the atmosphere of the friendly little paddle-wheeler on the Oka. That spell was broken.' Yet there were still moments of magic, with Asiatic horsemen racing the steamer with high pointed hats with the brims turned up and red leather boots with the toes curled up. He described how people shouted insults at them from the boat:

All was so gay! Down there in that mass, almost mess, of mixed peoples, the accordions were going all day long. Gorky's *Lower Depths* – or like the East End of London – with all the rich, lovable, stinking humanity that prevailed ... that is one memory I shall always carry with me from nearly five years in Russia. The deep, hopeful humanity of those river steamers – in those halcyon days of unimaginable freedom. (It was too good to be true, of course, yet no seer could have foreseen the grim aftermath.)

I read this again on my bunk, trying to keep abreast of our two contrasting journeys, reflecting on the coup which could prove the grimmest aftermath of all. The usual martial music blared from our loudspeakers as we sailed from Samara and I sympathized with the animals caged in the small zoo near the landing stage with disco music at full blast, their food probably stolen by the keepers as in other zoos in Russia. Poor, poor creatures!

At least there was no spectre of Death to greet me in the market place of Samara, nor, apparently, the KGB. Back in my cabin, I wondered if it was possible that they had decided to leave us alone. Then came the proverbial knock on the door – but this time it was Vladimir, grinning.

'Great news!' he cried. 'This is very important day. Now we have big changes.' He laughed with joy, as he revealed that Gorbachev was back in Moscow. 'This,' he announced, 'is the Second Russian Revolution!'

CHAPTER SEVEN

'The Englishman is Mad!'

APART from the personal relief at knowing we were safe from further investigation by the KGB it was glorious news that Gorbachev was free. With his genius for walking the tightrope and reaching the other side, I had dared to hope that this would be the outcome, unaware that he was finished as the Soviet leader. He had opened Pandora's box when he gave the Russians their freedom, with all the resentment that grows so paradoxically with independence. Not that the Russians were ever free, nor will they be; that is one of our misconceptions. Another reformer, Peter the Great, offered men a glass of vodka if they shaved their beards, and women a cup of coffee if they visited the galleries which displayed the art he brought back from the West, yet he had no qualms in ordering the death of every malformed child despite the pleas of the parents. It has always been '*Niet!*' in Russia, with the twin powers of the church and their negative commandments, and the Tsar's belief in the divine right of kings, followed by the oppression of Communism after that first hopeful decade from 1920 to 1930. If Gorbachev could have broken the mentality that craves for domination even if it takes the fiercest form of anarchy, he would have succeeded against the odds.

Vladimir was ecstatic with relief, yet disillusioning. 'Gorbachev makes one big mistake. He believes it is possible to reform Communism from the inside. It is impossible.' This proved remarkably perceptive. He had just heard the announcement on his radio that the leaders of the coup – a general, the head of the KGB and the new Prime Minister – had been arrested. 'These silly old men with their bulldog, Brezhnev faces,' he snorted. 'They deserve medals, for they have achieved more in three days than Gorbachev in three years. They are celebrating in Moscow, all over Russia, though not on *Pipkin!* You are lucky to be here at such a moment.'

At dinner I contributed a celebratory tin of anchovies, unearthed unexpectedly when I repacked one of my cases. Vladimir recoiled – 'too salty' – but they proved to be a favourite of James's and the sharp taste enhanced our squashed tomatoes. Our two beers were concealed on the floor after we learnt from the battered waitress, Lou, that one of the passengers informed on us to the Kapitan, for even a glass of beer is begrudged on the *Pipkin.* James tried to spot the informer, but it could have been anyone; they stared back unflinchingly. I asked Vladimir how the passengers had reacted to the news of the coup's failure, for they looked despondent; probably they were the very class who clung possessively to their minor perks which were now in jeopardy.

Vladimir shrugged. 'I think they do not believe that things will be better. In their heart they might have hope, but they do not believe. Remember they are slaves for seventy years, but now with the Second Revolution, maybe great changes.'

'Real change will take time,' said James cautiously, and I agreed. When a machine breaks down from corrosion it cannot be repaired overnight. Then I remembered the flare-up in Eastern Europe when one country after another caught fire and regained freedom in a matter of weeks. It was possible that great changes were taking place at that very moment.

Intoxicated by the news, our bottle of beer and nightly ration of Cognac, James and I started to fantasize, and Vladimir caught on quickly as we divulged our plans to liberate the small boy with the exaggerated gestures, Vladich, who befriended us when we boarded the *Pipkin* and had not been seen since, doubtless incarcerated on the bridge for helping the English spies. After we freed Vladich, we should arrest the mad Kapitan and Vladimir would replace him. He would make reassuring announcements on the loudspeaker to the passengers as we changed direction and sailed south-west to Rostov into the Black Sea – 'The Volga is now *very* wide!' Istanbul would pass for Astrakhan – 'You will notice the Ottoman influence on the skyline' – and James and I would go on shore, returning with delicious food and drink for the passengers, getting them so paralysed on *raki* that they would finally lose their senses and assume the Suez Canal is the Volga–Moscow canal on the return journey. It would be only when we sailed across the Indian Ocean to New Zealand that the Russians would find it surprisingly hot and start to ask questions. As they lived in a constant state of charade anyhow, believing every loudspeaker announcement fed to them, our fantasy contained a hideous truth.

'The *Pipkin* will be famous!' cried Vladimir. 'The *Potemkin* – the *Aurora* – the *Pipkin*!' To find a Russian who shared our surrealist sense of humour was miraculous. The last passengers left the saloon with stern faces, and Lou looked at us baffled, but she had been good to us in her way, allowing us to linger, and we rewarded her with Marlboro. I was fortunate to travel with two companions who appreciated the absurd.

At eleven thirty in the evening we docked for ten minutes at the small town of Khyalynsk, which is famous for its apples, and sure enough a circle of well-wrapped *babushkas* with baskets of apples crouched in the gentle rain on the landing stage. Motionless, they might have been the cast of an opera waiting for the curtain to rise and spring into action, as they did when the first passengers scampered down the gangway and started to bargain. This was how I had imagined the voyage throughout, with peasants selling their wares as they did to my father.

'This would not have been allowed ten years ago,' James reminded me, for I had forgotten that Communism had stamped out such initiative as my father had seen when he sailed down the Volga sixty years earlier. Vladimir and the jovial woman with her son bought apples from different

baskets and gave some to me: hers larger and redder, his small
and green yet tastier. Neither were particularly nice, belying
Khyalynsk's reputation. As always, Vladimir advised us not to
hurry: 'Longer you wait, better the bargain.' He disappeared,
returning a moment later – 'Come Daniel' – and led me to a
stall at the back with a few smoked fish almost blackened in
the process, and the fisherman seated phlegmatically behind.
James discouraged me from buying one and I am sure it
would have caused a mess and tasted filthy, though I was
sorry afterwards that I failed to find out.

Our last major stop was at Saratov at nine o'clock the next
morning. The shipping office was attractive, with lamps topped
by glass bowls which lined the promenade. Going on shore we
found a church bright from restoration and a market with
plums and melons on open stalls, though Vladimir swept us
away saying they were no good and would be better in Baku,
ignoring the fact that everything would be more plentiful
there. There were a few surprises: fresh herbs, horseradish,
pale green peppers and even a stall which sold chicken
gizzards and flat fresh fish, so it seemed that some survive in
the Volga and nearby tributaries in spite of the pollution,
caught by the fishermen we had seen who cast swirling,
voluminous nets from their boats. With a little effort, the fish
could even be saved from extinction, which was their fate in
parts of the Black Sea where chemicals disgorge from the
rivers.

It must be hard in the winter when fresh produce is
priceless, and it was hardly a riot of fun in the hotel where
coffee was forbidden in the large dining-room on the ground
floor; nor was it available in the upstairs restaurant, where two
young men were drinking a bottle of Russian wine labelled
Sauvignon which had little relationship to the genuine stuff, as
I realized when they were kind enough to offer me a glass. A
shelf displayed small plates of seaweed and little things
mounted in heavy aspic. The usual games were played as we
were directed to another eating place upstairs in our search
for a cup of coffee, a smaller room where it was a speciality,

only to have the waitress place a chair firmly in the doorway as she closed down – '*Niet*'.

Disgruntled, we returned to the sun deck on the *Pipkin*. James believed that the overcast weather was due to the smoking oil-wells of Kuwait, but as we sailed the clouds gave way to reveal a blue sky and a river mist which dissolved in the heat.

The *Pipkin* responded, breaking through the water jauntily, leaving a wake behind us as if we were sailing along a Mediterranean coast. This fantasy was realized by the sunbathers in startling costumes: one attractive though Amazonian young woman had a skin-tight outfit from which she burst provocatively. Her smile was innocent but she oozed sensuality. In contrast, a pinch-faced woman with one curler in her greying hair, a sour mouth, sagging breasts and black spots dotting her white flesh, changed benches so incessantly as she tried to sunbathe, followed by her equally hideous daughter, that she defeated her objective of a tan, for in her ceaseless game of musical benches she was never still enough. Yet they were enjoying themselves.

The strange-looking man who was still heavily wrapped in scarf and raincoat, peering angrily through his bifocals as he stalked around the deck, was in the church earlier and may well have appreciated it more than I did. Perhaps the disagreeable-looking lady with the artificial loop of henna hair now shrouded by a net, and her one-armed husband, would have proved fascinating if we had been able to understand each other. I doubt it, but I accepted that we were not much fun for them.

New arrivals who boarded the ship at Saratov included a young couple, plainly sophisticated, who recoiled with horror as they entered the dining-room and saw the food. Uncontrolled children raced round the deck. Radios in the cabins played a cacophony of conflicting music with a preponderance of ballads, and the *Pipkin* assumed a holiday atmosphere at last, though it was hard to tell if this was due to the end of the coup or, more likely, the sun. At dusk, when the passengers retired to their cabins, there was a new sense of peace as the ship glided over the water with scarcely a murmur from her engines. The river was wide again, several miles across, and so smooth that the bow caused just a ripple as she cut through. Occasionally a patch of ruffled water, sometimes weed, creased the surface as if whipped up by a passing gust or disturbed by some mysterious element below. The steppes were stupendous, stretching 'without border' as Vladimir put it, on either side, with no sign of humanity. They were not flat but undulating, dust-coloured with occasional clumps of trees, once inhabited by the fox, ermine and sable which drove the hunters eastwards as the wretched animals were exterminated in the search for further pelts – the 'soft gold' which prompted the colonization of Siberia, the Russian equivalent to the Klondike's gold rush.

Vladimir and I leant over the rail and absorbed the view in a moment of rapport, with the advantage of silence, so I was spared the usual platitudes of football, pop and weather from those who wish to practise their English. Our journey would have been insupportable without him, especially at such a critical moment. Vladimir belonged to the new Russia with no hesitation in expressing his contempt for the old. A symbol of the future, he ran the risk of constant trouble but he would survive. His reflective mood induced by the dusk and passing shorelines changed at once as two Russian girls joined him and he started to flirt outrageously. I was pleased to know that he would have their company on the journey back, and left him laughing. That is how I remember the *Pipkin* at her best, sailing down the Volga jauntily as if she were heading for the open sea.

Our last supper on board was uneventful and I went to my cabin at eleven. James told me that after I left, a passenger arrived in the dining-saloon and started to flirt with Nina, the sexy waitress with sores. I had noticed that the older, battered Lou was staggering, and apparently she was in high spirits when Vladimir was joined by the two girls who insisted on dancing with him to their transistor on the deck outside, oblivious to the bridge directly above them.

A few minutes later the Kapitan descended in his usual state of fury to find Lou slumped in a chair, and Nina smoking our Marlboro on the knees of a Russian passenger who had brought a bottle of Cognac, the first sign of alcohol on board apart from our own nightly treat, and was swigging it down while the others frolicked outside.

Speechless, the Kapitan caught sight of Lou's simple little 'passenger's book' which I had signed earlier, so accustomed to the nickname of *Pipkin* that I forgot to use the proper name of *Clara Tsepkin*. He seized the book and glared at it suspiciously, sending Nina for Vladimir so that he could interpret, as Lou was incapable of answering his questions.

Vladimir looked at the page and translated my inscription automatically: 'I SHALL ALWAYS REMEMBER MY LOVELY CRUISE DOWN THE VOLGA. THE *PIPKIN* IS UNFORGETTABLE.'

'The *Pipkin*?' cried the Kapitan, exasperated to hear this word again. 'What is this "*Pipkin*"?'

Lost for an explanation, Vladimir tried to calm him down. 'I think the Englishman is mad!'

1. My father and a Karachaite in 1929, outside a low stone *kosh*. Surprisingly, he called him 'a superb creature . . . a Mongol aristocrat'.

2. Wicker – Alexander Wicksteed – my father's travelling companion, with white beard and stick.

3. Khassaut in 1929 before its destruction, with 600 households and the mosque and minaret on the far right (and see 23).

4. My mother, Eve Stoker (sixth from the right in the front row), with the Imperial Family at the opening of the Anglo-Russian Hospital in St Petersburg.

5. Myself, aged three, in a Cossack costume bought by my father from Russia.

6 and 7. James and Vladimir leaning over the rails of the *Clara Tsepkin*, nicknamed the *Pipkin*, on the Volga.

8. Myself with black-market hustlers in Yaroslav, one of the first stops on the Volga.

10. Vladimir in front of the
Fantastica restaurant in Kostroma.

9. The thirteenth-century wooden
church inside the monastery at
Kostroma, one of the riverside
ports.

11. Kazan during the coup – 'Where
is our President?' Anxious Russians
wait for news outside the office of a
newspaper. Myself with a carrier
bag; Gorbachev's poster boldly
displayed behind.

12. Schoolchildren on parade, 7 May, in Pyatigorsk, with the statue of Lenin waiting at the top of the steps.

13. The man in the blanket during the midnight commotion in the hotel in Tbilisi, confronted by the floor lady and the security man.

14. Babushkas selling flowers in Pyatigorsk. Food may be short; somehow there are always flowers, as if to compensate.

15. Hospitality at the dacha outside Baku in Azerbaijan, near the Caspian Sea.

16. *Four Townsfolk Carousing*, by Pirosmani, the primitive artist whose naivety captured the simple joy of Georgian life before it was contaminated by civil war.

17. Mikhail Lermontov, the author of the sardonic classic *A Hero of our Time*, the story of a young Tsarist officer exiled to the Caucasus.

PART TWO

To the Caucasus

CHAPTER EIGHT

The Lies of Volgograd

THE travel brochure lies because that is its job. The camera lies because it is by its nature selective, sparing you the din of traffic and the eyesore round the corner with a single image. The artist comes closer: Constable tells you the time of day; Monet's *Antibes* shimmers in the afternoon, around three forty-five I should say, with the murmur of pine trees and the scent of resin. Inadvertently, the travel writer lies because his first impressions are bound to be prejudiced by personal experience; the weather makes a difference, even the time of his arrival.

If you reach your destination jaded after the ordeal of airports in the early afternoon when the shutters are down, the restaurant closed, the sky grey, and the hotel over-booked, and then have the luck to meet a stranger who volunteers to help and carries your luggage ahead, never to be seen again, your opinion of the place will be less than generous. Arrive at six in the evening to be welcomed by a friendly hotel manager and sit at a pavement café to watch the nightly promenade as a molten sun slips into a pewter sea, and you will relax.

I digress like this to try to explain why Volgograd came as a shock. It was one of two cities, the other was Baku, which I did not recognize from the descriptions.

I had been misled by Bruce Chatwin's *What Am I Doing Here* which recounted his journey in September 1982 on an Intourist ship filled with Germans making the macabre pilgrimage to the former Stalingrad to see where their fathers, sons or brothers had died in the siege in the last war. '*Mein Mann is tot in Stalingrad*,' they told him.

This discouraged me from travelling Intourist, but I had been tempted by his tantalizing glimpse of the 100-year-old paddle steamer with a raking funnel which had tied up alongside the Intourist ship at Kazan. 'Her cabins were freshly varnished,' wrote Chatwin, 'and there were swagged lace curtains in her saloon.' Chatwin's captain told him that she was 'the ordinary passenger boat from Moscow to Astrakhan on the Volga Delta – a journey which took ten days'. It was this which inspired me to take that steamer. The *Pipkin* could hardly have proved more different.

As for Volgograd, as Stalingrad had become, no one had a good word to say for it. Chatwin described it as a depressing city of

> stucco and marble where Soviet veterans are forever photo-graphing one another in front of war memorials. Rebuilt in the 'Third Roman' style of the forties and fifties, it rises in layers along the European bank of the Volga ... you can look back past another Doric temple which serves as an ice-cream shop, across some sandy islands, to a scrubby Asiatic waste with the promise of deserts beyond.

Factually this was correct, but it led me to expect a new city with soaring façades and broad piazzas similar to the eerie emptiness of London's rebuilt docklands. In Moscow, a Russian woman shook her head when I asked if I should stay longer than my planned day and night in Volgograd and raised her eyes to heaven as if to say that five minutes would be too long.

Certainly that was the view of my father in 1929, who left his boat there as I did. He and Wicksteed continued by train to Rostov, though they learnt that it had not run for the last thirteen days. Sitting in the dirty square, my father concluded that Stalingrad was 'the last and worst of the depressing Volga cities'. Forced to stay there in the hope that the train might leave the following day, he knew this accounted for some of his depression, but not all of it.

It is difficult to define just the quality of dreariness of these Russian provincial towns. The old ones, like Old Novgorod, have inherited a romantic personality from the past, early churches and monasteries. But these Volga towns, marking the eastward expansion of the Slav, have, until very recent times, been nothing more than Cossack outposts.

Before it became Stalingrad, the city was known as Tsaritsyn, held by Stenka Razin, the pirate of the Volga, and for three months during the Red and White wars after the Revolution it was held by General Denikin, until the Reds drove him out in the bloody summer of 1919. Plainly, the situation always had strategic value, but it did not become important until the British arms manufacturer, Messrs Vickers, built an artillery works there, in 1914.

By 1929, my father found dirty, dusty, cobbled streets and a paper-cluttered square:

Stalingrad plagues you with the awful desperation of a hot, sultry, summer afternoon, when you have nowhere to go. People just sit – and talk.

Returning to the railway station in the hope of buying tickets for the midnight train, he encountered a funeral for a child, with a little girl balancing the lid of a tawdry coffin at the head of a procession.

The silver-painted bound box was decked with flowers made of wood shavings, dyed yellow and pink to imitate roses. It was carried by four other girls who had it slung in silk ribbons. We tramped with it to the outskirts of the town, where among unpainted board shacks some church bells were clanging crazily and a factory band was practising the *Budeney March*. And there we left it – with the priests chanting before the modern icons of a redbrick church. Death, somehow, among such surroundings did not seem so sad.

In the evening a band played inside a garden of cool acacias opposite the station with most of the population hanging over its wire fence, but when my father tried to go through he was stopped by a young Communist. '"Was I a member of the Railway Transport Workers' Club?" this impertinent young girl demanded.' Turned away, he joined the other envious citizens, pondering on the ideals of a democracy that turned a town park into an exclusive club: 'Oh, freedom! That was Stalingrad 1929. Heroic Stalingrad.' He left thankfully. This is why I expected the worst, always an advantage to the traveller.

Perversely, I loved the place. This was partly because of the relief at leaving the *Pipkin*, where our departure ran true to type as a mix of aggravation and farce. The large *babushka*, who had not touched my cabin before, pushed me aside as she seized the sheets. Spotting a packet of Marlboro in James's cabin, she seized that too until she discovered it was empty and threw it away in disgust, raising her fist to his face. I cannot say I felt a pang at disembarking, though I was glad to do so without bitterness. A blonde lady and her friend even called out '*Dosvidanya*' (goodbye) as I walked down the gangway, and I was particularly pleased when the jovial woman and her son passed me on the quay where we all shook hands with mutual cries of '*Spasibo*' (thank you). It was raining heavily, at seven in the morning and there was no taxi in sight, so Vladimir ran off in search of one, returning defeated. As at the major ports, a group of passengers prepared to board the bus which had been arranged to take them to the churches and most important monuments, though the jovial lady confided to Vladimir that the guides herded them like sheep and she would not go again. However, I saw her join the forlorn queue which crossed the car park with their umbrellas to the waiting bus. This was the wrong one, so they trooped back to the shelter of the landing stage looking more dejected than ever. Acting on impulse, Vladimir splashed across, spoke to the solitary bus driver, and raced back with his broadest smile, saying to us, 'He take!' So we piled into the empty bus with all our luggage and drove off, to the pop-eyed amazement of the queue at this ultimate insult by the English spies. As I looked back, I saw the jovial woman and the boy as they ran a few steps into the rain, their faces beaming with amusement as they waved us goodbye.

As our private bus wound its way laboriously to the top, I became increasingly absorbed in the crowded streets on the way to our hotel. Far from an empty de Chirico vista, the hotel lay snugly beside a square with a central garden dense with trees. Admittedly the atmosphere was sombre, reminding me of cities from my childhood travels like Zagreb, but this was partly due to the heavy rain and even then it was not unpleasant. I had been thinking of a fairly recent reconstruction, but the city was rebuilt after the Battle of Stalingrad which ended in 1943, nearly fifty years earlier. Half a century! Instead of the impersonal Intourist hotel which I feared, I was delighted to find it cheerfully old-fashioned, in the style of Stalinist imperial baroque which is more sympathetic than most Soviet architecture and, paradoxically, less brutal. There was even that rare decadence, an aged porter to carry our bags. In the marbled green dining-room with Corinthian columns, we ordered breakfast which Vladimir ate heartily, and I climbed the carpeted stairs to my bedroom which had makeshift planks over the battered door but proved spaciously old-fashioned inside with a balcony overlooking the square. This first impression was totally at variance with everything I had expected from what I had read.

We continued to James's bedroom, where Vladimir closed the door and opened it again sharply a few moments later to check if there was anyone listening outside. This was our last chance to say goodbye. James gave him a T-shirt emblazoned with the name of some pop group I had never heard of, though Vladimir recognized it at once. 'If you give it me, I will sell,' he said with a surprising lack of sentiment, asking James to carry it out of the hotel in a carrier bag in case the KGB searched him as a Russian dealing with two foreigners. Already, he was acting with more suspicion on land than he had on board.

Throughout our journey it had been difficult to thank him, though we did our best to pay for his meals. When he needed a comb at one of the river ports, pointing to a plastic horror in a kiosk, I was glad to give him the spare I kept in my sponge-bag. Still in its pristine folder, the Kent was a posh comb and Vladimir studied the price tag with disbelief. As far as I remember it cost £2.50, the equivalent in roubles of an average week's salary. No wonder he shook his head.

When we gave him the fifty dollars we had decided on, he was equally direct: 'Are you sure this is not too much for me?' It was too little for all he had done for us. Curiously, I do not think that he had expected anything in return.

Vladimir still had a couple of hours left on shore, so we took a bus to the monument which commemorates the Russian defence of Stalingrad. Its immensity is overwhelming. A winged figure of Victory comparable in size to the Statue of Liberty without the plinth, it can be seen on its suburban hill for miles around. From the Volga I had already seen the solitary, shell-shocked mill which Stalin left intact as a reminder of the devastation of the surrounding buildings, but the monument had been created especially in honour of the Fallen Dead. So long as the Russians held this particular hilltop, Stalingrad was safe, which explains its symbolic position.

The statue depicts the Motherland armed with a sword. Like that of the Soviet worker and peasant girl clutching the hammer and sickle designed by Vera Mouchina and reassembled for the Paris Exhibition in 1922 where it caused a sensation (it is now back in Moscow), the monument is in the heroic style of Stalinist statuary which is easy to deride until you are dwarfed in its presence. It is both awful, in the sense that it is full of awe, and deeply touching.

Yet the approach was muddy, with no signposts, and when we reached the steps we were blocked by a barrier and had to detour over rubble and a railway line before we were able to resume our ascent to the platform at the top, a well-designed courtyard with a man-made pool flanked by statues of armed soldiers, known as the Court of Sorrows or Fallen Soldiers Square. The atmosphere was heightened by the scream of bombs, the rallying cries of officers and the cheers of charging soldiers relayed by loudspeakers. It was absurdly melodramatic and certainly surreal, but this was the imitation of war and it was magnificent. Making their pilgrimage in the rain, the Russians, women and men draped in medals, were understand-ably tearful. In the vast carved cave at the far end, I climbed the circular staircase and looked down from the balcony on to the gigantic hand which held a perpetually flaming torch, and the children and young men who laid their flowers below, flanked by two soldiers impassively on guard.

Here was a salutary reminder that the Second World War is more symbolic to the Russians than to us. For them it is the Glorious Patriotic War, and, as A.N. Wilson wrote in his life of Tolstoy, the Russians find the Western indifference incom-prehensible, with many of our young people unaware of the causes and protagonists:

> Whether this is because until very recently it was, by and large, a gerontic state ruled over by men whose finest hour was during the last war, or whether because of the huge numbers slain, or whether because the shock of being invaded when you live in an uninvadable country takes several genera-tions to live down, who can say. What a twentieth-century Russian feels about the Glorious Patriotic War against Fascism was felt just as strongly by the nineteenth-century Russian about the invasion of Napoleon. It was the great moment of national trial and national deliverance, analogous to the defeat of the Spanish Armada in Elizabethan England, exercising a similar appeal over the popular imagination, the sort of collec-tive experience in which a nation finds itself.

When I discussed this with Andrew Wilson on my return, we laughed at the thought of the Russian reaction to such flip-pancy as the television comedy *'Allo! Allo!'*, which mocked the Germans and the French Resistance too.

'And think of *Dad's Army*!' he countered. How marvellously

British that we had the strength to show our Home Guard as a group of delightful, elderly, shambolic misfits.

To mock the last war would be inconceivable in Russia. Her sacrifice and suffering was greater than our own – one reason why the eventual victory and 'national deliverance' was seen as a personal triumph for Stalin, acclaimed as the saviour of the Motherland, blinding his people against the harsher reality of his tyranny.

Even fifty years later, the reverence shown by the Russians at the memorial was almost tangible. You would need to have been heartless not to be moved as well.

James relishes Stalinist kitsch and admired every detail, but when we reached the foot of Motherland we were worried that Vladimir might miss the *Pipkin* and splashed our way back hurriedly over the railway track to the main road. No bus in sight and not a car would stop. I gave Vladimir a packet of Marlboro, but as more cars whizzed past I realized that he was clutching it in his hand. The moment I told him to display the familiar red carton a car screeched to a halt and we climbed inside. Vladimir gave the directions to the driver, a pleasant young man who laughed a lot, and we said goodbye near the landing stage where the *Pipkin* waited to leave on the final lap to Astrakhan. Vladimir gave James a phone number to ring on future visits, while I sent a final message to the Kapitan, screwing up my face and wiggling my ears with my fingers as if to say 'yah boo', which Vladimir understood at once, convulsed for the last time by my well-meant if schoolboyish humour. I was saddened when I said I would give him my address and he replied, 'You do not understand. It is bad if the KGB search me and find it.'

With smiles and waves he ran back to the ship. Our rapport had been extraordinary. I know I shall never see him again.

The laughing driver dropped us at our hotel offering us roubles for more cigarettes but by now we had none with us and roubles would hardly have been an inducement if we had. Purged by our visit to the Motherland, our duty done, while James unpacked his special towel for a long soak in his bathroom I wallowed in the infinite luxury of a long hot shower. We joined up for a stroll before lunch. It was Saturday, the leaders of the coup in Moscow had been overthrown, and the crowds were celebrating. After the glum faces on the *Pipkin* the happy holiday atmosphere was a lesson not to judge the Russians by their *petite bourgeoisie*. The rain had lifted and the park was spotted with girls in identical white wedding dresses photographed with their awkward, best-suited grooms in front of statues. After welcoming smiles, we explored the streets beyond, which were filled with people, and decided to forgo the solitary memorial of the mill with its adjacent museum of the siege, deciding it was time to enjoy ourselves.

Back in the Intourist hotel, which was blessedly free from tourists, we indulged in treats which had been day-dreams on board ship: soup, not only drinkable but tasty; black caviare; ice-cream with a touch of honey; an indifferent bottle of white wine followed by furious vodka; and coffee – all paid for in roubles at the equivalent of two pounds for both of us. At that rate I could have consumed a bowl of caviare, though this was not the finest. How could it be at such a price? It remains one of my regrets that I was unable to buy a huge tin of Beluga and consume it on my own, the only chance I should ever have. Caviare could be bought on the black market – not that I was offered any, and in any case it is suspect now that the sturgeon poachers of the Lower Volga are so organized that they build their own canneries and produce tins with labels forged so well that it is hard to tell them from the genuine article, such as Beluga, though they are really of an inferior quality. The sturgeon, a noble fish which can live for ninety years, does not stand a chance. The construction of the dams below Volgograd in 1930 prevented the fish from returning to their natural spawning grounds, and by 1991 the lower reaches of the Delta were contaminated by the pesticides which leaked from the rice fields, adding to the general pollution. Any fish that survived were found to be contaminated. Today a sturgeon has to be crazy to leave the Caspian and brave the river. The giant Beluga, the size of a shark, is extinct and all

the fish in the Volga are threatened. Due to the greed of man
the Volga is dying and no one cares. Referring to the merciless
scale of development in Siberia with dams drowning whole
villages to create the largest reservoirs in the world, polluting
the air as well as the water, it has been claimed that these
dams 'embody man's conquest over nature' as if nature is at
fault. With the Volga and parts of the Black Sea virtually
lifeless, and the Aral Sea turned into desert, it seems that
nature is losing.

All this should have made me ashamed to enjoy my few
spoonfuls of caviare in the hotel, but it didn't.

We were joined at our table by an aggressive, spotty tart
who looked at me, thought better of it, and coiled herself
around James, seizing his cigarettes and fighting back fiercely
when he refused to hand over the packet. She became so
insistent that in the crisp tones of a man from the Foreign
Office he asked her to leave him alone, and she flounced back
with a show of indignation to the men at another table who
greeted her annoyance with roars of bawdy laughter and
waved to us sympathetically. By contrast, a grand wedding
was being celebrated in the next room, the tables laden with
dishes of colourful food as if for a magazine. A tiny bar
opened at the other end of the dining-room at two o'clock and
James, spotting a photograph of Annie Lennox tacked to the
wall, declared to the barman he knew her well and would
bring the singer here on his next visit. This was a palpable
untruth but the barman's attitude changed from sullen resentment to smiling indifference. Meanwhile, I became involved
in incomprehensible conversations with Russian businessmen
who forced vodka down my throat as they explained their
interminable 'commershial associations' in the belief that I was
a businessman too, until I staggered up to bed exhausted by
my first day's freedom on land.

With his greater resilience, James ended up in a bedroom
with some of the toughest men he had seen and one astound-
ingly beautiful girl of twenty-two who had taken him upstairs
but then disappeared with a sailor who was red from alternate

swigs from bottles of Cognac and vodka. Another sailor offered James her friend for four dollars – 'an incredibly ugly, plump girl with dyed blonde hair' – who invited him to her room and looked miserable when he refused. Then the beauty re-appeared and held James's hand, but she looked unhappy too and James behaved like an English public schoolboy and went to bed on his own.

In the taxi to the airport the next morning, he seemed to regret it. 'You know, she really was a beauty. She had knock-out eyes, as if they were set halfway back in her head. I've never seen anyone so beautiful.'

'Weren't you tempted?'

'Oh yes. She asked me, "You want?" There was no ro-mance.'

'Well, it's too late now. You'll never see her again.'

'The awful thing is, I might. When I gave her my card I told her to come to England where I could make her a top model.' He sighed softly, though it was hard to tell if this was apprehension or hope.

Soon we were heading south to Baku on the Caspian, the capital of Azerbaijan. Though warned in Moscow that it might be difficult to get a flight, due to 'the political unrest in the area', we had no difficulty in buying seats and I had time to reflect on the reason for my journey – the Caucasus. It was only now that James warned me of the dangers ahead, re-counted by his friend in London who had told him that far from strolling beside river banks in fertile valleys, we would spend most of our time clinging to narrow mountain ledges with sheer drops on the side. Like an echo, my father's words came back to me: '. . . one of the worst trails I have ever seen. It went down in slippery little surfaces along the sheer sides, and then became merely a series of footholds among the chaos of glacial waste.' And this was *before* his ascent of the Klukhor Pass. I wondered if I was up to it.

CHAPTER NINE

Falling Statues

WHAT does one hope for from a city? With luck, the unexpected. I assumed that Baku would be hilly, whereas most of it is as flat as a war-game on a card-table and equally forbidding. I gained this false impression from an old history book rather than from a brochure, for no package tour would dare to suggest that you go to Baku for a holiday. Admittedly the curse of Television Travel reaches the distant corners of the world – I once heard a pert little presenter gurgle in the Congo 'I am now in Africa, *au naturé*' – but even she would have found it hard to be so gushing in Baku. The oil wells are that, for the area still provides 15 per cent of the world's petroleum reserves, though supplies are running out. Oil has always been the reason for Baku's existence, strategically placed with Persia and India on the far side of the Caspian.

Oil and the threat to India made Baku a place worth fighting for.

There were several routes which the Russians considered for their planned invasion of India during the last century. One was by sea from the Persian Gulf, which would have left her troops too vulnerable once they landed. Another was over the deserts and mountain passes, a pitiless march which would leave them depleted and exhausted. A third was across the Caspian Sea to Krasnovodsk on the eastern shore, across Afghanistan to Khiva north of the Karakumy desert, south to Bokhara and Samarkand, and from there to Herat and Kabul. The River Oxus was also seen as a means of ferrying Russian soldiers by local fishing boats to Balkh, from where they would march to Kabul and the Khyber Pass. Various forays were undertaken and at one point a few Russian outposts were within twenty miles of the Indian border. Understandably, the British became obsessive over this threat to the riches of the East Indies, which they regarded as their own. Young officers on both sides displayed exceptional courage as they disguised themselves as holy men or native traders and literally spied out the land, making maps of the little-known territories in between, risking and sometimes sacrificing their lives in doing so. Others sought alliances with local emirs with such surprising bribes as a beautifully carved carriage drawn by massive shire horses which managed to survive the heat and were transported part of the way up river on a raft. Their arrival caused a sensation as such large horses were unknown.

That spendid book *The Great Game* by Peter Hopkirk describes the secret war between Victorian Britain and Tsarist Russia (though there were periods when they were ostensibly allies). One of his delightful, true stories concerned the journeys of William Moorcroft to Bokhara and Tibet to discover how far the Russians had advanced in their bid for the markets of the northern states of India – 'a monstrous plan of aggrandisement' said Moorcroft – with the certainty that Russian traders would be followed by Russian troops. Arriving at a remote village in the Kailas region of Tibet, he was astonished to be greeted by two dogs, a terrier and a pug, breeds unknown to Central Asia. Recognizing him as a European, the dogs licked him excitedly and performed 'a passable imitation of military drill'. Moorcroft understood at once: the dogs had been abandoned by Russian soldiers who had got there first!

Having read Hopkirk's book only after my return, I was unaware of the importance of Baku in the game played between the two powers. Such was the British suspicion that Russia's threat to India continued to be believed into this century. Even after the Revolution in 1917, when the Bolsheviks had still to occupy the region surrounding the Caspian,

Baku was seized by counter-revolutionaries. Baku was one of the threads of torn allegiance which are so hard to unravel. The conflict was religious as well as political. In *The Victors' Dilemma* John Silverlight wrote that the Azerbaijans were 'Muslim in religion, Mongolian in origin, and closely related to the Turks'. At one point the Turks occupied Baku, though rumours that the troops were British were so prevalent that Stalin, then the Soviet Commissar for Nationalities, denied them indignantly on 28 May 1918: 'No British troops have appeared in Baku, if only because the entire Baku government and the entire east of Transcaucasia are guarded by Soviet troops, who are ready at first call to come to grips with an external force . . .'

In fact there were two British attacks led by Major-General Lionel Dunsterville, who crossed from Baghdad with forty-one Ford Model T cars and fifty-five officers, to find the port of Baku temporarily in the hands of a Bolshevik Committee, so he turned back.

The First World War was still being waged and the main British aim was to stop the German–Turkish forces from capturing the oil wells and, even more important, to block their advance towards Afghanistan and India. The Russians stopped fighting after the Revolution and their commander in the Caucasus made a private armistice with the Turks which they regarded as an invitation to continue, gathering the Muslims of the Caucasus, Transcaspia and Turkestan into an 'Army of Islam'.

I have gleaned these facts from the excellent *The Day We Almost Bombed Moscow* by Christopher Dobson and John Miller, who stressed the point that with the surrounding rivalry of the anti-Bolshevik revolutionaries, Baku was 'a Bolshevik island in a non-Bolshevik sea'. It was to foil the Turks and Germans rather than oppose Bolshevism that Dunsterville returned to Baku on 17 August, crossing the Caspian on the *Kruger* from the Persian coast, for Baghdad had been captured by the British the year before. Describing the conflict as 'a glorious tangle', Dunsterville referred to himself as 'a British general on the Caspian, the only sea unploughed before by British keels, on board a ship named after a South African Dutch president and whilom enemy, sailing from a Persian port, under a Serbian flag to relieve from the Turks a body of Armenians in a revolutionary Russian town.' That summed it up exactly.

To add to the comic operetta, his tiny force of 900 men consisted of Tommies in shorts and solar topees, who complained of their rations of 'herring paste', as they referred to caviare. They were marched up the streets twice to give an impression of greater force but were hopelessly outnumbered and withdrew. For six weeks they had held off a Turkish army ten times their strength and suffered 71 casualties compared to the Turkish 2,000, but after they left the Azerbaijans took over Baku under Turkish control, raped and looted, and killed 9,000 Armenians.

This became excellent propaganda for the Bolshevik agitators who warned that English capitalists had concluded an agreement with the local counter-revolutionaries: 'The Bourgeois and their despicable dependants are in favour of the English. The Workmen and Sailors are in favour of the Russian Revolution.'

Baku's loss was irrelevant, for it was becoming obvious that Germany had lost the War. When Turkey withdrew from the area the British landed again, on 17 November 1918, led by Major-General Thomson at the head of 2,000 British and Indian Gurkhas who were welcomed by cheering crowds and the Acting Foreign Minister of Azerbaijan who proclaimed the start of 'a new and luminous era of solidarity'. Major-General Thomson acted as the Allied representative, with his ships flying the flags of France, Russia, the USA and Britain, and declared himself Governor General in charge of public order, insisting that he had no intention of interfering in internal affairs. Then war broke out between Armenia and Georgia and he was promptly involved.

Simultaneously, British forces landed from Salonika on the Black Sea, the vital exit for oil transported by train from Baku, and occupied Georgia. Today it seems almost incredible, but, for a short time, Transcaucasia was under British rule until the Allies sorted out their new position with the Bolsheviks who were now virtually in charge of Russia. The Bolsheviks made private deals with the Germans, who were prepared to leave Baku to the Bolsheviks in return for a quarter of the oil production and the expulsion of the British.

Unfortunately, in the confusion of the British retreat from Baku under Dunsterville, twenty-six Bolshevik Commissars had been taken across the Caspian where they were shot by counter-revolutionaries, to the disgust of the British Major-General, Wilfred Malleson, in charge of Central Asia – 'In my opinion you are all alike, Red or White.' But the British reputation was diminished by the unnecessary executions for which they were blamed. The following year, Stalin wrote of 'the lawlessness and savage debauchery with which the English agents settled accounts with the 'natives' of Baku and Tran-scaspia just as they had with the blacks of Central Africa.' His suspicion of the British was sown at an early date and was generally shared. When the remains of the Bolshevik 'heroes' were cremated in Baku, the local newspaper referred to 'our twenty-six comrades who were savagely shot to death by British executioners and White Guards'. Consequently, the Commissars entered Soviet legend as martyrs, victims of British imperialism, and remain so to the present day. In this way, the British were used as convenient scapegoats, enabling the men who were really responsible to escape the blame. Ironically, the rumour that Beria, Stalin's brutal head of the secret police, had worked for the British in Baku, helped in his disgrace and execution, so some good came of it at the end. None of this would have happened, but for the oil.

Driving from the airport was weird because of the derricks which dotted the landscape in their thousands, rising from a blighted landscape. Instead of being regulated in lines behind a high fence or modern compounds, they sprouted at random to various heights in back gardens where there was not a trace of greenery left. They were both surreal and alien, as if planted there by visitors from outer space, with still some signs of life as they heaved up and down with the rhythmic sound of heavy breathing. There were pools which were odiously black and I wondered what would happen if someone threw a lighted match on the surface, though the oil looked too sluggish to catch fire.

Discovered at the end of the last century, oil has been the wealth and curse of Azerbaijan, for the country was unable to control the boom which resembled a gold rush, with new millionaires building Italianate palaces and importing their own harems. As usual, the maelstrom of nationalities led to violence and everyone was armed; the millionaires built funk-holes protected by steel doors where they could retreat with their women while the riots waged outside. When foreign workers poured into Baku at the start of the century, there were strikes because of their living conditions, which Maxim Gorky described:

> a black hell painted by a brilliant artist, the workers' huts close to the ground around the chaos of the oil-rigs, the long barracks quickly knocked together from red stones, piled one on top of the other as they were found, these barracks looked like nothing so much as the lair and caves of prehistoric man.

Baku remains a ruthless city with little time for the niceties of life. I liked and feared it. After the outskirts we passed tall-turreted and stern-faced buildings which suggested the former splendour bought by oil. A boulevard embraced the sea with a sweeping arm and a Maiden's Tower on the slope at the end where the old quarter begins. Built in the twelfth century it was largely spared by the Mongols who swept in a hundred years later and destroyed only part of the city. Baku has always been a vital stepping-stone between the east and west, finally ceded by the Persians in 1813.

With the enticement of the encircling Caspian beyond, Baku looks attractive in a colour photograph but the sea proves as hostile as the city. Oil pipes reach out for 62 miles into the so-called sea which is really a landlocked lake at 60–92 feet below sea level. There are parts which are so shallow that my father was astounded on his first crossing after they had been sailing for two hours, to see a man walking on water, like Christ at Galilee, but of course the ship was passing through a channel and the man was fishing for shrimps. The Caspian is the world's largest inland water (Lake Baikal is the largest freshwater lake) and though pollution is increasing there are still sturgeon breeding there, now reluctant to return to the Volga delta north of Astrakhan. The water is too salty for enjoyable swimming, though there are beaches with huts at little coastal resorts further south. I hoped to try one until James told me of a French fashion designer who caught an infection in the Caspian and died, though it was rumoured he had been murdered by his Russian lover, a top official who feared a scandal. I had not realized that such things happened in Russia – not the infection, but officials with male lovers from the West.

Baku means 'the city of wind', and neither that nor the smell of oil can be conveyed in a photograph. The sky was overcast when we reached the main square, which was dominated by the gigantic figure of Lenin thrusting an outstretched arm in front of a governmental building. This proved to be the Municipal Department of Health, with a top floor decorated with towers and turrets; in fact it remained a mere façade after the funds ran out, like so much in the USSR.

At either end there were two identical hotels. The Intourist was full but the Azerbaijan allowed us in, though the receptionist insisted that we pay in dollars, a hundred each, which James settled with his Access card. This was an astronomical, guilt-inducing price, the equivalent of 3,000 roubles each for the luxury of our private rooms. If we stayed for three nights, the cost would equal a six-months' salary for a Russian; however, once we started to equate expenses like that it led to madness. At least the rooms were available, though my door failed to lock and no water sprang from the tap. Nor did the lift stop at the dining-room floor, as we learnt after various attempts to have a late lunch, to be told at last that we were too late. It struck me as typically Russian that the lift refused to stop at the one floor where it was needed most.

The numerous bars on different floors were unmarked and shut simultaneously, so I could not buy the mineral water which obsessed me as never before after the *Pipkin*. Instead, we explored the narrow, sympathetic and balconied streets near the Maiden's Tower and passed the evening on our own after we were unable to phone our two contacts. Instinct led us to stop at an open Caravanserai which echoed the eastern magic of those ancient resting places for caravans along the trade routes, once filled with the clamour of merchants with their servants and camels. Now it was quiet with pale cream stonework and a series of arches around the open courtyard, containing the separate cells where the merchants once slept and which are now used as private dining-rooms. The food was excellent – we had Azerbaijan pilau – and we returned to the hotel contentedly. We actually found an open bar where we talked and laughed with a freedom denied us on the *Pipkin*. Disillusionment came in the morning when I was told it was impossible to have either coffee or mineral water for breakfast, even though I waved an imperious dollar bill. I was given the smiling excuse: '*Big* problems. Difficult political situation. *Democratization*.' So that was the new alibi.

Wandering into the square, which was empty in the early morning, I photographed Lenin's statue as a crane drew up beside the outstretched arm, presumably to clean it – a nice visual touch. Suddenly a limousine swept up, several policemen converged on James and myself, and others who must have been watching near by jumped out of bushes. Like the crazed Kapitan, the senior policeman was hysterical with rage, though we could hardly have looked more harmless and were plainly tourists. The more he gibbered and pointed to the crane, the more I smiled and nodded benevolently in order to enrage him further. After the KGB this was child's play, until I was grabbed by two of the plain-clothes men and hustled into the back of the black limousine with darkened windows.

James surrendered his film at once but I refused and they started to shake me as if I were a cocktail.

'For God's sake,' muttered James, peering through the window, 'give them the film. Why do you always have to cause trouble?'

I looked at the policeman who was shaking me. He was plainly nervous and uncertain what to do.

'No,' I replied emphatically, 'it might be interesting to see the inside of a Russian prison.' At this point I was left with no choice. Recognizing a potential trouble-maker, the senior policeman seized my little Japanese Konika from my grasp and opened it with the speed of long experience, ripping out the film, which was was half-exposed. After that there was no point in protesting further so I got out of the limousine with as much disdain as I could muster and returned furiously to the hotel with James following, equally angry but for different reasons: 'If you think it would be fun in a Russian prison, then you really are mad!'

In my bedroom I checked to see if the camera had been damaged, as indeed it had been, and it took two wasted films before the third agreed to work. It was never the same afterwards, which accounts for the lack of photographs in this book, although my old Rolleiflex came gallantly to the rescue.

I took my fury out on the floor lady, padding along the corridor to complain that there was still no water in my room so it was impossible to wash, and the lock refused to lock. Far from being intimidated, she responded with the usual argument which led to a shouting match and left me ashamed of such pettiness, producing a packet of Marlboro as an apology. Instantly she offered me a better room, but the fight had gone out of me and I gave in like everyone else. I doubted if the water would run in the new room either.

Going on to my balcony on the fifteenth floor, I was puzzled by the growing crowds gathering in the square below, for there seemed to be no cause for celebration or public holiday. After the failure of the coup, it seemed more likely that this was a demonstration against the Azerbaijan regime. So far it was peaceful and it did not occur to me that I might be in danger if I returned to the square. By the time I did so, a line of police with helmets and riot-shields were lined up in front of Lenin's statue and it dawned on me that it was being pulled down, as statues of Lenin had been in Moscow a week earlier. The crane was not for washing but for toppling. I blessed my luck at being in Baku at such a moment.

By mid-afternoon there were ten thousand people in the square and the police abandoned any attempt to control them as the tanks rolled in. I crossed the line of riot-shields to photograph the statue again, and this time there was no interference. Paradoxically, the atmosphere had changed completely with the arrival of the army. The demonstrators thrust carnations into the gun barrels of the tanks, and the young, oh so young soldiers helped to pull the children on top, or stood there laughing, their arms around each other's shoulders. The leaders of the demonstration tore down the flimsy barricades which blocked the steps to the municipal building, and started to proclaim, demanding the independence of Azerbaijan from the Kremlin, with the irony that they were still dwarfed by Lenin on his massive plinth behind them. Briefly a separate country in 'the glorious tangle' of 1918–20, the Azerbaijans were by now proudly nationalistic, as so many states were soon to be. The speakers demanded the dismissal of the President, who was regarded as a hard-line Communist, in favour of military rule continuing under Russian control. I learnt this later, for I could only guess what was happening at the time.

Caught up in the excitement, with smiling faces all around me, I found that people were anxious to speak when they realized that I was English, but it was hard to understand their volubility. I felt foolish when a hush fell on the square and they raised their right arms in silence as a gesture of solidarity. I did so too, aware that this was highly emotional and slightly theatrical, but I felt it was ruder not to join them.

That night, at one thirty under the cover of darkness, the crane did its work at last and Lenin was toppled. When I looked out from my balcony in the morning there was no trace, just a few bricks from the plinth and plenty of dust.

*

It must seem ungrateful to say so, and it is, but one of the punishments of travelling in the Soviet Union was the over-whelming hospitality. The knowledge that our hosts had gone to infinite effort and inconvenience, spending money they could ill afford, created acute guilt. This was aggravated because you dared not refuse any of the dishes placed before you with such pride. For the host family this was an event. The wide-eyed, well-behaved children stared at the foreigner – the *nemsi* – with wondrous curiosity as if one had stepped from an alien world, as indeed I had. The parents relished the chance to exchange views and exercise their language, which could have been invaluable in learning about their country except that they were more interested in learning about England. They loved to laugh and a few had the appreciation of the ridiculous shared by Vladimir, and they felt they had failed if they saw you looking glum. Consequently, you were both the entertained and the entertainer, which can be hard work with strangers. Not only did I have to listen ten times as hard to someone whose English was eccentric, but I had to struggle to make myself understood. Hospitality in Baku proved a double penance – first on my unfortunate stomach, then on my tired brain.

We met the first of our contacts on the second evening. They were related to an official in the Union of Artists known to James who felt justified in phoning the man's brother. In my turn, I had Susan Richards's book as a gift for her friend Togrul, though she implored me not to take advantage of his hospitality, which he could ill afford. As usual, this was hard to avoid without insulting his pride and it was only at the end of our visit that I was able to persuade him to accept a few dollars, which he did reluctantly, even though I stressed they were strictly to buy a treat for the children.

The first family took us to dinner in the best restaurant in Baku, which proved to be the Caravanserai where we had strayed instinctively the night before. We continued afterwards to the old quarter and a wooden house where their friend had a splendid studio upstairs, rich in heavy atmosphere, draped with the magnificent Azerbaijan and Persian carpets he dealt in professionally. Sweet champagne was produced, finer than any I had tasted in Russia, but the gauntlet of vodka toasts at dinner had taken their toll and the ride back to the hotel was a blur. We arranged to meet in the morning to go to the friend's *dacha* in the country near the Caspian. The friend was not only gracious but wealthy.

Having foisted ourselves on our hosts I almost resented their generosity, which is so irrational as to be Russian. James was better at socializing because it was an integral part of his background. These are occasions I avoid in England and I would have been happier to idle around and observe the mix of nationalities conducting their business so seriously in the ground floor foyer of our hotel – men with hooked noses and liquid cattle-eyes, scratching their balls as they talked and seemingly so tough that they would knife one with indifference. Unable to speak his language, I would have been content to sit in silent rapport with the huge though gentle wrestler from Kazakhstan without the barrier of language but with the smiling courtesy of mime and the occasional break-through if a word was mutually understood. I would have preferred the company of ordinary people, however incomprehensible, to that of the intellectuals. This was one level where James and I differed. However, even I was aware that in doing nothing I might see nothing, so I was pleased when our hosts collected us.

We drove through dusty streets of uniform dereliction to the strange fire temples built by the Zoroastrians as shrines in the fifth century harnessing the untapped oil and gas underneath the ground, where flames burst out spontaneously. They are among the most sinister objects I have seen, suggesting that human life is worthless compared to religious belief. Standing or crouched inside were desiccated dummies, corpse-like figures draped in turbans and sheets, while another blackened shape wore a loin cloth and chains. Flames still flared from the corners of the Inner Temple, the area surrounded by a wall with the incongruity of a few modern derricks swaying outside.

The fire temples were confirmation of how close we were to India.

We continued out of Baku along atrocious roads to the *dacha*, which was not situated in a wood on the shores of the Caspian Sea as my inane optimism had imagined, but was more of a shack erected on flat ground devoted to vines. This might sound derogatory, but it was close to paradise in Baku for the vineyards produced clusters of small sweet grapes and the fig tree was ripe with delicious green figs. This would have been reward enough, but the family and their friends had devoted the morning to preparing a banquet for us of classical Azerbaijan dishes which would have been the envy and the dream of Muscovites. An unfamiliar green soup called *diusbara* with miniature ravioli and a spoonful of vinegar, and kebabs from a smoking barbecue in the surrounding garden where the trees provided shade, were served at a large table on the open-air verandah protected from the sun by a sloping roof. Though Baku is called the windy city, air is a blessing after the stifling, overcrowded apartments. Throughout the afternoon we consumed water-melon, more grapes, the specialities followed by cakes, our every mouthful watched by the eyes of the family eager to share in our enjoyment. They could hardly have been kinder and it was difficult to break away without seeming rude; and as there was no telephone it was impossible to warn Togrul, my contact in Baku, that we would be an hour late. Returning to the hotel at five, we found him in a state of despair, having thought he had lost us.

'Hurry!' he cried. 'Dinner is waiting! We must leave at once.'

Togrul was a charming man, highly intelligent and humorous, delighted to use his English phrases such as a startling exclamation of 'Flibbertigibbet!' He shared the apartment with his beautiful daughter (for he was separated from his wife), his sister and her children, and their father, who rose to make a brief speech of traditional welcome when we arrived before he returned thankfully to the TV set in the corner which is rarely switched off in a Russian home. Togrul's sister was aggressively intelligent, pouncing on evasions, determined to correct my misconceptions. She proved invaluable in helping me understand the issues which divide Azerbaijan, echoed in different forms in many of the Republics.

Two hundred thousand Armenians lived harmoniously with the Azeris in Baku until 1990 when the Kremlin made a deliberate attempt to whip up rivalry between the scapegoat Armenians and the Azeris. She had witnessed the first of the calculated murders when men burst into an apartment block near by and ransacked the homes of Armenians, throwing their possessions into the courtyard where they smashed them to pieces. Then she saw them lift the apparently lifeless body of a young man and heave that over too. This premeditated action provided the army with the excuse to move in. Altogether fifty people were killed, including Azerbaijan nationalists, but the Armenians were blamed for the trouble and most of them fled from Baku to their own state of Armenia or the disputed borderline territory of Nagorni Karabakh where, ironically, they formed a powerful army of their own, while the Azerbaijans were dependent on Moscow, despite their fictional 'independence'.

When I asked her why the Kremlin had deliberately provoked a civil war, she looked at me as if I was idiotic. 'To make us forget our hopes of freedom and national independence,' she explained patiently. 'Of course the Kremlin is clever.' Since then the Azerbaijan threat to Communist rule in Moscow has faded but the conflict continues with the Armenians claiming independence too. The number killed in the disputed Nagorni Karabakh is larger than people realize: 25,000 since 1988, and it is probable that the original Communist provocation will rebound with a horrible cost of life. James saw a parallel to Chernobyl which he believed was instigated by the Kremlin in a similar attempt to divert the threat of nationalism in Ukraine. I found this hard to credit, but Togrul's sister shook her head furiously in agreement: 'There will be nothing but trouble,' she declared, returning to the conflict between the Armenians, whom she liked, and the

Azerbaijans to whom she belonged. 'Our country is heading for a hurricane.'

Course followed course throughout the discussion and it was plain that this had cost them dearly, for they had no resources like our lunchtime hosts. Just as I thought dinner was finished and settled back with an inward groan of relief, the main course of chicken wings and pilau was laid before me with further cries of pleasure. My stomach had contracted on the *Pipkin* but this was clearly a case of *noblesse oblige*.

'You are hungry, yes,' demanded the sister who had been displeased that we had kept the dinner waiting. She looked at my bulk and decided that I needed an extra large helping.

'Yes,' I replied weakly.

I woke early in my bedroom with the light glaring through the flimsy curtain. The day was stifling already as the heat rose from the statueless square, unless it was descending.

I lay there in that uneasy torpor which is neither sleep nor balm for contemplation but a halfway limbo prey to doubts and masturbatory fantasies. I opened my eyes suddenly to see a man's face peering down at me from a foot away. I rarely lock my door and in this case it would have been impossible: he must have crept in like a cat.

For a second my brain did not connect with the visual affront. Then the shock hit me. Furious and vulnerable, wrapping the sheet around me, for I slept naked, I shouted at the man and gestured him out. He was nondescript, not a typical swarthy Azerbaijan but a balding middle-aged man with furtive eyes.

'*Tovarich!*' he pleaded, raising his hands apologetically in the face of my anger as I hurried him out. I slammed the door after him and it bounced back until I succeeded in shutting it. I dressed quickly, shaking from the incident.

'Probably a case of mistaken rooms,' I told James later.

'You're mad if you believe that and madder still not to lock your door.'

'Easier said than done,' I pointed out, 'with this one.'

In retrospect I assume the man was checking the room and if I had been fast asleep he would have taken such possessions as my watch on the table and my cameras. It was seven o'clock, so if I woke he could have pretended he was looking for a friend to tell him it was time to leave.

Whatever the explanation, it left me more unnerved than I had been by the KGB or the police who confiscated my film in the square outside. It would have been so easy for him to have killed me.

CHAPTER TEN

'You are in Serious Trouble!'

THE journey from Baku to Tbilisi led to our first argument. In spite of his saintly forbearance, a necessary ingredient when travelling with me, James could be just as obstinate as I could. Until now everything had gone to plan, surprisingly so in view of the coup though it would have been problematical if that had succeeded. Bound together on the *Pipkin*, branded as 'spies', we scarcely had a cross word, which was remarkable considering that few friendships survive the hell of travelling in each other's breathing space. Now, unable to reach Astrakhan, I was anxious not to diminish our journey further by taking short cuts. Also, I have an aversion to airports and flying over land where people are invisible seems to me to be the negation of travel. I wanted to take the bus from Tbilisi stopping overnight at Kirovabad at the hotel near the bus stop, and was tempted by the villages we would pass through, like Shamor which was famous for its dry white wine, and Tauz for its market. However, the road ran perilously close to Nagorni Karabakh with the risk of being stopped by Armenians and shot. James thought it was better to live. I was not so sure.

An alternative was to take the train, a fifteen-hour journey costing less than fifty pence, but the lady at the Intourist office in our hotel – a curious anomaly as there were no tourists – expressed the irritating though logical view that as we should be travelling overnight there would be little to see. James agreed wholeheartedly. He had taken a train from Moscow to Kiev the year before and warned me that Russian trains are tedious, airless and foodless. I reminded him of his remark that a train was the one place where Russians spoke freely, knowing they will never meet again, but he countered this with a reference to the hijack of the train from Tbilisi which had taken place a few weeks earlier.

'That could be fun!' I said. He shook his head pityingly with his annoying 'When will you ever learn?' expression and booked us on the Aeroflot flight on Wednesday, displaying the iron will that lay behind the flopsy façade.

Airports are airports everywhere but Baku's is worse than most. It's the enforced rigmarole which I detest: the insistence that one should arrive hours in advance only to be met by delays and utter indifference. The bossy Intourist lady had arranged a car two hours too early – 'to be on the safe side' – so we waited interminably in the turmoil of the terminal in a swarm of shouting people trying to find out news of their flights while their tearful wives and bawling children guarded their sacks and boxes with stares of dismay. Eventually we left this inferno, which was colourful at least compared to the dreary rooms upstairs reserved for the few Intourist passengers, a service evidently used by richer Russians too.

My temper had not been improved by the stranger in my room and after we lugged our luggage on to the small jet – there were no such creatures as porters or baggage-handlers – I looked down on the eastern ranges of the Caucasus, undulating mounds with a trace of road and glimpses of small settlements below, and thought how interesting it would be to be *among* those hills and valleys.

It is part of the penalty game at Tbilisi airport that Intourist passengers are taken to the grand terminal building on their arrival but the taxis are lined up at the far end of the tarmac for the ordinary passengers several hundred yards away. By the time we reached the modern Iveria Hotel I was tired by the accumulation of small aggravations rather than any major set-back, with the added annoyance of learning that this was a public holiday for godmothers, which meant that all restaurants and bars were closed. Plainly, godmothers were not supposed to eat or drink on their special day. While James tried to telephone our contact, a distinguished publisher who was a friend of James Butterwick's, I told the lady at the Intourist office that we wanted to drive on to Ordzhonikidze, formerly Vladikavkaz, and cross the military highway to Kislovodsk. As if I had made an improper suggestion, she raised both hands in horror: '*Very* big problem. Impossible. Difficult political position.' This was confirmed by the publisher who hurried to the hotel though extremely busy, and arranged for us to pay in roubles which meant a huge saving. Then he showed us around the old part of the Georgian city with wooden houses tumbling over the banks of the swirling river which eventually flows into the Caspian Sea. As I had hoped, James was delighted by the elegance, the space and air, and the plane trees which lined the spacious Rustaveli Boulevard named after the theatre. Needing a visa for Georgia, we were in a different country. In my ignorance I had not fully appreciated how separate the Republics were and have proved to be. Georgia is one of the proudest, with her own language and culture. It is a fertile land with vineyards and orchards; the name 'Georgia' is nothing to do with St George but a translation of the ancient Greek for 'land of the free farmer'. Frescoes showed St George killing the Shah of Persia rather than a dragon.

Rustaveli Boulevard was a pleasure to walk through. It started with the Iveria Hotel and the post office; then we went past a municipal building with a sculpture of Stalin's face, so high that it was only partly destroyed, the splendid façades of the old Tbilisi Hotel and the Rustaveli Theatre famous for its Shakespearean productions, and the government building on the other side where twenty people, mainly women, were struck down by Soviet soldiers as they staged a demonstration. This was commemorated with plaques and flowers laid on the steps, explaining why the Russians were no longer welcome in the Georgian capital. Yet I heard a conflicting view a few days later from a young conscript who had been there that night with orders to protect a top Communist official and claimed that the Georgians started the trouble – 'My best friend was killed beside me. That is not good.' He was nineteen, one of Yuri's students, and asked me not to mention his name.

Nowhere in the world approximates the *joie de vivre* of a Paris boulevard, but the Rustaveli was a Russian runner-up, ending in Liberty Square, formerly Lenin Square before his statue was toppled. Near by is the Museum of Georgian Art, with jewellery and twelfth-century enamels from the rule of Queen Tamara, and the wonderful primitive paintings of Pirosmani which convey Georgia's past better than any history book.

Pirosmani led a miserable existence but his affection for the Georgian countryside is expressed joyfully in such scenes as the panoramic *Kakhetian Epic – The Alazan Valley* and simple observations such as the *Family Picnicking*. I had not seen his work before and fell in love with it. Hardly known to the outside world he is revered in Tbilisi. A street is named after him, ironically where he was found unconscious in 1918 in a damp basement after lying there for three days without food or water, and was taken to a hospital where he died a few days later, certified as 'X, beggar of some sixty years'. A friend identified him and gave the more dramatic epitaph: 'He had an angel in his breast.'

Pirosmani was a true primitive, an innocent who was self-taught, basing his work on the sign paintings with which he made a living, and traditional woodcuts. He was 'discovered' in 1912 by three artists on holiday from Moscow, much as Alfred Wallis was noticed in his backyard in St Ives, painting on the backs of cardboard boxes, by Ben Nicholson and Christopher Wood.

Pirosmani's *Woman with a Tankard* was a *succès fou* when exhibited in Moscow and he was taken up by intellectuals who were charmed by his lack of sophistication. This was the death of him if not his talent. A newspaper cartoon ridiculed him publicly, showing him with bare feet painting a giraffe; this pleased his former supporters, who were now envious of his fame, but wounded him. Pirosmani was an easy target, but this was the cruelty of shallow judgement. He had always been odd, rambling incoherently in the street after too much vodka, robbed by a partner during a brief period when they set up a business, but he harmed no one. Admittedly, he had the pretension to ape the appearance of the artist by wearing a fedora hat, but this was soon abandoned as his fortunes sank and he became nomadic, sleeping wherever he could, leaving walls of barns covered with his pictures. He travelled with a wooden box which held his equipment, and the black oil cloth he used for canvas. The few roubles earned from his signs were spent on the best brushes and paints, before the vodka. Finally he lost his box and replaced it with a sack, carrying his tubes and brushes in his pockets. He continued to paint until his death. He asked for so little: 'What we need, brothers, is this. Right in the middle of the city so that we can be near to everyone, we ought to build a big wooden house where we could gather. We ought to buy a big table and a big samovar and drink a lot of tea and talk about painting and art. But you don't want this. You speak of other things.'

Of a possible two thousand paintings only two hundred survive but these provide a celebration of Georgian life in less violent times. His pictures are full of fun and gusto, befitting the primitive: *Night-time Revelry; Doctor of a Jackass; Fisherman Amidst Rocks; Church Fête* and *Threshing Floor at Dusk*. He recorded both the people and their animals: the Iranian lion, a she-bear with cubs, divine service in a village, a man led off in chains by two soldiers, and above all the Carousels with the tables laden with food and drink while musicians played their drums and flutes. Without the guile to impress, Pirosmani was devoid of artifice.

I happened to dine in the Daryal Restaurant in a basement off the Rustaveli Boulevard which was lined with reproductions of Pirosmani's work, like the woman with her tankard of beer; they were so well done that I mistook them for a moment as the real thing.

A simple, cheerful place, it was crowded with Georgians who vied in calling me over to their tables, where hesitant talk became the stranger for vodka: 'What is real friend, a really friend and lasting friend, this is the man who comes with you, some bullets, someone tells you some good thing, this is the friend who comes with you.'

A rasping of feet as they stood up, clashed glasses, and knocked back the vodka in one of their toasts.

'How many children do you have?'

Disappointment when i ʰdmit I have none, for it seemed wrong to lie to them.

A moment's silence, then an eager alternative: 'How many childhood friends you have? If you know this, we will drink also.'

I remembered my dear friend Anthony West with whom I went to numerous schools and rose to my feet: 'To my old schoolfriend, Anthony West.'

Seizing any opportunity for a toast, the entire restaurant followed suit, clashed glasses again and cried out, 'To Anthony Vest!'

Unlikely though it may seem, the men at my table were called Tango and Nongo. They continued their toasts to 'Lovely people and lovely wives'.

'I think of you as my son,' said Nongo, when he learnt I had no children. 'I shall play your child's role though I am thirty-eight.'

Tango joined in – 'And I shall be your brother!'

Tango and Nongo were now my new family and with a wistful anxiety to please, they toasted, 'Let us drink to *everyone!*' and followed that with the final flourish: 'To Georgia, this God-blessed country!'

God-blessed! A hideous irony, for since then Tbilisi has been torn apart by civil war, Rustaveli Boulevard is in ruins, and for all I know poor Tango and Nongo are dead.

I have no doubt that there are places which go through periods when they are blessed or cursed: think of Belfast. Tbilisi was about to enter that dark phase. Already, as a sort of warning salvo, the famous cable car which took one to the top of Mount David, from which there were panoramic views of the sprawling city, the industrial outskirts and the shining Caucasus in the distance, had crashed to the ground a few months earlier, tumbling down the mountain side, killing several children trapped inside. Admittedly, such a contraption suspended in air by a slender thread is a risk to be avoided, but this disaster could be seen as an omen by the superstitious.

A curious instance occurred on our visit to Mtskheta, the ancient Iverian capital in the fourth century BC fourteen miles away, at the junction of the Rivers Aragri and Kura which wander into the distance together. In the historical relay race which exchanged power in these areas, the Persians, in the third and fourth centuries AD, and then the Byzantines and Arabs invaded Iveria until King David united the western parts on the Black Sea with those in the east, and it was under his grand-daughter Queen Tamara, who ruled from 1184 to 1213, that the region saw the peak of Georgian culture with the exhibits now in the museum, and the work of such artists as the poet Shota Rustaveli whose romantic epic *The Knight in the Panther's Skin* is still revered and who gave his name to the Boulevard. I tried to read the sluggish verse but it must have suffered hideously in the translation.

Queen Tamara seized control of the Caucasus from the Christian empire of Trebizond (now Trabzon) on the Black Sea, extending her rule to Armenia and Azerbaijan on the Caspian. After her death the region was disrupted once more by Tamerlane, the Mongol who claimed descent from Genghis Khan and invaded Russia from his capital in Samarkand. He was followed by the Turks of the Ottoman Empire, and the Persians, until the Tsar took over in 1795 after Tiflis (the old name for Tbilisi) had been raided yet again. This led to the taming of the Caucasus and the mountain battles with their leader Shamil which ended in his defeat. Even in this century, the relay race was revived with the short-lived independence of Georgia after the Revolution in 1917, before Georgia was annexed by Moscow as a new Soviet Republic in 1921. Now she has won her independence again with her nationalistic fervour sown a thousand years ago, at the cost of civil war inside her own territory.

Queen Tamara and the Kings of Georgia, including the last who signed the peace treaty with the Tsar, are buried in the great cathedral of Mtskheta, which was built around an original Christian church (575 AD) and remained open for worshippers throughout the centuries, even spared by Stalin out of deference to his formidable, God-fearing mother who lived to be almost a hundred. There are legends concerning a fragment of Jesus's robe and a cross from the Virgin Mary brought from Cappadocia by St Mina, and you can see the tiny ancient church inside.

But what amazed me on my earlier visit on my way to the Caucasus were what were undeniably two flying saucers depicted on an altar at eye level on a fresco which showed the crucifixion with a space craft below each of Christ's outstretched arms. I might have dismissed this until I saw another flying saucer high above an archway, and made a sketch which resembled a floating squid with its tentacles hanging down as if it were landing. The implication that a space craft might have landed in this part of the world centuries ago was so stupendous that I told James, who found it hard to believe, so I took him there now, armed with my camera and its built-in flash. When we entered the cathedral I led him to the altar to prove that I had not imagined it, and thought for a moment I had made some mistake. Then, with bitter disappointment, I realized that the frescoes both on the altar and above the archway had been covered over with cement. Possibly they were gaining a notoriety which was unwelcome. Later I mentioned them to some Georgians who confirmed that they had existed but seemed reluctant to discuss them, though they told me a girl had received national publicity a few weeks earlier with her claim that she had seen a flying saucer near Tbilisi. As I have no evidence, I doubt if anyone will believe me and I could tell that James was unconvinced, but they were flying saucers, unmistakably.

The hospitality in Tbilisi proved even more high-powered than in Baku. It was so beyond the call of duty, prompted by a chance, brief encounter in the Groucho Club the year before, that I felt my customary guilt at being the excuse for such special occasions. I was left with an irrational feeling of indebtedness, especially as the Georgians were so determined to please that they seized prized possessions from the sideboard to present to me as gestures of friendship. This landed me with two gifts which could hardly have been more difficult to carry on the journey ahead: a fragile vase and a large copper plaque. I still have the vase but I left the plaque in the back of a taxi, probably out of a subconscious wish to rid myself of such an encumbrance. This added to my guilt. Obligation is a wretched emotion.

James's contact was a film producer so successful in her own right that she had little need of us, yet she entertained us in her spacious living-room the length of a squash court where we listened to the latest developments of the coup on her television set which had the CNN news. Imperious with her dark hair swept tightly back, she was a natural hostess who arranged everything in moments with no apparent effort and still had time to talk and laugh while seeing that everyone's glasses were full. Yet I felt she was concealing a private tension and was making a heroic attempt to do so. In different circumstances we might have forged a marvellous rapport.

After several hours of intense intellectual chat, at which James excelled, I broke free and returned to the basement bar in the Iveria Hotel where I had an argument with a German engineer who took offence when I told him that Hitler patted me on the head when I was eight in Garmisch-Partenkirchen. This is true, but seems so unlikely that it causes a frisson of dismay whenever I mention it to Germans, which is probably why I do so. For good measure, I added that the Führer said I looked like a good Aryan child. This went down so badly that I had to be rescued by three jolly Turks who were in Tbilisi to initiate a tie-factory, of all unlikely industries. After this I was thankful to go to bed.

I was woken soon after midnight and it took me some moments to realize why. Voices were reaching me from the next room. They were raised and the walls were thin. As the shouting reached a crescendo, I banged with my shoe hoping to quiet them, but the noise increased. Plainly, several people were having a furious row. Paradoxically, now that I am slightly deaf, I am more susceptible to noise and always irritated by a loss of sleep. Doors along the corridor were opening and when I peered out I saw several men in vests. Slipping on my shirt and trousers, I went out to investigate, to find that the people next door had erupted into the corridor as well. The floor-lady was remonstrating, several men were gesticulating, and a prostitute, who was plainly the cause of the fracas, was struggling into her voluminous, golden clothes. Another man emerged from the bathroom wearing a shower-cap and a blanket and said nothing, his face expressionless. Then they started to fight each other, the last man naked as the blanket fell to the floor, while the floor-lady looked at me helplessly before running down the corridor for assistance. By now the corridor was thronged with people in their night-clothes as if a ship was sinking. Casting myself into the role of a third officer who rallied the passengers while the orchestra played, I distributed a box of chocolate biscuits intended for the Caucasus, which were accepted with tiny cries of pleasure from the ladies, after which I recited the opening lines of Tolstoy's *Resurrection* which went down less well because I did so in English. Then I went back to my bedroom and emerged wearing my Stalin mask which I had bought in Moscow. This raised considerable laughter and, gratifyingly, a small round of applause, even from a gigantic, smiling man who arrived with the floor-lady and looked the very model of authority. A few moments later the girl was escorted to the lift where she waited dismally, shaking her head. Peace was restored, though angry voices continued to echo from the next room until I fell asleep.

I woke up instantly. This time it was due to the insistent blare of a motor-horn in the car park right below. I looked at my travelling clock — it was four o'clock. The din continued with the aggravation of an occasional one-second spasm of silence and a sense of relief until the horn started again. I went on to my balcony and shouted down, wondering why no one else was doing so. The appalling noise continued relentlessly, but the surrounding windows in the hotel remained darkened. I yelled again without success. Finally my patience, which was running low by this time, snapped, and I came out of my bathroom with a glass which I aimed at the offensive car far below. I could hear it shatter and this time there was an answering cry, but the noise continued, so I threw another. It stopped abruptly. I went back to bed and fell asleep instantly.

I was woken again. This time it was light and I heard an angry knocking on my door, which was locked on the inside after the incident in Baku. I opened it to find James, white-faced, aiming his outstretched hand like a rifle. '*You — are — in — serious — trouble.*' The words came out like staccato gunfire. Then I noticed a policeman behind him.

'You'd better come in,' I said pleasantly, though I felt like hell.

'No! What have you been doing?' James demanded through tight lips. He actually wagged his fingers at me, provoked this time beyond endurance.

'What do you mean?' I tried to look innocent, and failed.

'You threw some glasses from your balcony last night and hit someone who is now in hospital. For all I know, he's dying.' I did not believe this but it was shattering news. I realized I was starting to sweat.

'How do you know I did anything of the sort?' I was trying to find out how much evidence they had against me. 'It could have been anyone, from any bedroom.'

'The floor-woman reported you.'

Damn! For a moment I wondered if James was taking his revenge for his awful experience on the dry-ship *Pipkin*, for he seemed to be enjoying this.

A grim relish was detectable as he told me, 'They are waiting for you in the managing director's office. The police have sent me to fetch you and bring you down at once. I expect the public prosecutor's there too. You must come at once.'

His expression proclaimed my guilt, though I noticed that the policeman behind him was smiling, which gave me new-found confidence. I turned on the offensive.

'Look, James,' I told him, 'Your very tone of voice is denouncing me as effectively as that horrid little boy who shopped his parents. Please *stop*!'

James flinched at this reference to the Soviet boy scout, Pavlic, a national hero who received the Order of Lenin after accusing his mother and father of being enemies of the State. His father was shot and the boy was murdered by members of his family though still honoured by the Pioneers today.

'Don't play Pavlic with me,' I warned him. 'Don't say a thing. With you as my self-appointed defence counsel, I don't stand a chance. Now I am going to have a shower and put on my best clothes and *then* I'll go down and see them.' I shut the door with a confidence I did not feel. I realized that I reeked of hangover and looked dreadful. Half an hour later, shaved and showered, with a clean shirt and tie, I had improved dramatically in appearance as the kindly policeman led me down that familiar corridor to the lift where the prostitute had waited, and downstairs to an office where a surprisingly large number of Georgians waited behind a side-square of tables for my interrogation to begin. It was daunting. I looked hopefully for the smiling man in authority who had laughed at my Stalin mask, but there was only the floor-lady who stared at me impassively, though she had been so friendly the night before. James looked aghast.

Then I had my first stroke of luck as I laid out my documents on the table to create as much distraction as possible and to give me some moral support. An attractive lady with a mane of lustrous, tawny hair took me aside and explained that she was the interpreter. Speaking firmly though softly, she confided that no one else could understand a word we were saying.

'If someone really is in hospital,' I began, 'I'm only too happy to pay a hundred dollars towards ...'

She cut me off sharply. 'That is not good idea. If money should be necessary,' she shrugged, 'that is different. What do you remember about last night?' Before I could reply, she continued, 'I suggest you remember *nothing*. You were too *drunk*.' She had given me my defence and I nodded gratefully.

The interrogation began. When the managing director of the hotel wanted to know who I was, I produced an article I had written after my previous visit the year before, which was published in the *Telegraph* under the heading 'Georgia Stays on my Mind'. I knew from experience that Russians are fascinated by cuttings even if they cannot understand them, especially if there are photographs. This had a striking silhouette of Lenin standing in Lenin Square – not that any trace of him remained now in Liberty Square, as it had been renamed. They studied it as if they were diamond merchants in Amsterdam. Then I had my second stroke of luck as the interpreter read my flattering reference to the Iveria Hotel and the managing director looked up, apparently impressed by this surprise witness for the defence. James came forward but I knew that if I was going to resort to a subterfuge of lies and bribes it would be hard to do so if he was present, and so I asked him tersely to wait outside the 'courtroom'.

Seizing the advantage, the interpreter spoke at some length on my behalf with occasional translations for my benefit. 'As he remembers nothing that happened, he cannot really be held guilty.' That was roughly her argument and to a degree it was unanswerable. I smiled and tried to look serious at the same time.

It worked. There was a volley of discussion and then the interpreter turned to me, tossing back her hair in triumph. 'The director says he sees you are reasonable man but fears this could happen again which would not be fair to the next hotel. However, if you promise ...' She assured him that I was leaving Tbilisi the next day for the Caucasus and would not be causing further trouble in Georgia, a pledge confirmed by

James who had crept back into the room and declared he would be responsible for my good behaviour, for which he received a dirty look from myself, while the others considered their verdict.

The managing director rose with obvious relief and shook me warmly by the hand. The others did so too, one by one as if I were a visiting ambassador. The floor-lady laughed, the lady interpreter kissed me on both cheeks, and later, as I drank a cup of coffee, and never had I needed one more, the smiling policeman came up and kissed me on the cheeks as well, refusing my tactless offer of a few dollars with a pained expression and a gentle wave of protest. Throughout the day people in the hotel greeted me as if I had done something heroic. Understandably, James was furious.

Of course I was guilty, totally in the wrong.

I had been through a roller-coaster year before I arrived in Moscow and I had reached a point in life where I was drinking more heavily than ever, as if I wanted to be found guilty. My hopes for a restful cruise down the Volga had been dashed and my expectation of a gentle stroll across the Caucasus was starting to recede as well. So I felt an overwhelming relief at being acquitted. Even I did not relish a spell in a Georgian gaol, interesting material though this might have been.

In any other country I would have been arrested and should have been arrested, but there is one aspect of life, and probably one aspect only, where the Russians do not dissemble, and that is drink. Drinking is something they understand and tolerate because it is the one unification.

'It's so *unfair*!' muttered James. 'It's typically Russian that they didn't even have the decency to arrest you.'

I nodded. 'You know, James, I'm rather shocked myself.'

CHAPTER ELEVEN

Over the Georgian Military Highway

I WAS on course again, heading towards the Caucasus, the ultimate aim of our journey.

When you think of Persia and India to the east, and the Black Sea and Europe to the west, you appreciate how vital it was to forge an access across the mountain range and keep control of it. The Georgian Military Highway over the Krestovyy Pass (7,695 ft) was the key to the Caucasus. When little more than a track, this was the ancient route from Asia into Europe, when caravans from India and Persia, laden with carpets and tea, climbed their way slowly over the mountains to sell their goods to the west.

Yet I should explain at once that we were doing the journey the wrong way round. We had crossed the lower-eastern Caucasus on our flight from Baku, now we were re-crossing the mountains on our way to Kislovodsk, and from there we would attempt to climb the Klukhor Pass and descend to Georgia again, to the eastern region and the Black Sea. The immensity of the mountain range, with 125 miles of glaciers and 20 peaks over 14,000 feet, makes such a zig-zag process more comprehensible. It was roughly what my father set out to do, though he took the train to Kislovodsk from Rostov-on-Don, then the capital of the northern Caucasus. (If this sounds complicated, please bear with me and look at the map.)

Guilt-ridden after my disgraceful behaviour, I was happy to leave Tbilisi, and elated at the prospect of crossing from

Tbilisi to Kislovodsk, a distance of 130 miles, over the Krestovyy Pass which my father described euphorically as

> one of the most sensationally beautiful mountain highways in the world. In the gorges of the wild Terek you see the river smoking among its black rocks a thousand feet below, the walls of sheer rock rising thousands of feet straight over your head; and beyond, in the gap, the eternal snows of Mt Kazbek looming under their cap of clouds. From the crests of high passes you catch glimpses of other snows on the main range, running high along the sky. But you never get near them.

Whoever held the Krestovyy Pass held the mountains and the crucial region of Kabarda on the southern side near Tiflis (the old name for Tbilisi). If Shamil, the Muslim leader of Daghestan, the eastern Caucasus, had secured the Pass he could have held out for longer than the twenty-five years of his struggle against the Tsarist troops from 1834–59. Fighting was in the Circassian blood – they lived to fight and fought to die – but the Russians had the practical objective of their expansionist policy which included Georgia, who had asked for Russian support. The Caucasus mountains lay in between so they had to be subjugated. Also, Shamil guarded one of the routes to India.

Conversely, resistance was natural to the mountain warriors who wrote love letters to their daggers and dealt in severed heads and hands as coinage, proof of a vassal's subservience, for the tribes were often divided among themselves. Girl babies were of no significance, but a boy had a cradle with a dagger laid beside it to instil an early reverence for war. Writing of these mountain tribes, Lermontov exulted:

> In friendship firm, in vengeance firmer still –
> Not theirs the Master's teaching from above –
> They render good for good, for evil ill,
> And Hate with them is limitless as Love.

The Russian aristocracy were equally heroic. My father wrote,

They rose to deeds of valour, of comradeship, and of self-sacrifice in the Caucasus that they have probably never equalled in all their courageous history. If it is true that 'mountains make the man', the Caucasus provide many noble examples.

Indeed, as far as it is possible, this was a noble war, certainly compared to the conflict in Georgia today.

Russian officers led their men up the cliffs, hand over hand, to take the villages which were built on the edges like eagles' nests. At times they formed human ladders as they climbed on each other's shoulders, and had themselves lowered in baskets to get at the tribesmen on a ledge below. The savagery was sublime. They fought sword to sword; one was inscribed with the words 'No braver man, no keener blade', for the Muslim fighters asked or gave no quarter. When the women of an *aoul*, a cliff-top village, saw that all was lost, they threw their children over precipices and jumped after them. I find it hard to credit the claim that they actually threw their children at the soldiers as if they were boulders, but in such a struggle all things were possible. Otherwise, they worshipped their children, if they were boys. When a chieftain's son was killed in battle, he cut his body into sixty pieces and sent them with horsemen to his vassals across the mountains, demanding the tribute of an enemy's head in return. When Shamil was forced to hand over his beloved son as a hostage, he fought the harder. His sister threw herself 600 feet into a torrent when he told her to; his mother was beaten unconscious on his orders when she pleaded for mercy for a defaulting tribe. Yet Shamil was capable of sentimentality, adoring his huge, ugly cat whom he fed with delicacies. When the cat died he took it as an omen – 'This is the end of me!' – and, thus dispirited, he was surrounded and captured soon afterwards. The Russians were generous in their victory, allowing him to make the pilgrimage to Mecca. Afterwards he returned to Russia with his favourite wife, a Georgian aristocratic beauty, and ended his days in St Petersburg as a white-bearded patriarch honoured by his former enemy, who recognized his bravery. Shamil's exploits became legendary: he was said to be able to jump twenty-seven feet, and he travelled with his own executioner, who threw Russian officers into pits where they were kept like wild animals, even flayed alive. His father was a drunkard, which so offended Shamil's religion that he warned him that the next time he saw him drunk he would kill himself in his father's presence. The old man knew he meant it and never drank again.

With such exploits it is tempting to regard the war as a sport, but it went deeper. The Caucasus divided the Christian and the Muslim worlds, so this was a jihad, a holy war between the cross and the crescent. Religion was the cause worth dying for among the mountain tribes; and politics the cause worth fighting for on the part of the Russians, for the Caucasus was seen by the Tsar as the stepping-stone to Delhi. In 1800 when Georgia was first united to Russia by the Emperor Paul, he contemplated the invasion of India.

This was not so fanciful as it seems today. The Tsar even suggested an alliance with Napoleon whose determination to seize India from the British grasp was undeterred by Nelson's destruction of his fleet at Aboukir, in Egypt, on 1 August 1798. But even he rejected Paul's undertaking that an army of 35,000 Cossacks should advance across Turkestan, while a French force would sail down the Danube and cross the Black Sea in Russian ships, down the Volga to the eastern shore of the Caspian, and continue from there through Persia and Afghanistan to the River Indus. Joining up, the two armies would advance on India together.

Napoleon was unconvinced, asking how his army could march across 'a barren and almost savage country' over a distance of nearly 1,000 miles. Paul argued that the country had 'long been traversed by spacious roads ... Rivers water it at almost every step.' This absurd assurance failed to change Napoleon's mind so Paul decided to continue on his own.

On 24 January 1801 he placed an embargo on British ships entering Russian waters in the Black Sea and ordered General

Orloff to raise 22,500 Don Cossacks and to march on India via Khiva and Bokhara to the Indus, which would take them three months. 'You are to offer peace to all who are against the British, and assure them of the friendship of Russia. All the wealth of the Indies shall be your reward. Such an enterprise will cover you with immortal glory, secure you my goodwill, load you with riches, give an opening to our commerce, and strike the enemy a mortal blow.'

The explanation for the foolhardy venture was Paul's confused state of mind, bordering on madness, but, as Peter Hopkirk points out in *The Great Game*, no Cossack thought of doubting the Tsar's wisdom, let alone his sanity. Ill-equipped in mid-winter, the Cossacks drove their 44,000 horses (two for each man), their food and twenty-four guns, across the frozen Volga and reached the Aral Sea, a distance of 400 miles, a month later. It was there that a lone, exhausted, galloping horseman caught up with them to bring the news that the Emperor Paul had been assassinated. His son Alexander, anticipating the certain loss of the Cossack army, ordered an immediate withdrawal.

Even so, and sixteen years later, the lure of India lingered and the Muslim tribes under their religious leader Shamil were seen as an unacceptable interference. Their subjugation became a necessity, with repercussions in the west where Shamil, a wild figure in a far-off land, was acclaimed as a resistance leader able to thwart the Russian army if the Tsar dared to revive his father's plan to march on their beloved India.

Questions were asked about Shamil in the House of Commons and the proposal was made that a British fleet should sail to the eastern border of the Black Sea to lend him moral if not military support.

A seductive figure to the ladies, Shamil was celebrated on the covers for sheet music such as the 'Shamyl Schottische' for the pianoforte, and the 'Circassian March'. Surprisingly well informed, Shamil wrote letters to Queen Victoria appealing for help against the Tsarist tyranny, and the fear that Russia might invade India gave him a brief importance. This misled Shamil into believing that Britain was an ally prepared to send him arms and ammunition: a nice idea, even to the British, but the Caucasus were too remote, too unknown a quantity. Nothing happened.

This was the turbulent though gallant background to the Highway I was hoping to cross. Now there was a new conflict which had caused the inevitable response of '*Niet*' when I tried to arrange transport. Georgia was suffering from the running sore of Ossetia, which the Kremlin had used as an excuse for refusing Georgia's independence. Though the region declared itself a sovereign republic at the end of 1990, preferring to stay in the Soviet Union, the Georgians insisted that south Ossetia belonged to them. Fighting was continuing at that moment, and though the casualties were numbered only in hundreds, rumours of mutilation were appalling. Another bewildering case of separate factions tearing each other apart in the new-found 'freedom' of the whole.

No one was prepared to drive us over the Pass until I offered a bribe of 100 dollars and a surly man turned up on the Sunday morning outside the Iveria Hotel in a car which looked so battered I doubted if it could manage a hill, let alone a mountain. Sure enough it broke down because the driver had forgotten to fill the radiator, which screamed in pain and boiled over when he fetched mugs of water from an icy stream. This gave us ample time to appreciate the views.

Because of the history and my father's tantalizing account, I expected the Krestovyy Pass to be wildly romantic with a tortuous road which looked down on gorges so deep they had never seen the sun. I had ignored the obvious: that as it is the *only* highway across the mountains there was bound to be heavy traffic. Also, and perversely, the weather was too clear, stripping the Daryal Gorge of the mystery it might have kept if shrouded by swirling mists. I expected too much. Of course there were dramatic views of mountains and valleys, and a jolly 'stop' at the foot of one ascent where local peasants sold provisions and fur hats, and the lorry drivers filled their flasks from the water trough, but they and I were firmly planted in the twentieth century.

I looked forward instead to the town of Vladikavkaz, now called Ordzhonikidze, the major town in north Ossetia. It was built on the banks of the River Terek in 1783 as the vital link in the Caucasian chain between east Daghestan and the west. Before that there was little more than a dangerous bridlepath at the mercy of falling rock. In 1772 a force of 600 men with two guns had only just succeeded in rescuing a party of Russians besieged by the Ossetians. It was this provocation which encouraged Count Paul Potiomkin, the Commander in Chief of the Caucasian Army, to convert the track into a military highway covering a distance of 145 miles, rising to nearly 8,000 feet. With startling skill, his 800 soldiers worked so swiftly in forging a way through the rocks that Count Paul was able to drive into Tiflis in a carriage drawn by eight horses in five years' time.

In 1799 Vladikavkaz was abandoned, destroyed and rebuilt. For the third time a Russian force crossed the Caucasus to Tiflis and in the following year the Emperor Paul placed Georgia under Russian protection.

By then established as a Russian military base, Vladikavkaz was an exciting place to be posted. Though it was rough and tough, the town was a trading point between Europe and Asia whose bazaars were rich in rugs, sheepskins, Persian silks and spices, with camels snorting beside the prized horses from Kabarda. There were Tartar mosques, an Orthodox church, a bank and a bureau de poste as symbols of civilization; a military band played in the park every evening; and the boulevards were lined with trees. Lesley Blanch, whose *Sabres of Paradise* describes the Caucasian war, says that faded belles came husband-hunting in pursuit of the young officers: 'The bluest blood, the greatest names were now to be found concentrated in the Caucasus like some miraculous, accessible well from which ambitious matchmakers might hope to hook a golden fish.'

From time to time the routine would suddenly be shattered

by news of a Muslim threat and the civilians and their servants would be evacuated. Yet some of the women entertained the fantasy of being captured by the handsome brigands and forced to submit: one Russian lady who was rescued from such a fate escaped and returned to her captor. For the officers, their fate was to be thrown into one of Shamil's pits and left to die. With Shamil controlling large areas of the eastern Caucasus from the Caspian to Vladikavkaz, the town faced the constant threat of siege as he struggled to join up with the tribes to the west and seal the Caucasus off.

In 1846, with this objective in mind, Shamil attacked the Daryal Gorge but the Russian general exploited his small force with such brilliance that he convinced the other tribes of his superiority and held the Pass. It was a fatal moment for Shamil, who was eventually beaten, though not for another thirteen years.

No wonder that I yearned to enter the cobbled streets of the old town of Vladikavkaz. Instead I found a modern town of such stupefying ugliness that I could smell the discontent. I was confronted by the most depressing conglomeration of concrete building that I have ever seen, far worse than the worst city in Romania, true to its uninspiring modern name of Ordzhonikidze, called after a Soviet 'hero' who has much to answer for. I can remember no colour, no greenery, no attempt at decoration except for the grim, monumental square. To live there happily, you would need to be slightly mad or constantly drunk, or to indulge in incessant vice. As for the threat of violence, what a welcome distraction that would have been – though I suspect that the people kill each other from boredom rather than political passion. I heard no gunfire, though one angry man raised his fist against me at a garage when I took a photograph of a car literally stuffed with live white chickens, while our despondent driver queued interminably for inferior petrol.

Staring the angry man in the eyes, I spoke to him in the clipped tones of Noël Coward:

'Twas brillig, and the slithy toves
Did gyre and gimble in the wabe;
All mimsy were the borogroves . . .

'Oh, do get back in!' cried James impatiently.

And the mome raths outgrabe.

The man's arm dropped.

In Russia there is so often a sense of *déjà vu*, that I was not surprised by the account of an overnight stay in Vladikavkaz by Archibald Forman, in his book *From Baltic to Black Sea*, published in 1932:

Everybody declines to be answerable for anything that goes wrong; suggestions that the rooms of the hotel are more or less alive with insect life are regarded as the wanderings of a lunatic, or at most the caprices of the mad English, who must be humoured. '*Nichevo*,' they say to themselves. 'Tomorrow the English will have gone and the next people will not be so fussy.'

There appeared to be an open-air restaurant in a shady garden, and rather than face the airless dining-room, we strolled into the little arbours, where there were small tables covered with soiled tablecloths; upon each plate was a small piece of torn paper some seven inches square, and further investigation showed that this was expected to serve as a table napkin. Nothing happened for twenty minutes. Ancient old men, who in another land would be seated at their firesides putting the world in order and resting after life's battles, are given the job of waiters, presumably because they are useless for anything else. Occasionally one of these feeble creatures shuffled past, but either owing to defective eyesight, was unable to see us, or was too dull-witted to understand that we wished to be served. Eventually our little interpreter could stand this inaction no longer, and seizing a senile-looking old man with a week's growth of beard on his chin by the arm gave him our order. As nothing appeared for over forty minutes, and was unlikely to do so in the future, she proceeded to the kitchen and brought the meal along herself.

As most travellers in Russia will testify, it is astonishing – in an *Alice in Wonderland* way – that the more cataclysmic the change, the more everything remains the same. Or less so. At least Archibald Forman saw some 'wild and villainous-looking men lounging about with short daggers in their belts ... with rows of cartridge cases across their chests', with an odd collection of types in the numerous wine shops. 'Much wine,' he commented, 'is being drunk in this district', the final refuge of the Russian.

Of course it is crass to form an opinion of a place on a first impression, with the very glibness that my father despised. It is conceivable, that those who live in Ordzhonikidze love the place, though I doubt it. It was not the squalor which depressed but the absence of any colour. I had been hoping all along to find a Pirosmani or Chagall landscape, a primitive but happy scene with wooden houses and indignant geese marching along a muddy track bullied by peasant women in brightly coloured shawls.

This was not altogether fanciful, for I had found such a place in Kars on the border of North-eastern Turkey which I had visited a few years earlier, though advised not to. I take this literary detour because Kars was everything I had been expecting here. It is a tough place, a town that changed hands constantly in the last two hundred years, still dominated today by the great citadel which was defended during the Crimean War in 1855 by a British force led by General Wilson who became a national hero in England even though he lost. In 1877 the town was occupied by the Russians until Lenin restored the province after the Revolution, as a gesture of solidarity towards his fellow republican Kemal Atatürk.

Kars is so wild that even Turks hesitate to go there. There was no need to impose an official curfew at night, for only knaves and fools would venture out. I did so, and though there were fights and arrests around me, I felt as safe as I always do in Turkey. This sounds arrogant, but if you feel no fear of violence you are unlikely to exude the musk which attracts it, unless other people are out of their minds from drugs as they might be in New York or Glasgow.

Apart from the hideous new governmental buildings, Kars remains a frontier town, which took me back to the turn of the century; and though the back streets are derelict, the low houses bear the influence of the Russian occupations with unmistakable decoration. I would not have been surprised to see a troika racing past; instead I side-stepped into the mud as herds of sheep were driven through the main street, dodging the hissing geese that waddled with sublime hauteur along the cracked pavement. (Why is it, I wondered, that you find geese in every village venue, yet never once upon the restaurant's menu?)

Guide books shudder at this 'armpit of Eastern Turkey' and tourists rattle through askance on their way to the ghost city of Ani twenty-five miles to the east, but I found the atmosphere was positively cheerful, and though the two small hotels have been condemned by the Turks themselves as among the most dreadful in the world, I found mine bearable, though the carpets seemed soaked with urine and the place reeked of boiled cabbage. At night I found a bar with massive murals of hunting scenes, a friendly restaurant, and a café where some noisy Turks insisted I join them for copious glasses of *raki*, after which they whisked me off to a brothel on the outskirts of town which we never reached because they got out and started to fight instead, before returning me punctiliously to the café where they were arrested by the patrolling policemen when they started to fight again. A jolly time was had by all.

By comparison, Ordzhonikidze was dead, and we drove on to Kislovodsk in grim silence. Though it had proved disappointing, we had crossed the Georgian Military Highway and were reaching our objective.

CHAPTER TWELVE

Reunion with Yuri and Ali

SEVERAL of the spas of the Caucasus rivalled Baden-Baden in their heyday: for instance, Zheleznovodsk, a mud treatment centre which is more attractive than the name suggests, and Pyatigorsk, the oldest 'balneological health resort' in the former USSR. Brochures offer cures for nervous, locomotory and gynaecological disorders, though their illustrations suggest that the cure can be more frightening than the ailment. With their promise of rejuvenation and longevity, and with the alpine freshness of the air and the prettiness of the green undulating foothills, it is natural that these resorts are popular with the Russians. Though little known to the world outside, the spas are bound to become a tourist attraction in the future unless the Caucasians tear themselves apart like their neighbouring republics. Indeed, the hotels are there already in the form of the sanatoriums, though many of them are now in a state of decline.

Of the fifty natural springs in the Caucasus, the most famous is the Narzan, which means 'strength-giving', in Kislovodsk. My father wrote that a White Russian in Paris would have given his last franc to drink it.

This had been a favourite drink of the wild mountain tribesmen long before a Russian ever set foot in the Caucasus. 'The drink of heroes' they called it. And bathed in it for centuries. Some, it must have been, for the sheer delight in wallowing in such exciting stuff (it is the most amazing feeling) but most because of the ancient, and still held, belief in its magical qualities.

These included a cure for venereal disease, as Wicksteed discovered when he shared a pool with two swarthy men who explained why they were there and showed him the evidence.

'Great God!' Wicksteed told my father. 'I won't feel safe for weeks.'

When we arrived at the Kavkaz Hotel in Kislovodsk I was delighted to see bottles of the stuff on a table near the lifts. The three baboons at reception from my previous visit had been replaced by women who tried to be agreeable though none spoke a word of English. Possibly because they had no yardstick to go by, or because they fell in love with him, James persuaded them to accept roubles, which proved a saving of at least two hundred pounds over the next few days, for the roubles amounted to little more than five pounds. Armed with bottles of the Narzan water, I tried the lifts and found they were temporarily out of order, as I suspect they had been for the last decade, stopping at the first floor and refusing to go higher. James vanished down interminable corridors while I guarded our luggage as he tried to find our rooms, returning with a man who showed us to another lift which was curiously full, considering that the hotel was empty. At last I struggled into my bedroom and found to my surprise that everything worked.

'Dear James,' I wrote in my diary, 'what a hellish travelling companion I must be, totally unable to adapt, though this is the essence of travel.' 'Every step a problem,' he had remarked at one stage on the *Pipkin*, but as I stared forlornly into the mirror I realized that I was the biggest problem of all. I am at my best when travelling alone because I have to make more effort; in this case I knew I could rely on James, who was well-behaved and universally liked.

That night in the hotel we watched an astounding Sunday cabaret. With a stamping of feet and flashing eyes and tawdry, startling costumes, and a gallant band of three musicians, it might have occurred in Constantinople in 1910. The musicians' loudspeakers were turned up full blast and the heavily made-up male leader of the troupe of dancing girls changed his costume more frequently than they did, though he was less skimpily clad. He made his first entrance in a white suit and black fedora as he introduced flamenco, Apache and Cossack dances and a sexy ballet. These were followed by a camp version of 'Putting on the Ritz' with high kicks and bright smiles as the girls removed their clothes – arch to the very end – while he dropped his trousers, to the consternation of the Russians in the dining-room, and a few hisses.

It was plain that the floor show had succeeded in making them very randy indeed. The show was over and the customers started to dance, formally to start with, though this soon gave way to solo turns who performed with a skill the cabaret might have envied. One young man, tough and athletic, danced in an apparent frenzy making steps with the speed of machine gun fire. When he was joined by an ample lady with no waist dressed in red who attempted to match him, he was cheered on by his friends. Everyone laughed and clapped as the young men replaced each other like a relay race in surpassing speed. There were echoes of Greek *bouzouki* in the delicacy of the movements – though that would have seemed slow motion by comparison. Ultimately the dances were Caucasian and Cossack, delightfully abandoned after the coy contrivance of the gallant cabaret.

I went to my room smiling in spite of the lifts, and the phone rang almost at once. Yuri had just returned from his visit to England and was back in Kislovodsk. This was good news, for it meant that we could set out for the mountains without any delay. I was eager to start immediately.

When we met him in the morning, Yuri was still elated with the short-lived joy of the returning traveller with much to tell. It was bizarre to learn the details of the Moscow coup and realize how little we knew by comparison. While we were thrust into limbo on the *Pipkin*, fed scraps of information by

Vladimir, Yuri had learnt the truth over breakfast in his bed-and-breakfast in Scarborough, watching it blow for blow on British television.

Yuri described the three young men who were killed as they defended Yeltsin's White House against the tanks, including a Jew who was now a national hero. 'Another fought in Afghanistan, yet he died on the streets of Moscow.'

'I was very worried for you,' he told us. 'I had no idea what might have happened to you, especially when the British government advised all English peoples to leave Russia.'

James revealed his horror at the thought of what might have happened to us if the coup had succeeded, and we told Yuri of our visits from the KGB. In fact, since our visas were in order, I doubt if there was any danger at all, except there can always be misunderstandings in such circumstances. At best we could have been deported back to London and Moscow; at worst we might have been held somewhere until an authorization was received, or possibly forgotten, though I would have raised such a stink that they would have been happy to see the last of me, unless I had the proverbial 'accident'.

Yuri was certain that our Caucasian attempt would have been prevented if the coup had won: 'Everything would have been regulated and foreigners placed under constant suspicion. Your visas would have been revoked.' He told us that his mother, a charming, civilized lady who lived in Pyatigorsk, had little idea of the truth during the coup because the media were controlled by the State Committee for Extraordinary Situations – a chillingly Orwellian title – and they played *Swan Lake* on television throughout the crucial day.

Yuri is the most intelligent Russian I met, with Vladimir's intuition and an additional wisdom of his own. He has a good turn of phrase and his English is remarkable except for grating Americanisms such as 'He is good guy, I think.' His teacher of English at the Language Institute in Pyatigorsk, where Yuri now taught English himself, lives in Scarborough and looked after Yuri. He arrived with ten pounds yet managed to see Oxford, London, Liverpool and York where he took the bus to

Whitby. There he climbed the steps to the graveyard at the top where Count Dracula first drank English blood. When the coup failed, the local pub in Scarborough, which adopted him during the 'emergencies', presented him with a bottle of vodka. Loving England with a passion rarely displayed by the English, he learnt the intricacies of pub etiquette quickly in the 'Joelee Roger' as he called it. He was greeted on his arrival with 'The usual, Yuri?' as the barman poured him his draught Guinness. When they heard it was his twenty-eight birthday, they invited him to stay after hours: 'The lights are turned out and a girl enters with big cake and candles and they sing "Happy Birthday, Yuri" and drink to my birthday and the end of the coup.' He was immensely gratified, and so was I in learning that the people in Scarborough had been so nice to him, especially when the immigration officials in Heathrow can be so hard on a foreigner who arrives with only ten pounds in his pocket, and turn him away.

My hope of a quick departure was dashed when we tried to contact Ali, our Karachaite guide who had no telephone. We took a taxi to his home on the outskirts of Kislovodsk but he wasn't there, and after waiting for an hour managed to hitch a lift back, in exchange for Marlboro. While Yuri searched for him in the centre of town I took James to the tea garden where students were celebrating the first day of term which, perversely, was a school holiday. Always in Russia the young redeem the worn-out parents. The girls were dolled up with ribbons and bows, guzzling coffee, cakes and ice-cream as if this was Vienna, though the food was poor by comparison. I coincided with a group of boys with cheerful, open faces, dressed in well-cut uniforms, as they poured into the public lavatory near by where I was startled to see an apparent giant rising several feet in the next cubicle until I discovered that the students climbed on to the top of a Turkish-style mound which brought them level with the door, allowing them to look down on each other and talk. Not much privacy for someone with the runs like myself, but jolly nevertheless.

In the afternoon I retired to my bedroom, wilting, while

Yuri took James to meet his mother. I asked the floor-lady for tea, and she brought me an ancient samovar corroded with calcium and filled with water which looked alarmingly brackish. I gave her a large piece of Cornish fudge in exchange. Quantities of kaolin and morphine supplied by James did not allay the runs but the tea left me calmer as I lay on my bed reading while the rain cascaded down outside.

Ali was traced and we met him at seven in the evening outside the white colonnaded entrance to the park which looked ghostly in the fading light. Silently he led us in the drizzle through a formal garden redolent of John le Carré intrigue until we reached a grand sanatorium reserved for top Communist officials, which explained why it seemed empty except for a pop group rehearsing deafeningly in the ballroom. The floors were parquet and the furnishings and mirrors luxurious which confirmed that all animals were equal under Communism though some decidedly more so than others, among them Boris Yeltsin who had stayed here in the old days.

With instinctive taste, Ali had chosen the sanatorium's bar – which served Cognac but no mineral water, a discrepancy which was now familiar – where we could be alone. Something was wrong and he looked disgruntled. To this day I am not sure what had upset him, but he was devoid of guile and his mood was transparent, though he cheered up visibly when I produced the bottle of scent for his girlfriend, and especially when I showed him photographs I had taken near Khassaut the previous year, of himself on horseback. These prompted the familiar grin; I have always found that photographs are the most welcome and personal gift one can bring. Yuri wondered afterwards if Ali had been upset by our few glasses of Cognac, for he was a Muslim and did not drink in public, but if that was the case it was foolish to bring us to a bar in the first place.

Now he started to relax as I laid out my maps on the table and we settled down to discuss our route. I intended to follow in my father's footsteps as far as possible: first to Khassaut from where we would strike out across the mountains until we reached Utsch-Kalan on the headwaters of the Kulan river. Once this was the capital of Karachay, but it too had been decimated by Stalin and only a few houses remained. A short distance from there we would enter the Hurzuk valley, where 500 Karachaites held out against 20,000 Tsarist soldiers in 1828 until after several months they were forced to surrender, which they did with honour, each side respecting their enemy. Then back to the Kuban river, which we would follow to Teberda and finally to Dombay at the foot of the mountains.

Instead, Ali suggested going by car to a village two hours away where we would get our horses and walk with them for seven days until we reached the base of the Klukhor Pass which he said he had crossed, and I saw no reason to disbelieve him. The actual crossing might take two days with a further day for our descent to a point where we might be able to find transport and reach Sokhum on the Black Sea.

Ali explained that the horses would have to be left behind before our ascent of the pass since it was too narrow for them, which made me wonder how I could manage if a horse could not. Ali added that we would have to carry our luggage. He assured us that this was no problem for the distance was only twenty-six kilometres.

James gave a sort of yelp. 'Twenty-six kilometres? But that's about sixteen miles!'

Ali smiled, assuring us that he and Yuri could carry the luggage or hire a local guide to help us.

Everything suddenly seemed straightforward, suspiciously so in retrospect. But after we agreed that we should allow eleven days to make the journey, possibly twelve in case of bad weather, Ali horrified me with the alternative suggestion that we could make the journey by car by a more obvious route, walking during the day and meeting up with the driver at an overnight stop in the evening. Undoubtedly this would have been easier and Yuri nodded his approval. I had to stress immediately that the whole point of the journey as far as I was concerned was to leave the beaten track and enter the solitude of the Caucasus and go where few had gone before. I sensed that they thought this perverse, but I was adamant. I did not wish it to be easy.

Then we compared lists of equipment. We had our own sleeping bags and Ali said he would arrange for the two tents for bad weather and the final ascent. Ali's fishing-rod was added, with the flies I had brought with me of the type used by my father when he fished the Kuban River.

Apart from the brown trout which Ali was certain to catch, food presented more of a problem than I had realized. There was little chance of buying *smetana*, the sour cream devoured by my father and Wicksteed, nor eggs or even fruit as we made our way, though Ali promised to kill a sheep for us at his home before we left. As for drink, Narzan water could be taken from the natural springs. We had been given five bottles of Georgian wine in Tbilisi, but we decided to give them as presents for return hospitality in Kislovodsk. I suggested it would be a good idea to bring several of the small bottles of Cognac as a night-cap, especially in bad weather. I sensed that Ali regarded this as a self-indulgence and in the event we took only one small bottle which was three-quarters full and was rationed nightly with our mugs of tea. Ali's attitude to alcohol varied, for he was to welcome that nightly treat as much as we did. Now, in the sanatorium, his friend the barman, a wistful, bearded poet, produced a special Cognac, which Ali drank with the rest of us. The taste was so superb it encouraged me to forsake vodka altogether unless it was pressed on me as a hospitality impossible to refuse.

Yuri declared euphorically that Ali was the best man in the district to guide us on such a journey. 'Why!' he enthused, 'he is worth 5,000 dollars!'

I winced, hoping that Ali did not understand this, for the moment had arrived to hand over the money, 500 dollars instead of 5,000. Ali was not a man to be effusive but appeared satisfied, and so was I.

CHAPTER THIRTEEN

'Of Arched Eyebrows Plucked
by Pretty Fingers'

ALI was a Karachaite – but who are the Karachaites? I had little idea of their background, for they are rarely mentioned in the history books and Stalin did his utmost to erase their past, which was why Ali and his friends were so appreciative when they learned that I wanted to know of their importance in the Caucasus.

The conspiracy of silence, encouraged by the Russians as if the Karachaites are not worth mentioning, is bewildering, for they go back centuries to the tribe with the prosaic name of Alan. Their graves have been discovered as far north as Rostov on the River Don, dating from two thousand years ago, and Pliny, writing in the first century, described them crossing the Klukhor Pass with climbing irons and toboggans, sliding past the glaciers on their way to the ancient city of Dioscurias, now Sokhum on the Black Sea.

The Alans were heathen rather than Muslim. At the end of the fifth century they travelled from the Black Sea to Rome with the Goths, who continued to Spain and Africa while the Alans returned to the Caucasus, where they were known for five hundred years as the Alan State. As autonomous republics emerged claiming a nominal independence, the most important in the western Caucasus were the Karacheyvo, whose capital was Karachyvosk; and the Cherkessians, or Circassians, the people of the Caucasus, whose capital was Cherkesskaya. The complex nature of these tribes with their different religions and backgrounds makes those of Bosnia and Serbia seem simple. When he entered the mountains, my father wrote of the various conflicts:

> Over the ridges of the lower mountains to our right lay the country of the Kabarda-Balkarians, people of Turco-Tartar and pure Arabian blood. Their capital had once been the commercial centre for Byzantium. It was these sophisticated, softened, trading people who had refused to join the great Shamil, in his last wild guerilla campaign against the Tsarist Russians, and thereby forced his surrender, and the end of 160 years' Caucasian war between Cross and Crescent. Flanking us lay the Ossetes, who, lying across the centre of the main chain, sold the key of the Caucasus to the Russians – the Mamison Pass.

In the same way, Ossetia preferred to stay in the Soviet Union when Georgia declared independence in 1990. As for the little-known Mamison Pass, at 9,265 feet, this was the other main pass across the 125 miles of the frozen chain of mountains, though more impenetrable than the Krestovyy, or Georgian Military Highway. As for the Klukhor Pass, historically a military track to Sokhum and the Black Sea, that was no longer practical due to erosion. It had virtually disappeared.

At their peak in the last century, the Karachaites (descendants of the Alans) numbered 300,000. Ali estimated that two-thirds were killed, or died in their Stalinist exile, before Khrushchev allowed the survivors to return. They have been the greatest survivors of all. Somehow in all this bloodshed and intrigue, the Karachaites continued because of their isolation. In 1820, the English explorer Douglas Freshfield wrote that 'the fierce tribes of the Karatshoi [confusingly there are numerous spellings] prevented any attempt to penetrate their fastnesses', and they preserved this measure of freedom after the Russian Revolution until Stalin's soldiers swept into the western Caucasus to take their revenge when the Germans withdrew from their occupation of Kislovodsk. It is odd that their survival should go unnoticed when so many tribes were

18. Shamil, the formidable Muslim leader of the Eastern Caucasus, who fought the Tsarist troops from 1834 to 1859 when he was captured. He became a popular hero in England, where songs were named after him.

19. Ali skinning the sheep outside his home in Kislovodsk.

20. James Birch with admirers in Khassaut – the few young people left. The 'smiling woman' holds her hand to her face.

21. The uncle, waiting to be greeted with due respect
in his capacity as head man of the village of Khassaut.

22. Myself on horseback – a ridiculous sight – and the unfortunate animal's owner, a Karachaite shepherd.

23. Leaving the ruins of Khassaut, we set out with our horses to climb the Caucasus. The remains of the mosque, though not the minaret, can be seen in the background on the right.

24. Hadji devouring my scraps outside the *kosh* opposite Mount Elbrus, our first overnight stop.

25. James, Yuri and Ali in the *kosh* at the top of the hill where we bedded down for the night.

26. Ali (Hadji's head), James Birch and myself, with a sweep of the Caucasus behind.

27. Ali, our Karachaite guide, who rose to the occasion when our porters deserted us.

28. Ali rescuing my shirt beside the refreshing river where I hoped to stay the night.

29. Ali diving into the glacial water of Lake Turie, at Dombay. Rashly, I followed, at the risk of dying from the shock.

30. Lake Klukhor. In the foreground is a memorial to Russian soldiers killed in resisting the Germans. A photograph cannot convey the cold evil of the place.

31. My father's Karachaite guides, with Lake Klukhor to the right and the pass in the distance, centre left.

32. Made it! I reach the top of the Klukhor Pass. The descent has yet to be faced.

33. Descending from the Klukhor Pass over several furious rivers. Even Ali looks apprehensive, while I am utterly exhausted.

34. The massive statue of Lenin outside the municipal building in Sokhum.

35. Final destination. Reaching the resort of Sokhum on the Black Sea, as my father hoped to do. A gentle scene, devastated since then by civil war.

liquidated, like the Kalmucks who came here in the thirteenth century with the grandson of Genghis Khan, whose republic was dissolved in 1943 after they, too, sided with the Germans. It is estimated that 200,000 Kalmucks were deported to Siberia, though a few escaped to Paraguay after fleeing with the retreating Germans.

Once there were separate tribes in almost every valley; one of the most romantic was the Khevsuours who claimed descent from the Crusaders and wore chain-mail until the end of the last century and are now extinct. The Romans needed 134 intepreters to make themselves understood. Frequently they fought among themselves and betrayed each other instead of uniting against the Tsar. When Peter the Great tried to conquer the Caucasus in 1772, unsuccessfully despite his 82,000 veterans of the Swedish war, he was joined by 70,000 Kalmucks, Cossacks and Tartars. The greatest resistance came later from Shamil and the Chetchens who were early masters of guerilla warfare until their defeat in 1864 when many of the Circassians escaped to Turkey rather than submit, the men joining the élite janissaries of the Sultan's army while the women entered the harem where they were appreciated not only for their beauty but also for such culinary delights as Circassian chicken, with pounded walnuts, which became the Turkish national dish still prepared today.

As the greatest survivors of all the tribes, the Karachaites are free once more and gaining strength in the western Caucasus where they are admired yet also feared as wild mountain gypsies who ride into Kislovodsk, where they frequently get drunk in spite of their Muslim religion. The rougher lot are also known as rapists and there is some truth in the accusation. Ali was one of their élite.

The day after our discussion we went to his home where he killed a two-year-old sheep for us. His disgruntlement had gone and he was beaming. Compared to the claustrophobia of the tenement blocks, his home was splendidly open, a ramshackle cluster of farm buildings with a steep hill behind and no other houses to get in the way. A wooden verandah ran

round the main house with tables on which were strewn
drying fruit beset by flies. Ali's old brass bedstead was also
placed outside, though taken in during the freezing winter.
There was neither a television set nor a telephone but there was
air and space with views across the valley up to the opposite hill
with the white palace where Brezhnev had his dacha.

The slaughter of a sheep is a Muslim tradition which many
Christians view with horror, especially those on holiday. This
is irrational when you think of the horror of abattoirs, or our
own stag-hunting, unless it is crudely done. Ali performed it
scrupulously, though I suspected that the elaborate details of
the ritual were partly for our benefit. Nothing is thrown away;
the choicest cuts are reserved for special friends and the bits
and pieces given to the poor. Muslims are supposed to wear
headgear throughout as Ali did, and the sheep's head must
point to Mecca in the south-east before the animal is killed.
Every drop of blood must be drained and in this case it
poured out in a vibrant stream of pillar-box red as Ali made
his first cut across the animal's throat. However, if the sheep is
killed instantly the meat tends to be tough, so you should let
the sheep die before you cut again. Presumably the animal
was too far gone to mind Ali's delay, though this could be
wishful thinking. It was tied up and seemed resigned to its
fate, for it offered no resistance, and when it was dead the
carcass was hung on a pole which supported the house and the
last of the blood was drained off into a bucket. If fresh blood
remains in the heart, this means that the sheep was good-
natured. Apparently this one was sweetness personified. Ali
then proceeded, with an axe and a sharp knife, to cut the legs
off at the joints, which he did effortlessly. He admitted it had
been difficult physically when he killed for the first time
though never psychologically for he had known the ritual
since childhood. Delighting in his prowess, he peeled off the
skin with his hands rather than a knife, for you should not cut
too much or else the meat will suffer. While the skin was
taken away by his mother to have salt spread on it, the horns
and the head were placed on a table, the eyes still open,

seeming to follow me. In spite of all this butchery there was surprisingly little mess; even the guts were removed carefully to avoid the smell.

Ali's father, a tough, apparently old man – in fact two years younger than myself, took the bucket of blood for his dogs. 'Good dinner, Da!' he exclaimed, lifting James off the ground to prove his strength. Ali's mother served us a massive breakfast with their homemade *ayran* of sour milk accompanied by honey and wild raspberry jam. At last I was eating healthy food, though this was followed by gargantuan portions of the national Karachaite dish of *khichin*, a crisp fried dough filled with melted butter, potato, eggs and cheese which ooze out when cut like an immense chicken Kiev, but it is a hundred times superior. It was too delicious to reject, though my stomach rumbled warnings of indigestion which proved all too accurate. I ate it in other parts of the Caucasus, but nowhere was it half as good.

To wash it down we drove to a Narzan spring which was walled to prevent people climbing in, but a pipe spouted the sparkling water which I drank copiously, splashing my feet and hands. Between the two wars, when they were at their peak, Narzan water was piped directly to the sanatoriums until they realized that they were exhausting their greatest asset. Today it is guarded more carefully.

This pleasant outskirt was a modest Karachaite settlement with attractive wooden houses in different colours; one, half-hidden by trees, resembled a tiny chapel.

Yuri revealed that we were close to the Ring which featured in Mikhail Lermontov's *A Hero of Our Time*, his sarcastic title for the most sardonic of novels. This is a book which I give to friends. Lermontov's name might be unfamiliar outside Russia, but he evoked the bitter-sweet lure of the Caucasus as dramatically as Tolstoy, who saw it through more boisterous eyes. It is fair to say that if you do not know and love *A Hero of Our Time*, you can neither know nor love the Caucasus.

Lermontov captured the ennui of Russia, which is one of its

constants. Reading his work you sense the languor, the whispered assignation behind a gloved hand, the buzz of insects on a hot day, the stab in the back with a measured word. Lermontov was exiled to the Caucasus for political meddling, like his hero Pechorin who is posted there following the uprising of revolutionaries among the aristocracy, who were put down savagely in St Petersburg in 1825. Pechorin is blessed with good looks, money and education but suffers from the cynicism of the generation of free-thinkers who were disillusioned after the failure of the uprising though too young to be involved. He forswears anything so easy as happiness. He has been described as 'psychotic' yet is all too reasonable. In today's terms, he is 'world-weary'.

The Russian revolutionary Alexander Herzen described the ten years that followed the revolt as 'not enough to make them grow old, but enough to break them. They became stifled in a society without any real interests, wretched, cowardly and servile.'

A hero? Lermontov explained in his foreword: '*A Hero of Our Time*, my dear sirs, is indeed a portrait, but not of one man: it is a portrait built up of all our generation's vices.' He wrote it when he was twenty-five following his first exile to the Caucasus for his poem 'On the Death of a Poet' which, dedicated to Pushkin, expressed his contempt for the court surrounding Nicholas I and the corruption of his rule. Three years later he became involved in a duel, the pretext for his second exile.

On my previous visit I had been to the little Lermontov Museum near by in Pyatigorsk where he was stationed. 'Little' is not meant disparagingly. These are the quarters of an army officer in a low white-washed house with shutters and a thatched roof. Inside, a narrow bed lies beside a colourful red carpet on the wall, and his uniform and white forage cap hang beside the wardrobe. It is all basic, though there are touches which indicate that these were the billets of an exceptionally civilized young man: a wooden chair is placed beside a circular table prepared with paper, ink and quill, in an alcove on the outside balcony with fir trees a few feet away. An easel stands in the other room with one of his paintings, for Lermontov was an accomplished watercolourist and the walls are hung with his pictures. These include a self-portrait which reveals him as a slight, dark-featured man with wide eyes alert with suspicion, and small black moustaches which curl up at the end. He excelled with the drama of his watercolours of the Daryal Gorge, *Mount Elbrus at Sunrise* and *The Environs of Pyatigorsk*, then scarcely more than a village with snow peaks in the distance. He records them lovingly as if he belonged there. And this is the spell of the Caucasus, that he *did* belong. The exiles, voluntary or conscripted, found a solace which redeemed their loneliness.

Even in the remote garrisons described by Tolstoy, where men were prepared to die and whiled away the days by playing cards, drinking bad champagne and pursuing the few available women, they found a freedom of expression denied to them in St Petersburg, and if they were posted to Kislovodsk they could have the best of both worlds, the town's sophistication and surrounding beauty. Even Pechorin, who nurtured his loneliness, joins the evening ride to the Ring on the outskirts, a strange rock formation like a solitary jutting cliff above the River Podkumok where a freak of nature has bored a hole through which the last rays of the setting sun can be seen. The evening excursion had romantic motives too: 'A large cavalcade set out to watch the sunset through the rocky window. To tell the truth, though, none of us thought of the sunset. I rode next to Princess Mary.' Crossing the river in mid-stream where the current is swiftest, she sways and Pechorin quickly bends down and puts his arm around her waist, tightening his embrace. 'What are you doing?' she protests, but he pays no heed to her quivering confusion and his lips touch her soft cheek. She speaks at last: 'Either you despise me or you love me very much.'

Pechorin makes no reply and when they rejoin the others the Princess is unnaturally gay, though he knows she will spend a sleepless night weeping, and realizes that 'The very thought gives me infinite pleasure; there are moments when I understand the Vampire ... And yet I have the reputation of being a good fellow and try to live up to it.'

But this is the incident which antagonizes his fellow-officers, provoking a reluctant rival Grushnitsky into challenging Pechorin to a duel.

The duel is the great moment of the novel.

'Pechorin must be taught a lesson,' declares the captain of dragoons. 'These Petersburg whippersnappers get uppish until they're rapped on the knuckles! Just because he always wears clean gloves and shiny boots he thinks he's the only society man around.'

'And that supercilious smile of his!' exclaims another. 'I'm certain he's a coward.'

To test his courage, they agree that Pechorin's pistol will not be loaded. They are unaware that he has overheard the conspiracy and calls their bluff with his customary indifference, agreeing to fight it out on the top ledge of the Ring, which assumes a symbolic importance. He tells Princess Mary the truth: 'without trying to justify myself or to explain my actions. I do not love you.' Afterwards, he wonders why he has done this:

> Sometimes I despise myself; is that why I despise others too? I am no longer capable of noble impulses; I am afraid of appearing ridiculous to myself. Another in my place would have offered the princess *son coeur et sa fortune* but for me the word *marriage* has an odd spell: no matter how passionately I might love a woman it is farewell to love if she as much as hints at my marrying her. My heart turns to stone, and nothing can warm it again. I would make any sacrifice but this; twenty times I can stake my life, even my honour, but my freedom I shall never sell. Why do I prize it so much? What do I find in it? What am I aiming at? What have I to expect from the future? Nothing, absolutely nothing. It is some innate fear, an inexplicable foreboding.

Knowing of the deception, he approaches the duel in a state

of resignation – 'The world will lose little, and I am weary enough of it all' – but as he reaches the Ring he cannot remember a morning bluer or fresher: 'The exultant ray of the new day had not yet penetrated into the gorge; now it gilded only the tops of the crags that towered above us on both sides … I remember that at that moment I loved nature as never before.' The spell of the Caucasus yet again. They reach the top of the projecting cliff to find the ledge covered with fine sand as if laid there especially for the duel.

> All round, wrapped in the golden mist of morning, the mountain peaks clustered like a numberless herd, while in the south Elbrus loomed white, bringing up the rear of a chain of icy summits among which roamed the feathery clouds blown in from the east. I walked to the brink of the ledge and looked down; my head nearly swam. Down below it was dark and cold as in a grave, and the moss-grown jagged rocks hurled by storm and time awaited their prey.'

It is agreed that the first man to face his opponent's fire should stand at the edge of the abyss. Grushnitsky is filled with shame at killing an unarmed man, and Pechorin's doctor begs him to reveal that he knows of their deception. 'Certainly no. Perhaps I want to be killed.' Grushnitsky's bullet grazes his knee but he keeps his balance. As they change places, Pechorin assures his opponent, 'Don't be afraid. Everything in the world is a pack of nonsense. Nature, fate, life itself, all are worthless.' He gives the man a last chance to retract and then calls his bluff. 'Doctor, these gentlemen, no doubt in their haste, forgot to put a bullet into my pistol: I beg you to reload it – and well.'

'It can't be, I loaded both pistols,' the captain protests, but they know he is lying. Pechorin fires.

> When the smoke cleared, there was no Grushnitsky on the ledge. Only a thin pillar of dust circled over the brink of the precipice. Everybody cried out at once.
> *'Finita la commedia!'* I said to the doctor.

He did not reply, but turned away in horror.

I shrugged my shoulders and bowed to Grushnitsky's seconds. As I came down the path I saw Grushnitsky's bloodstained corpse between the clefts of the rocks. Involuntarily I closed my eyes.

The affair is hushed up.

I have been to famous literary sites and been disappointed, but not by the Ring. It is both tremendous and delicate. If I were a watercolourist I would have painted it interminably, with its infinite variety of colours and contours. A camera cannot do the subtlety or perspective justice. Partly, of course, my emotion was due to the knowledge of Pechorin's duel. Also, of the aftermath. Lermontov was killed a year after his second exile, in a duel at Pyatigorsk. It is said that he rode to the meeting place savouring every moment of the natural surroundings he loved, as if he was taking leave of them. As the seconds primed their pistols, a thunderstorm erupted and the skies were torn by lightning as Lermontov fell, killed by the jealous fellow-officer, though Lermontov merely raised his pistol into the air himself, a detail suppressed in the enquiry. He was not yet twenty-seven. Dispossessed, he had found his destiny here, seduced by the voluptuousness of mountains. Behind his cynical façade, Lermontov was in love with the Caucasus.

This was the atmosphere my father expected too, naively, in 1929, with echoes of the spa used by the Tsarist officers and their camp followers, a place of 'rendezvous, lovers' trysts, of picnics on horseback into the wild ravines of the mountains, of arched eyebrows plucked by pretty fingers; the mazurka, gold epaulettes – and duels.' He was looking back nostalgically, but these romantic days belonged to a distant, Tsarist past. In 1929 the Communists were taking over, and my father was dismayed:

Now all that was over. Romance was gone, beauty was dead. And Wicksteed and I, wandering in our search for horses, felt as alien in that hostile existence as if we had been invaders from another planet. The faces of even the old buildings had changed – and refused us admission. The Grand Hotel, the Park, etc ... these had become the Red Stone, Red October, the Karl Marx Sanatorium, all reserved for responsible Communist Party workers – and no arched eyebrows plucked by pretty fingers or any bourgeois nonsense about being drowned in love for the factory lads and lassies (if such there were among that lot) who now inhabited them. Love had been put on a 'natural' basis; like an animal going on heat. It was about as unappetizing and vexatious an atmosphere as I ever want to breathe. Even old Wicksteed, indefatigable champion of the proletariat, had to mutter as we stared at the odiously arrogant, happy and hostile faces all staring at us, in the Narzan Gallery. 'This is a *beastly* place! Already ruined by tourists! I would not want to spend a night here even if I *could* stay!' I had to smile; that he should call his beloved Bolsheviki tourists!

It was unusual for my father to indulge in such impetuous hyperbole. His objectivity as a foreign correspondent was impeccable, but this was the start of his disillusionment with Russia. Until that moment he regarded 1929 as 'unquestionably the high point of the Russian Revolution – the Russians were still human (as they will be again some day). In roving about Russia I had met Communist after Communist whose devoted self-sacrifice and zeal had aroused my envy.'

But after his 'long, lazy and hopeful trip' down the Volga, he was furious to arrive at Kislovodsk and find

the old boring Moscow atmosphere again: all the suspicions, and politically indoctrinated hates ... It can be understood why the faces in the Narzan Gallery struck me as odiously happy: they were mutton, sheep. And their ignorance about the outside world was invincible. The clear streams, the snowy mountains, the deep pine and fresh beech forests, all the ever new and radiant beauty of nature – these idiots, with their materialistic conception of life, would deny anything but utilitarian values: what they could get out of them. Staring at them, I thought that while the mountains themselves, the sheer rocks might defy them, the mountaineers could not: this spring of 1929 was probably the last when one could ride up among the tribesmen in the higher Caucasus and still be among free men . . .

In 1991, the Caucasian spas had entered a third phase. The irony did not escape me that when my father came there the Communists were moving in; now they were on their way out. For once in my life I was delighted to reach a contrary opinion to that of my father, for I was one of the 'odiously happy' faces who drank the Narzan water in the Gallery when I joined them in Kislovodsk sixty years later. After Moscow where it was virtually impossible to eat or drink in the open air, it was a treat to eat an ice-cream in the shaded tea garden, albeit beside a dirty pool. As for the Gallery, it was still abounding with 'sheep' bringing glasses or cups to drink the prized water which spouted from marble stands in varying strength. Mine was 'moderate' and the sulphurous water tasted as foul as anything which is meant to be good for you, though I have drunk gallons of the delicious stuff from natural springs since then and realize why it arouses such passion.

Blocked by officialdom at every attempt, my father was unable to get horses and finally sought the help of a Circassian, with cartridge-covered breasts and a silver-handled dagger, who sat at a kiosk in the park as an 'exhibit', selling postcards.

'It would be better,' he told my father, leaning forward in case they were overheard, 'if you got your horses inside the Caucasus.' There was an old Kuban Cossack who could usually be found sleeping off a drunken bender with his back against the wall of the old Tartar mosque, and he had a *lineaka*. So my father left Kislovodsk thankfully on this springless cart led by two remarkable little horses with Uncle Yeroshka frequently lashing the wheels with chains so that he could slide his cart like a sledge down the steep ledge that led into the valley, crying 'Steady, my darlings!'

I was impatient to be on my way to Khassaut myself, exasperated by Ali's well-meant indifference to schedules or clocks. Determined to introduce us to his Karachaite friends, he drove us out of town in the late afternoon, passing a bold, new sign which announced that we were entering the Karachay region. That this is an autonomous republic is wishful thinking but already there were foundations for modern settlements and for two mosques – signs of the Karachaite recovery. The Muslims may be in a minority but they help each other out with a network of relatives. Ali, however, was pessimistic in spite of the new religious tolerance, telling us that the old traditions had been destroyed by progress and there were too many cases of rape of Russian girls, even though former laws condemned any violence against women, or the bullying of the old and the weak. Formerly a rapist would have been killed on the spot with no fear of a vendetta when women were left alone in their huts while the men went off to fight or hunt. Those harsher days are gone and there is no denying that the Karachaites are prospering – 'Under Stalin our shepherds were limited to twenty sheep compared to the flocks in Tsarist days. Now we can have five hundred. It's a really good time to get rich but it is difficult to restore the spirt of our nation. We may be richer but there is no more discipline.' Ali's lament was echoed throughout the new Federation of Russia where many look back fondly to the stricter days of Stalin. Memories of his cruelty are short.

Ali belonged to a Karachaite nobility and had a hundred relatives to call on. One was the boss of the local council, a rough diamond whom we collected from his village, and drove into the hills with a further stop to buy jars of honey from a man who wore the traditional gauze mask. With lush countryside and plump cattle munching on the green slopes, this was Pirosmani's landscape at last. Ali wanted to show us a wooden villa intended for top Communist officials, now planned as a hunting lodge for his friends though they had just run out of money for the last materials and it was empty. The lodge was placed romantically at the foot of a forest inhabited by wolves, hare, wild cats, boar and bear, and of course the eagles which glided above. Ali became like a bear himself, with the largest, strongest human paws I have seen. Completely relaxed, his face was creased by smiles as he talked excitedly, his eyes half-closed, laughing aloud with pleasure. I wandered outside as the mist started to fall with the descending dusk and large, friendly dogs followed the shepherds who carried logs for the open fire inside the unfinished hut. When the dogs barked with excitement, the sound echoed into the forest as if a thousand dogs were barking back.

The meal, prepared inevitably by Ali, consisted of chunks of refreshing water-melon which Yuri assured me was good for the kidneys though James warned me of hepatitis, followed by lamb soup with a pungent garlic sauce and not at all greasy, and finally with huge bony chunks of boiled lamb from the animal slaughtered that morning. I assumed that the chops and legs were being kept for our journey across the mountains. How wrong this proved to be, but where they were distributed remains a mystery.

With the seduction of food and fire and the strong wine we brought from Georgia, the Boss aired his views dogmatically. As ignorant as he looked, he was a rabid anti-Semite, infuriating Yuri as he recited an accusing and unlikely catalogue of Jewish guilt: the Russian Revolution was a Zionist plot hatched for 250 years; 90 per cent of the Bolshevik leaders were Jews and Lenin himself was partly Jewish; and they have been belligerent for the last two thousand years because 'they are so *nasty!*' This outburst was followed by the announcement that Oliver Cromwell was a freemason; Martin Luther a Jew who confessed on his deathbed; and one of Churchill's ancestors was bribed by a rich Jew to lose a battle. This last one was a poser. Frequently, in such outpourings of prejudice there is an unexpected truth, but neither James nor I could work out if he was referring to the Duke of Marlborough, and, if so, which battle. The Boss went on: as the Russians controlled 60 per cent of the world's natural resources, it suited the Jews to eliminate the Russian people and take over, which was why they had instigated the coup in order to make it fail and wipe out the generals – 'Ninety-five per cent of those who back

Yeltsin are Jews. Einstein stole his theory from a man called Gilbert ...' The welter of statistics continued, leaving Yuri fuming because they were too far-fetched to answer. This did not prevent him from trying to do so as we rattled back in the darkness, the primitive tracks scattering stones which scraped the underbelly of the car hideously. The car baffled me. Ali had bought it in Germany, and not only was it surprising that he could afford it, but it was even more curious that he chose a car so low-slung that though it might have run smoothly on an autobahn it was incongruous here, unless Ali was susceptible to status symbols like everyone else.

An angry argument broke out between Yuri and the Boss and whenever Ali wanted to join in he slowed down to 10 m.p.h., even when the road improved, and it was now after midnight. The Boss was dropped off at last, highly displeased with Yuri and his opinions.

As we drove on, Yuri apologized. 'But the man says something I cannot accept. He says Salman Rushdie's *Satanic Verses* is a bad book but he has not read it.'

Ali agreed that it was a bad book, while admitting he had not read it either.

'How is this possible?' cried Yuri indignantly.

I joined in for the hell of it. 'I *know* it's a bad book and I haven't read it.'

'I haven't read it either,' James chipped in. 'And I know it's bad as well.'

Yuri shook his head, almost in tears in the face of such prejudice. I suspected that his contradiction of the Boss had been tactless however justified, for he is not a Muslim. The argument came to an abrupt end as we were stopped by a police road block, the only one I encountered in Russia.

Next day I was woken by the piteous cries of a dog at dawn, a howl followed by a moan. I heard it yesterday. Was it trapped? The cries seemed weaker and I despised myself for not having found and freed the animal, though I had no idea what I would have done after that. Befriend it for a day, only to abandon it again? The cries reminded me of a dead black and white dog by the roadside yesterday, probably hit by a car, with an identical companion distraught with worry as it tried to nudge it back to life. I am too sensitive where dogs are concerned.

The day promised to be perfect and I itched to be away, exasperated by hours of further delay while our equipment was packed into a jeep to take us to the village of Gombashi where we were due to collect our horses. I begrudged every wasted moment, but eventually we left Ali's home in the battered, bursting jeep driven by Ali's cousin Khopay who declared, 'If God helps us, fucking hell, I have so much enthusiasm I could drive you to Elbrus if I have a good meal and drink.'

I was reminded instantly of the old Cossack's cry when my father set out in his *lineaka*: 'Me and my little horses can take you to the moon, if you want to go there!'

It was an exuberant start as at midday we drove out of Kislovodsk through the poplars, on our way to the mountains at last.

PART THREE

The Mountains

O, wild the tribes that dwell in these defiles;
Freedom their God, and Strife their only law!
                    LERMONTOV, *Ismail Bey*

The Caucasus – 'a gigantic ethnographic museum'
                    TROTSKY

CHAPTER FOURTEEN

The Uncle and the Bear

THOUGH Pyatigorsk and Kislovodsk are in the Caucasus, it is only when you reach the hills and mountains that you feel you have arrived. The landscape changed the moment we started to climb.

What are the Caucasus? How do I describe them? There are isolated details which look surprisingly familiar but the whole is on a more stupendous scale than I had seen before. Even the great Rift Valley in East Africa is dwarfed by comparison.

Yet it is not the size but the infinite variety which is so attractive. A ridge of land resembled a rocky formation in Crete overlooking the curved inlet where Zorba danced; black, hornless cattle, dubiously descended from Aberdeen Angus, suggested the Scottish Highlands; lawn-like slopes reminded me of the other Highlands, in Kenya; while woods with wild flowers peeping between the denser grass might have been transplanted from the West Country, though they contained bear and wolves. Ali claimed they were harmless except for attacks on wandering sheep, adding the universal lament, 'The only enemy in the Caucasus is man.'

These are the twin joys of the Caucasus: the peacefulness of the foothills belied by the sweeping panoramas on every side. Yet neither these nor the range of mountains which stretch back in various layers are in the least bit daunting.

Khopay, Ali's cousin, shouted, 'Have you ever seen gorges

or canyons like this?' translated by Yuri, who added that Khopay is delighted by my interest in Karachay.

'It is a pity that not many people know such a beautiful place exists. We must tell people in the West that the tribes have always been independent and are proud of this. Hard work is the most important quality, very dignified. If you have Karachaite friend he is very reliable.'

The jeep, painfully overcrowded with our equipment and ourselves, screamed in protest as it bumped along at 10 m.p.h. over stony tracks as we started to wind our way up passes carefully constructed on the sunnier side of the mountains, since the ice would take longer to melt in the shade. The additional din was deafening, for Ali and Khopay yelled at each other as if in violent argument though in fact this was proof of their friendship. Khopay looked at Ali adoringly, baring his golden teeth in which no normal tooth was visible, and the happier he became the louder he shouted. Outside the day was radiant while we were incarcerated in the shuddering vehicle. This was hardly the leisurely stroll I had been looking forward to.

I was additionally dismayed to learn that we were returning to Khassaut after all, apparently to give Ali's 'uncle' the photographs I had taken there the year before, when the 'uncle' himself was away hunting. His wife, the nice, smiling, round-faced woman who had invited us into their home for cool, refreshing *ayran*, homemade cheese and bread, with fruit bottled for the winter, tried to do so again but we had already eaten and were short of time.

We started up a different valley on a track no car would have tolerated, punishing our jeep so cruelly that at times it was only kind to get out and walk through the glades beside the river. At the top, the track disappeared and we careered over open fields, often to the edge of a perilous drop into another valley below. The best of the day was lost, the sky was lowering, the visibility almost gone and it was cold, but all this was part of the game. Khopay and Ali chattered excitedly when they spotted a farm in the distance and I wondered if we were lost until Yuri explained they were searching for the shepherd who was waiting with our horses. After an hour as the mists closed down, we found a lone, lean man with one dejected horse, an optimistic dog – as only dogs can be – and a flock of black sheep. But this was not our shepherd; he had departed suddenly to herd cattle into another valley. I had expected this. Ali's arrangement seemed too tenuous from the outset. Now there was no alternative but return to Khassaut. The smiling woman welcomed us back.

There is no hospitality to equal that of unsophisticated people who are nevertheless more civilized than those who live in towns, but that in the mountains is special. I had only experienced it once before with a peasant family in a remote part of Turkey. It is instinctive, the hosts take pride in it, and it is lavish. The smiling woman was the second wife of Ali's uncle (if he was his uncle), and considerably younger. There was a large room upstairs with rough beds and giant pillows where we could sleep, and after I had stacked my equipment I went outside and absorbed the warm-hearted moment at dusk when the village stirred briefly from its daily torpor before it went to sleep again. Women came back from the fields, one carrying a pail of red berries; Ali's uncle returned from hunting; and two horsemen cantered in as they herded cattle and calves along the road, while tethered dogs barked in furious frustration. A lorry drove up and stopped behind the houses, decanting a woman with a shopping bag, and a powerful-looking man with a carrier bag who was welcomed by an ecstatic puppy until he was kicked away by a small boy who craved his father's attention for himself.

I sat with Ali and his alleged uncle on a rickety bench with our backs to the wall of his house as the last survivors of Khassaut paid their respects to him, as the head of the village: one man with a kiss, a young nephew with a smile of obeisance, and a girl with a dutiful shake of the hand, all of which he accepted impassively. He was like granite except for his massive hands which shook convulsively; surprisingly, this did not prevent him from hunting, though I suspected that his aim would be erratic. His eyes were narrow and hard, his mouth unaccustomed to disagreement. It was only when we ate our supper that I began to realize what a remarkable man he was, probably younger than myself. I was relieved that I did not compliment him on his grandson as I was about to do, for the eight-year-old boy doing his homework in the corner proved to be his son by this second marriage. The red-haired nephew was about twenty, playing silent games with the boy with whom he probably shared the same mental age. It was an odd tableau as they talked lovingly in mime while Ali's uncle sat on his chair at the head of the table, apparently in angry silence. He was called Ramazan, after the Muslim fast of Ramadan, and broke his silence to make a short speech saying how pleased he was to learn that I was following in my father's footsteps and was paying him such respect. He declared, as if he meant it, that I was an honoured guest in his house and wished me health and a safe journey when I left. This was so surprising that I found it very touching and felt inadequate in the face of such courtesy as I attempted to reply. His son abandoned his homework and the game with the nephew, and squatted on his hands, listening in rapt respect as Yuri translated.

This was the best of the few remaining houses in Khassaut. It looked nothing from the outside, almost derelict, but inside the room was decorated with high kitsch – plastic flowers, Kewpíe dolls, and posters of four inquisitive kittens and a circus troupe in elaborate costume and heavy make-up. These contrasted with the good carpets on the walls, the skin of a jackal whose snout was pierced by an eagle's feather, dried white thistles, and the uncle's hat suspended on antlers.

Most astonishing was a framed portrait of Shamil, whom I recognized instantly. I had borrowed James's copy of Lesley Blanch's marvellous book on the Caucasus which had an almost identical illustration, and I showed it to the wife, asking why they had a picture of Shamil who defended the *eastern* range of the Caucasus.

'Because he was the Muslim defender of *all* the Caucasus against the Russians,' she replied.

Later, Yuri whispered the complaint, 'She says these things against the Russians, yet I am Russian.' Plainly he was indignant and hurt, while I was enthralled by this confirmation that we were outside Russia altogether, with this echo of the rebellious past.

Ali's uncle shot lynx, fox, bear, wolf, wild goat and jackal. Once a bear nearly killed him. He was hunting with a friend who had gone ahead when a young bear suddenly emerged from the trees and attacked Ramazan. As they fought, they rolled down the hill with no time for him to seize his gun or even call out to his friend. As the bear tore off his clothes in the struggle, he succeeded in reaching his knife and pressed the handle against him as he thrust the blade into the animal's breast. They stayed locked in this bizarre embrace until the bear died, fifteen minutes later. Apparently one of Ramazan's nerves had been severed in the struggle; this explained his shaking hands, which were not due to Parkinson's disease as I assumed. I looked at him with new respect.

Gradually I learnt the truth of the destruction of Khassaut, and the history of the Karachaites, from Ramazan who had been living in the nearby village of Hurzuk when the Germans invaded in 1942.

Altogether, Karachay had covered 11,000 square miles and the Russians had been the Karachaites' traditional enemies, since the occupation in 1828 when General Emmanuel entered the region with a company of Tsarist troops. After a strenuous march they reached the Kuban River where their guide, a Karachaite deserter, betrayed a secret route to their headquarters. At seven in the morning of 20 October the last battle took place near Kartdzhyurta at the foothills of Elbrus and by seven that night the Russians had won. As the older men realized the futility of further resistance, the Karachaites came down from the heights and surrendered. The Tsarist casualties were slight: a mere 3 officers and 41 men. It meant the end of independence for the Karachaites and the start of the long submission to the Tsar. After the Revolution, the Communists moved in and they proved worse though the tribe retained an independence in the remotest valleys. Even the Germans were preferable, which is why, when the Germans invaded in 1942, the leading Karachaite family presented the German general with the gift of a stallion, a saddle embroidered with silver, and a golden sabre – the hatred of Communism so great that the Germans were welcomed as liberators.

'They did not harm anyone,' Ramazan assured me, 'except for the Communists and the Jews.' The anti-Semitism in the mountains was startling.

When they withdrew, many of the Karachaites went with them and those that remained tried to resist the Soviets in the narrow Komba canyon, but by then the entire region was surrounded and bombed by heavy artillery and planes. At the end of the summer of 1943, the Soviets seized Khassaut after marching from Kislovodsk and Stalin took his revenge.

'Stalin punished the whole Karachaite nation,' Yuri explained. 'It was so unfair. He destroyed everything. Even before that he abolished private property, even though our economy was doing well under Lenin. Collectivization destroyed our agriculture. He tried to exterminate the free people like the Karachaites and all their records so that no trace of them should exist, which is why we know so little of their history. Stalin even destroyed their books.'

In November 1943 the Karachaites were forced into exile.

'Couldn't they resist?' I asked naively.

Yuri shrugged. 'What use is a dagger against a machine gun?'

They were given so little warning that Ramazan's father had to run with his boots to the Studebaker lorry, supplied by American lend-lease to the Communists, and put them on inside. Within twenty-four hours everyone had been taken to the nearest railway station at Tcherkess. Ramazan's family was sent to Kazakhstan rather than Siberia. He was fourteen years old, which suggests that he was born in 1930, and a strong boy. His father survived that first winter but not the disease and excessive heat of the following summer. The rest of the family survived by working hard and were such superb shepherds that the authorities in Kazakhstan asked them to stay when Khrushchev allowed them to return to their homes.

They were respected also for the sanitary conditions they brought with them – Ramazan built a big hole for a lavatory – and the revelation that Karachaites used separate bowls for different functions – eating and excrement – instead of just the one. Refusing the invitation to stay, the Karachaites made their way back to the Caucasus to find their villages empty and their houses not only looted but also blown up by explosives in case something of value, or a piece of incriminating evidence, had been hidden in the walls or the roof. This explained why my father's photograph taken in 1929 was a revelation to those who never knew the village when it was alive. Now it was a forgotten place; not even the reverberations of the coup had reached here. 'There is no danger of famine,' said Yuri, 'so they don't care as much as the people in Moscow. Life does not change, news arrives late, people are involved with work.'

I shared this sense of isolated torpor which was rather agreeable when I woke at six thirty the next morning and while the others were sleeping under their gigantic pillows, I walked with a towel and sponge-bag along the path to the open Narzan spring, where I washed thoroughly, shaved, and cleaned my teeth. I was joined by two dogs: a friendly little black mongrel with a wagging stump of a tail, and her lean brown friend who sloped back home after this early prowl while the jaunty mongrel adopted me and we walked down to the sparkling Khassaut River, as my father had when he crossed a foot-log for 'a good sponge bath':

It was a marvellous sensation, the bubbles bursting all over me, but the water was as cold as ice. The rising sun was casting long shadows from the peaks behind me and the cluster of mountains up at the far end of the valley was a pure turquoise blue. I had forgotten to bring a towel and was sitting there with my shirt off, drying off, until I finished a cigarette, when I noticed that I was holding up the day's work of the community. These Caucasian Muhammadans, according to their own customs, are very proper people; about half a dozen young girls were waiting awkwardly on the opposite side of the small river, until this half-naked man left their water-hole. They smiled and burst into outright laughter when they saw me nearly slip off the foot-log which was very slippery from the dew. Then they walked across it like cats on a fence. They were in bare feet, of course.

In contrast, there was an absolute stillness on this perfect morning; no young girls, for none were left in the village. A thistle near me moved only because of a grazing bee. Apart from the little dog, there was no sign of life. The ruins of the mosque lay further down, though still identifiable. In 1929 it would have been carpeted with small rugs coloured with local vivid dyes and no woman would have dared to enter inside. As the walls were intact, it was possible it could be restored, although there would have to be a new minaret for that was destroyed.

Apart from a couple of ugly, new-brick bungalows, the makeshift school, and the incongruous Culture Club built a hundred years earlier when every cornerstone was worth a lamb, there is little more to Khassaut today than the single track with the ruined buildings and a couple of houses still intact, like Ramazan's. Yet, what vigour there had been when my father came there in 1929:

Picture these horsemen in a little mountain village of thatched stone houses, with a minaret like a stick of chalk standing up against the blues and greys of some nearby limestone crags, selling and buying horses, galloping down the main road after wandering cattle, reaching down at full gallop to pick from the ground one of their sheepskin hats which they had thrown there in mere bravado, rounding up the grey cattle, smoking, gossiping, lying flat on their faces in the warm sun – you have a perfect picture of Khassaut on a Sunday morning. Friday is the Muhammadan day of rest.

And like all good Muhammadans they were letting the women do all the hard work. Outside another stone and plaster house, on whose roof was already growing a good crop of grass, an old crone was weaving on a handloom. Another hag sat beside her spinning thread from a plummet-like spindle, which she set whirling with a sharp rub against her old leg. The Fates of the Karachaites – of what battles with the Cossacks of the line could these old women tell!

After my father's dip he ate a ten-egg omelette, shared, I hope, with Wicksteed.

Ali had organized a 'light' breakfast for us before we set out with the horses, which were due to arrive at nine, though this seemed late to me because an early start is invaluable on such a day, before it grows too hot.

Far from 'light', the breakfast proved prodigious: porridge, which I refused; a bowl of soup refilled by the smiling woman before I could stop her; scrambled eggs, potatoes, cheese, *smetana* and tea – enough to last a Moscow family for days. Remembering W.C. Fields's mother, who remarked drily, 'Almost a meal in itself', when he tried to impress her with his voyage around the South Seas, and told her he had tasted whale, I asked Yuri if they ate bear. 'Yes, they do eat bear,' said the woman. Apparently it tastes like beef though it smells different.

I went outside to wait. A couple of old men squatted on their haunches waiting too, though it was hard to tell what for. Even the dogs seemed to be waiting or dozing, except for one leonine dog who toyed skittishly with a puppy, probably her own, which wandered off to taunt a kitten, which dashed into the nearest barn, leaving the puppy disconsolate and bored. Trees cast shadows on slopes so smooth that a distant hill dotted with clumps of trees might have been designed by Capability Brown. A dog barked. We waited.

Dawn and dusk can be magical in the mountains, but on this day the tedium in between was almost tangible as the hours drifted away aimlessly while Ali rode off in search of the second missing shepherd. By two o'clock, when there was still no sign of them, I was so exasperated that I walked to the top of a nearby hillock with my field-glasses to see if anyone was coming, but not a speck of rising dust was visible. This is too bad, I muttered crossly to myself, our fifth day since our arrival in Kislovodsk and we are stuck in Khassaut, which I had reached the previous year. In my impatience, I failed to adapt to the timelessness of the mountains; it was later that I realized how fortunate we were to be able to absorb the life of the village at our leisure, becoming a part of it ourselves.

Meanwhile, I complained to James when I returned to the bench, 'Do you think we are being conned?'

'I would never have thought otherwise,' he smiled.

I laughed, and started to relax. 'If Ali does return,' I pondered, 'he'll probably say he bought the horses from a market fifty miles away to add to the romance.'

'They think of us as tourists,' James explained. 'The killing of the sheep was for our benefit rather than food for the journey.'

'We haven't seen any of it,' I agreed.

'And I'm sure he wore that hat for camp rather than tradition.'

To take advantage of the delay, I visited the school opposite. It was a simple classroom with four pupils aged from three to eight, which added to the difficulties of their teacher, who was Russian and therefore ostracized by the villagers except for the children, who welcomed class as a distraction from the daily boredom. She taught them French, an absurdity explained when she told me she had passed in that language at university. She gave a nervous laugh as if she realized the incongruity of the children learning French, and lamented the lack of funds for books to teach basic Russian which she admitted would be more practical.

Judging by her grief-stricken eyes, I felt she would be thankful to leave this alien Muslim community – for ever. Meanwhile she was doing her best to make the classroom look cheerful.

Lying on my bed afterwards I tried to read Chekhov's short story 'The Wife' but it was hard to concentrate. I kept on thinking about the teacher, a Chekhovian figure herself, as well as wondering when Ali would return. The smiling woman told Yuri she was worried for his safety, which made me realize how disloyal I had been.

Sure enough, I had misjudged him. He rode into the village at six o'clock with two black horses, having searched for the second missing shepherd in vain, ultimately finding another. Before I could stop him, Yuri said I was furious about the delay so I made him translate, 'I had total faith in you throughout; I knew you'd succeed. Well done!' To Yuri's further annoyance, I smiled broadly and shook Ali's hand. My congratulations were a blatant lie, as I was sure Yuri would tell him, though my delight at Ali's return was genuine. He had returned with the horses. Nothing further could go wrong tomorrow – could it?

The air was fresher at dusk and now that Ali was back we went in search of the wild mushrooms in the hills which the smiling woman had mentioned, though the villagers refused to eat them. While Yuri bounded to the top like a mountain goat, I looked around with the experienced eye of a mushroom picker and noticed a white cluster a few hundred yards away on the same level as myself. By the time Yuri had slithered back, I had picked a couple of dozen beauties, large and pink. He looked at my bag incredulously, having found only two on his own, and was horrified when James ate one of them raw.

As we strolled back contentedly, the sheep poured down a cleft in the hillside like a white avalanche and surged into a pen with turkeys and chickens on one side and goats on the other. Their pen was dominated by a black ram with four curly horns, not a freak of nature but a throwback to an original Karachaite breed. The animal knew it was special and the nanny-goats eyed it with staring wonder.

Neither Yuri nor Ali had eaten field mushrooms before; they had had only the yellow-topped variety found under trees. Nor had Ramazan's family, probably because they mistrusted anything so abundant. Yuri warned me that I should boil the mushrooms first and I compromised with a quick rinse under the tap outside, but the smiling woman, Ramazan's wife, rose to the occasion as always. Acting as my assistant, she anticipated every move as if we had rehearsed for a cookery programme on television, even though neither understood a word the other said. First she produced a magnificent iron pan and put in a large slab of butter while I cut the mushrooms into chunks. After frying them gently I covered them with a lid in order to let the juices flow. When I removed it she handed me a quantity of peeled cloves of garlic, fresh herbs, and finally the crucial *smetana*, laughing out loud at my delight. I was tempted to add a dash of our Cognac but decided it was too precious. After it had simmered for a few more minutes, she handed me the salt and pepper. The result was a triumph. Even Ali had two helpings accompanied by homemade bread, while I prayed that the mushrooms were as harmless as their look-alikes in north Devon. The nephew watched us intently, always silent; at times he looked so bewildered that he might have been on the point of tears, though when the others smiled, he did so too. I could not make out if he was mute or simple-minded; either way he could not have kinder surroundings.

Ramazan's wife was extraordinary. True to the Muslim tradition that the women are the drudges, she did all the work. She cooked and cleaned, collected the eggs, even fetched water from the river. I never saw her look cross or even tired. Life must be hard without the men lifting a finger to help her, but it could have been this challenge and constant occupation which kept her smiling, though I suspect this was intrinsic. I admired her tremendously, and I was aghast when James presented her with a tape of 'rap' music, part of the 'soft invasion' from the West, and received a cassette of Karachaite music in exchange. It did not seem fair. Then it occurred to me that 'rap' would be such a novelty to them that they might find it fascinating.

Our gifts reflected the difference in our ages. James's were geared to mementoes of 'heavy metal' groups whose insignia adorned the T-shirts and baseball cap (that hideous head-gear worn by American presidents when they go jogging) which he gave to Yuri.

In contrast, I did my best with odds and ends knowing that the most surprising objects were appreciated. I regretted having given away all my sweets on the *Pipkin*; I had only a last small bag of Smarties, which I handed surreptitiously to Ramazan's son, who accepted them so grudgingly that it surprised me. When I told Yuri how I wished I could have given them more, he replied, 'The host has gained in respect because *we* have stayed here.'

I found this hard to believe, until I remembered that this was the hospitality of the mountains which my father had experienced before me. He, too, had his farcical delay in Kislovodsk before hiring his horses in Khassaut. Now we had them too, ready for our departure the next morning, so I slept well under my vast eiderdown.

CHAPTER FIFTEEN

Three Karachaite Horsemen

AFTER washing in the Narzan spring, I watched the cheerful preparations for our departure as Ali and another man saddled our horses. To my eye, one horse was disgracefully overladen. The balance looked equal but the other horse carried light equipment like our sleeping-bags. I decided it was best to leave such matters to the experts, for I am invariably wrong; but a few moments later the unluckier horse sank to its knees and the load had to be readjusted with a fairer distribution. It is always disconcerting when one is proved right, and even now I thought that both horses looked surprisingly shaky.

Ramazan appeared from his house, unrecognizable at first in a suit and grey hat. With a paradox which made some sense, they were off to celebrate the survival of a relative who was nearly killed in a car accident and now lay badly injured in hospital. A ram was shoved into the ramshackle mini-bus which drew up behind the houses, and unlike the slaughtered sheep this animal had no illusions about its sacrificial fate and seemed to be looking at me for help as it struggled to break free. Once the ram was rammed inside there was the usual flurry of goodbyes and the inevitable false start as Ramazan's wife remembered she had forgotten something important and ran back laughing into the house. As she returned she gave me a quick glimpse of the object she had recovered – the small bag of Smarties which her son had handed over to her. Obviously he had been overwhelmed rather than begrudging, as I had assumed, but I wished I had been able to give her something worthy of the kindness she showed us. I shall always remember her affectionately as 'the smiling woman'.

The morning was peerless as we walked out of Khassaut. I led the horse with the lighter load though Yuri warned me he was 'tricky', which prompted me to dub him 'tricky Nicky' – a term of admiration in my case, for I have always felt that in 'Tricky Dicky' Nixon the Americans sacrificed one of their more astute presidents. At least he did not wear a baseball cap. 'Tricky Nicky' seemed docile apart from stopping every few yards to munch the wild flowers by the roadside. It would have been hard to ask for a more radiant start to a day: walking with horses and dogs beside the pure and sparkling Khassaut River, with a zing in the air as fresh as my last gulp from the Narzan spring. The dogs were the two who had joined me at the spring the day before. They belonged to one of the houses we had left behind, though they seemed to be neither pets nor working dogs like the frustrated animal chained permanently outside until it was freed by Ramazan for one of his hunting expeditions, a liberation that it must have lived for. I never saw a dog inside the house, due to the Muslim fastidiousness which regards such animals as unclean. I remember the horror of a Turkish couple who stayed with me in Devon when I put the dirty plates on the floor for my dogs to lick after our meal.

When I asked Ali why we never saw a sheep-dog, though there were herds of sheep, he told me that the little black dog was in fact the sheep-dog of the village. He thought her name was something like Hodjee, and as I could not keep on calling her 'the little black dog' I gave her the name of Hadji, after Hadji Murad, the historical hero of the Caucasus, and the title of Tolstoy's story which I carried with me.

Whereas Tolstoy started to write his Caucasian epics when he was twenty-four and a volunteer cadet in the army, *Hadji Murad* was written when he was seventy-four, inspired by a meeting with the man himself in Tiflis in 1851. He described him in a letter as 'second in importance to Shamil himself'.

Hadji Murad was one of the most astonishing of the Caucasian rebels, a man of exceeding strength and bravery though erratic in his loyalty. Writing about the Caucasus, Tolstoy made constant use of such words as 'merry', 'bright' and even 'calm' to describe the nature of the mountaineers, and did so of Hadji Murad in particular; Lesley Blanch wrote that

> Again and again he insists on this almost innocent gaiety or the good spirits (no doubt born of an untroubled conscience and a perfect liver), till we sense the simple, animal magnetism of these men, so far from the cynical and over-sophisticated Russian officers. Or, for that matter, the dark force of Shamyl who broods behind everything, a mysterious and satanic majesty enthroned among his mountain peaks.

At one point Hadji Murad deserted Shamil and gave himself up to the Russians. If this was motivated by a jealous rivalry with Shamil, it proved a mistake, for he suffered the indignity of being chained to a gun for ten days, after which he was led along a mountain pass tied ignominiously to a soldier. At one point it became so narrow that he hurled himself off the precipice dragging with him his captor, who was killed instantly though their fall was broken by a snowdrift as Hadji Murad intended. Though he landed more safely, one of his legs was broken, which left him with a permanent limp, and his skull was cracked open. The Russians assumed he was dead but he survived and rejoined Shamil, who was prepared to welcome him back. For the next five years Hadji Murad was his trusted ally, leading a series of raids behind the Russian lines in order to capture hostages who could be exchanged for a ransom which would buy them guns and ammunition. With a force of several hundred men, these attacks were of such daring that he became known as the Red Devil, after his red beard. After one celebrated occasion, riding 100 miles in twenty-four hours, he diverted his pursuers by shoeing his horses backwards so that the Russians, seeing their hoofprints, charged off in the opposite direction. On another, he dared attack a ball at the Russian headquarters in Daghestan but mistook the lighted hospital for the Commanding Officer's home. He escaped with only one hospital orderly killed, though the rumour spread that he had murdered every member of the staff, cutting them into small pieces which were roasted like *shaslik* in the hospital's kitchen, and the remainders devoured by the Russian soldiers on their return, unaware that they were eating their colleagues. Though this was untrue it added to Hadji Murad's legend, which Shamil began to resent. There had been ill-feeling when he ordered Hadji Murad to free a lady hostage who was related to a chieftain he had no wish to offend, which Hadji did with extreme reluctance in view of his captive's beauty. Finally, in his jealousy, Shamil decreed that his successor should be his second son, for his first was held as a political hostage in St Petersburg, instead of his volatile rival. Hadji Murad heard of a plot to murder him and surrendered to the Russians for the second time. This time they honoured him as a valuable prize, but he was a captive and his wild spirit quickly tired of the pampered court in Tiflis, described by Tolstoy who found it overpowering too:

> those drawing rooms, those women with pomaded hair, through which the false locks appear, those unnaturally lisping lips, those concealed and distorted limbs and the prattle of the salons which pretends to be conversation ... Those dull faces, those rich marriageable girls: 'That's all right – but don't come too near me, even though I am a rich marriageable girl!' All that sitting down and changing places; that impudent pairing of people, that never-ending gossip and hypocrisy; those rules – to this one your hand, to that one a nod and with that one a chat, and finally that eternal ennui, deep in the blood, passing from generation to generation.

The great ennui of Russia! How insupportable this must have been to the wild man of the Caucasus. Though he was lionized at the court in Tiflis, Hadji Murad was denied the chance to avenge himself on Shamil and rescue his son, who was held in a ten-foot pit and possibly blinded. If he had succeeded in defeating Shamil the course of the Caucasian war would have changed with some form of alliance, but the Russians regarded him with too great a suspicion to trust him. Finally, Hadji Murad broke free with a few of his close followers, killed his Cossack guards and headed for the mountains. There he made the mistake of pausing in a copse where he was recognized by an old man who told the Russians, who arrived in pursuit. Tolstoy described his death; after he was shot:

> then he saw his son Yusuf, his wife Sofiate, and the pale red-bearded face of his enemy Shamyl, with its half-closed eyes. All these images passed through his mind without evoking any feeling within him – neither pity, nor anger, nor any kind of desire: everything seemed so insignificant in comparison with what was beginning, or had already begun, within him.
>
> Yet his strong body continued the thing he had commenced. Gathering together his last strength, he rose from behind the bank, fired his pistol at a man who was running towards him, and hit him. The man fell. Then Hadji Murad got out of the ditch and, limping heavily, went dagger in hand straight at the foe.
>
> Some shots cracked and he reeled and fell. Several militiamen with triumphant shrieks rushed towards the fallen body. But the body that seemed to be dead suddenly moved. First, the uncovered, bleeding shaven head rose; then the body, with hands holding to the trunk of a tree. He seemed so terrible, that those who were running towards him stopped short. But suddenly a shudder passed through him, he staggered away from the tree and fell on his face ... He did not move, but still he felt.

His head was hacked off and displayed in the military hospital in Tiflis to reassure the public, and duly pickled and sent to the Emperor. But the Russians recognized his valour and the Viceroy Voronzov gave his epitaph: 'Thus on 24 April 1852, Hadji Murad died, as he had lived, desperately brave. His ambition equalled his courage, and to that there was no bound.'

'Hadji' was my nickname for the little black dog, and she

was to prove herself worthy. There is a baffling sniffing-order among dogs in which the scruffiest mongrel is greeted with respect while an aristocratic pedigree might be scorned or even attacked. And some dogs simply know they are unpopular, like Hadji's brown friend. After two hours we reached a solitary farm-holding where several Caucasian guard-dogs descended and surrounded us, barking furiously until they were called off by their owner. Not as savage as they liked to pretend, they were a fine breed, large, woolly, brown and white. They welcomed Hadji as if she were visiting royalty in shabby disguise, while the brown companion crawled in obeisance and decided it was time to return to Khassaut, by now several miles away. Hadji remained; Ali threw stones at her to make her go back for her own safety, but she had decided to be our protector and was not to be deterred.

Photographing our tiny expedition I cursed James for bringing the heavy-metal T-shirt and baseball cap which had transformed Yuri into an American politician, destroying the wilder image I had in mind. My annoyance was aggravated by the knowledge that food could have been brought instead. However Yuri was so proud of these Western tokens that he wore his cap even when he went to sleep.

Yuri was invaluable as our interpreter, intuitive and intelligent; Ali was the strongman. I had warned him that it might be a good idea if our first day's walk should not be arduous, but what was easy for him proved hard for us as we started to climb a hill which was so steep it was almost vertical, with nothing to grip on the long grass as I made my slow zig-zag ascent. The grass was peppered with wild flowers and in one cluster of Alpine blue gentian I sprang back from a coiled black snake which slithered harmlessly away, the only snake I saw on my journey. I was relieved that James was equally out of condition and I did not protest when Ali came back as we neared the top to carry my camera case. As he did so, he pointed excitedly to the left. There was Mount Elbrus as if it had just appeared, its twin, snow-covered peaks shining in the sunlight. I knew from my father's experience that bad weather can obscure the great mountain for weeks on end, so this splendid view was especially rewarding. At the top of the hill, the panorama was more spectacular than any I had seen: Elbrus eighteen miles away; the furthest mountains thirty miles in the distance. There was a ridge of rock to the right with the deceptive suggestion that a vast sea stretched on the other side. A flat-topped ridge directly ahead of us was flanked by the series of jagged, pointed peaks of a child's imagination. The limitless Caucasus beyond were dark, and the closer, sprawling slopes, green hills and rivers had an undulating gentleness by comparison. In this expanse there was not a building to be seen. As for signs of life, I noticed a horseman, then a shepherd guarding a hillside flock, and then another – that was all in the hundreds of miles surrounding us.

After roughly six miles we stopped at a hut which catered for passing Caucasian shepherds, such as the lean, swarthy men who sat outside on a bench. Inside we had soup and a sort of doughnut stuffed with gristle. James proclaimed it 'prodigious', though it was too greasy for me so I went outside and slipped the rest to Hadji, who wagged that stump of a tail as if this was the most delicious morsel she had tasted, as it probably was. Yuri flirted with the two Russian girls who ran the place for four months only in the summer, complaining that their existence is hard and the shepherds demanding. When he gave them some of our apples and pears, I was shocked to find myself resenting his selection of the best fruit. The gratitude of the women made me properly ashamed of my meanness and greed.

We had left Khassaut at eight and it was now twelve thirty, which was good going, though Ali announced his intention to cover twenty-five miles before the day was over. Talking to the Karachaites outside he succeeded in hiring a third horse to relieve our own overladen animal who looked even more wretched than before.

I was relieved also that we were approaching a plateau, pronouced by Yuri as 'the plah-toe', which promised flat going after the hill which had left me gasping. As we set out again we passed a pond with five white ducks, prompting me to recite from memory,

> Five ducks on a pond
> The blue sky beyond
> A thing to remember for years
> To remember with tears.

I knew this was wrong, and was surprised that James could not correct me because he had never heard it before. Checking it since, I discovered how wrong I was:

> Four ducks on a pond,
> A grass bank beyond,
> A blue sky of spring,
> White clouds on the wing;
> What a little thing
> To remember for years –
> To remember with tears!

My apologies to William Allingham (1828–89), whoever he was, for my travesty of his perfect verse.

The 'plah-toe', as James and I now called it, was unlike any plah-toe I have known, in so far as it was hilly, like a road from the top of a hill which promises to go straight down, but never does. As we crossed a field, a handsome black stallion guarding his brood of mares saw us as a threat and charged, stamping his hooves as he tried to keep his frightened mares in order, though he frightened them all the more.

'Very hostile, I tell you,' said Yuri. 'He protects his wives.'

He looked startled when I replied, 'And quite right too.'

As we continued, the stallion followed, prancing in agitation, his mares close behind him. Hadji was equally protective of us and charged back, snapping at the stallion's forelegs, keeping just out of harm's way while keeping him at a distance too. I noticed that Ali regarded her with new admiration. It was a joy to have her with us, so jaunty.

As we proceeded across the hilly plah-toe, three Karachaite

horsemen swept down from the rolling grass hills. One of the men slid effortlessly from the saddle to shake my hand, a gold tooth glistening in the afternoon sun. He was not the finest specimen of mankind; his expression suggested craftiness, which was confirmed by a crooked smile and intense curiosity.

He nodded approvingly when Yuri explained that I was following in my father's tracks.

Did I like the Caucasus?

It was easy to answer that with enthusiasm.

What was life like in England?

That was more difficult, as I tried to explain that in the larger cities we had more food in the shops and more entertainment. 'But there is a wisdom in the mountains. You have a freedom denied to us.' This high-falutin response baffled him, as well it might. Yuri translated that I meant true freedom, not political freedom, which puzzled him even more, for they had that already.

Had I drunk the Narzan water?

We were on safer ground and I replied enthusiastically, 'Oh yes, in Khassaut that morning!'

Was I happy to be there?

I tried to describe my feelings for the Caucasus as best I could, ending with the simple truth, 'This is probably the happiest day of my life.'

Satisfied at last, he told Yuri that he was pleased to meet an Englishman in his country. He shook my hand and, with a resounding cry of '*Dosvidanya*, Daniel!', he slipped back into the saddle, flung out his arms in a farewell, and was off.

I stood there watching the three Karachaite horsemen race up the hill which we had left behind us, their dogs barking in pursuit. At the top they twirled and twisted their horses as if they were dancing, showing off in their exuberance. There was a second of stillness as they stood there in silhouette, and then they poured over the other side and were gone.

CHAPTER SIXTEEN

A Bad Case of Sarcasm

THE late afternoon proved less idyllic, though we seemed to be walking on the top of the world. This had the disadvantage of a rowdy, ear-battering wind which parched the lips and made it advisable to wear the canvas camouflage cap I had bought in Barnstaple for two pounds. Also, the immensity of the landscape started to be overwhelming: I longed for a detail like a clump of birch trees or poplars to which I could relate. As for Ali's promised river bank, where we were going to camp for the night, this should have been near yet seemed to recede as I continued to walk upwards and though I could see for miles ahead of us there was no glistening thread of water to encourage me. When I had climbed Triglav, the highest mountain in Yugoslavia, with my parents when I was a boy, we reached a rough wooden sign with an estimated distance and time to the top; someone had scrawled underneath '*Mit Benzin!*' I began to fear that Ali's sense of distance was equally erratic, possibly measured by previous journeys when he had galloped across on horseback. This would explain why it was taking us longer than expected though it could hardly alter the actual mileage. Ali kept on reassuring me that the river was 'only a few kilometres' away, but this was the wishful thinking of the Irish, who tell you what you want to hear.

Perhaps Ali was not infallible after all. I had another niggling doubt regarding the twenty tins of meat Ali was carrying, with a sack of apples strapped to Tricky Nicky which were starting to rot. Where was the lamb from the sacrificial sheep? We did not have a pan to cook anything on, nor a rod for the flies to cast into the trout-filled rivers. Those delightful barbecues with *shaslik* of lamb, the fish sizzling in butter over the open fire, seemed stuck wistfully in my imagination – unless Ali intended to skewer the meat on a stick and baste it over the naked flames. Most mysteriously of all, we had no water. This was so crucial that I should have checked but I was certain Ali would have bottled it in Khassaut, knowing his addiction to the sparkling Narzan spring.

As for our slow progress, this was due to our pack horses, which were not in prime condition and suffered on the stony roads because they were unshod.

James remarked, 'There must be few places so primitive in the world. Some horses have shoes, others don't, some have saddles and others just worn-out cloth. No place could be so primitive except for South America.'

I suggested that the horsemen in Paraguay were highly disciplined by comparison, and on reflection he agreed.

I struck out ahead developing a fine regular stride, assisted by Gilbert and Sullivan as I chanted 'I am an Englishman,' and then a more military step to 'Tipperary'. The singing went so well and I went so far ahead that I lay down on a slope for the others to catch up with me. When they did, Ali confirmed yet again that the river was now 'only two kilometres' away and we should reach it within an hour with enough time to unload and put up our tents before it became dark. The prospect of sleeping beside the river was irresistible.

As I walked on it looked as if there were only two hills ahead, so the river *must* lie on the other side, though Ali surprised me by saying that there was a *kosh* on the way where we could stop if we wanted to. The type of *kosh* my father and Wicksteed stayed in was a low, smoke-filled shepherd's hut:

There was no chimney, no window; the fire was just laid on the dirt floor against the stone wall. The smoke was sucked out through a hole in the sod roof. And as the flames rose I saw a ring of dark faces staring at me. An older woman, her head wrapped in a scarf like a turban; an oval-faced girl, who was leaning forward trying to pull off my boots; a row of children, dirty with soot beyond all description. And the face of my host! To see a face like *that* – lit by the flames; Semitic and savage, and – smiling. He had his youngest son between his knees. It had been eating sour cream, its face was covered with it – and the father was now cleaning its hands by rubbing them with his own. He sat there on a log beside his hearth, watching us intently for fear that we might not find pleasure in it, find it too humble, while his womenfolk brought us wooden bowls of sour cream, cheese, and slabs of soggy, pale Caucasian maize bread.

Their bed, the communal bed, was a litter of fibre, like sisal, piled in one corner from which the whole family had cleared so that we might lie down. They sat amongst saddles and tubs of sour milk, the women in the shadows, as we men passed the bowl of sour cream from mouth to mouth. We all drank deep. Not to have shown signs of enjoying it would have been the greatest discourtesy. And if I had not seen that child's face smeared with sour cream, I think I would have enjoyed it: but I could not get rid of the idea that its sooty face had been at this bowl of cream first. The soot dropped from the birch saplinged roof whenever we hit it with our heads. One has to crawl inside a *kosh*. As the flames mounted we had to lie farther back on our sleeping bags which we had spread out on the sisal. From being half-frozen we were now almost scorched. A craggy featured Karachaite sat beside me. His repose, so silent, was like that of a cat which sits beside you and begins to clean itself when it is content. Then a girl crawled across and held a copper urn while he washed his hands and feet. Then he knelt and began to pray. He bowed and touched his head to the ground, twice. Then he arose again, as much as he could do in the *kosh*, murmuring his prayers, and then got down on his knees and touched his head to the earth again. An orthodox Muhammadan, he had propitiated Allah – and now we could discuss our dinner.

I realize that I take a terrible risk in quoting such a

description at length, for I know that I can never emulate my father's freshness of style.

Whenever they stopped they bargained for lamb through their Karachaite interpreter, arriving at a fixed price of seven roubles, and agreed on that price all their way across the Caucasus, to be cooked on an open fire, smeared with the sour cream *smetana* as I was hoping to do. 'Mountain sheep are as sweet as nuts,' my father enthused, but I feared I should never know.

My father was strong yet infinitely romantic, adoring the Russian ballet, seeing Nijinsky in New York and Pavlova dance in St Petersburg. The Caucasus were more alpine for him – 'carpeted with wild flowers; buttercups, forget-me-nots, dandelions – and clusters of white blossoms like stars.' But that was in the spring, and we left the wild flowers behind us on the vertical hill.

And if I congratulated myself on following in his footsteps at nearly twice his age, I was brought up short by the reminder of his damaged leg and the constant need to prevent infection. While two girls made butter by shaking cream back and forth in a goat-bladder in the *kosh* he has just described, he changed the sopping wet bandages on his left leg: 'It was embarrassing, but I must say I enjoyed the awe, the consternation which I caused when I dropped a few crystals of potassium permanganate into the bowl of clear water. That fascinated them. This was magician's work!' My father carried a medical kit in a small suitcase together with five hundred sheets of paper on which he hoped to type his stories and justify his trip. Unfortunately the Karachaites assumed he was a healer and produced a small boy from a neighbouring village whose fingers had been crushed between a tree and a rock a month earlier. 'It was a shocking sight. The whole tip of the left index finger was a mass of proud, suppurating flesh – and out of it protruded the bone. I almost gasped.'

My father boiled some water and repeated the miracle of making it turn purple, feeling for the lymphatic glands in the boy's arm. 'The little hero was utterly impassive. He made me feel ashamed of myself for the secret satisfaction I had enjoyed by the potassium permanganate miracle. Their idea of sepsis was terrifying.'

After dressing the finger as best he could, my father threw the pus-covered rag on to the fire but a woman seized it, rolled it up and sat her baby, whose bottom was bare, on the gory mess, and started to rock him contentedly. My father asked his interpreter to translate that the boy might lose his hand, even his arm, if they did not get him to a doctor in Kislovodsk at once. This led to an argument, until the Old Man of the Tribe, the man who had been praying, silenced them with a few words and assured my father that this would be done.

My father thought he might have saved that one arm in the Caucasus. But it meant that from that moment on he travelled with the aura of a learned man and a great healer, and everyone who was sick was brought before him. When one tribe produced a woman who had no nose – 'just a rotting red hole in her face' – he almost needed a doctor himself.

Earlier on our own journey I had been shown a derelict *kosh*, a low hut, rectangular compared to the dome-like shapes made of mud which I had seen in the Masai Mara, though they shared the same claustrophobic atmosphere. The *kosh* confronting me now near the top of the hill was a different matter. Built by sheperds as a communal refuge in bad weather rather than as a home, it had ten separate cubicles with sheep pens opposite. I peered into the first and recoiled from the broken planks, stones, glass and excrement, which would have taken a team of ten men a day to clear, for it was knee-high in debris. There was no thought of sleeping there, so I strode on to the top of the hill to look for the river. To my astonishment there was still no sign of it, so I returned to the *kosh* and was even more surprised to find the others unloading, as if they were settling down for the night. The now-tethered horses stood dejectedly in the violent wind which had risen against us and banged the derelict doors and tore at the plastic sheeting flapping hysterically at the glassless windows.

'What's happening?' I asked, stupidly, for it was evident.

'We are staying here for the night.'

'Impossible,' I shouted back in the wind. 'I've looked inside.' Without thinking, without waiting for a reply, I announced that I would continue to the nearby river with Tricky Nicky, my luggage and a sleeping-bag, and sleep beside it, or stay up if necessary with an Evelyn Waugh book as my companion and my Scargill miner's flashlight strapped to my head. I had seen the first and last cabins of the *kosh* and this alternative was gloriously romantic by comparison.

The reaction was furious.

'Why are you always in such a hurry?' James demanded.

'Because I want to reach the river before it's dark.'

This seemed to me sensible enough, but Yuri shook from rage rather than the wind. 'It is not possible to reach the river before it is dark. If you wish, we'll repay the money and return.'

'Don't be silly!'

'Why do you always complain?' James joined his side, plainly fed up.

'The trouble with you is that you *never* complain!' I retaliated. 'About anything. Have you even *looked* inside?'

To my dismay, they had. Their anger became understandable when I saw the cubicle in the middle which they had singled out and was reasonably uncluttered. A further inspection revealed that the first and last cabins which I had seen were the only two which were unusable. I had been well and truly hoist by my own explosive petard. My insistence on continuing must have seemed wilful, especially as James revealed that his feet were hurting and Yuri said he was exhausted. I tried to make amends with cries of admiration as we settled into our *kosh*, though these were greeted with suspicious silence.

Soon the argument blew over and the wind calmed down as well. There was no water apart from a bilious brown liquid in one of the sheep troughs, so Ali went off to look for a spring in the valley behind us. He glimpsed twelve wild boar racing across it but found no water. Valiantly, Yuri explored the other side and returned with a kettleful of water from a small stream which ensured our tea, the staple moment of our nightly meal, while James and I gathered wood for the fireplace in our *kosh*. By now I was ravenous and could have eaten anything, though not the curious bits of meat which Ali warmed up in a tin. It was hard to tell if this was a part of the sacrificial sheep; certainly it was not a leg, nor fillet nor chop, but something intestinal. Even so, I filled my mouth, anxious to be courteous after my earlier bad temper, though it tasted so horrible that I went outside, as casually as I could, in order to regurgitate it for Hadji like a mother bird. Hadji consumed it instantly and wagged her stump with gratitude, and though I doubt if Ali was fooled he approved of her now because she would guard the horses during the night.

With Hadji beside me, I sat on the steps and looked across to Elbrus in the sunset. This was an absorbing moment, for as the light faded the contours grew more distinct, revealing that a sombre range of lower mountains which are almost black lie *in front* of Mount Elbrus, which rises like a sensational backdrop behind them, the snow peaks glistening pinkly. Through my ancient Zeiss binoculars which belonged to my father – conceivably he used them here as well – I was able to discern where the lower range connected with Elbrus, at the ridge where Douglas Freshfield presumably started his ascent in 1868, only four years after the Russians tamed the Caucasus, the first explorer to do so. But when I went back inside, Ali told me that Freshfield had approached the extinct volcano from the other side, as he had done himself. Ali was a veteran mountaineer, having climbed Mount Lenin and Mount Communism (presumably now renamed).

As we sipped our delicious tea, fortified by a few drops of brandy and a spoonful of my honey, I asked Ali, 'What is the lure of climbing mountains, taking risks and enduring extremes of cold and discomfort which most people would do their utmost to avoid?'

Ali smiled with the tolerance of a man obsessed who realizes that others cannot be expected to understand.

'It is like sex,' Yuri translated, looking startled. 'First you have all the excitement and anticipation as you go up; when you come down you feel a great sense of relief.' A keen comparison, but I was not entirely convinced.

I was able to reassure Ali that it had been a splendid day, which was true. We had covered twenty-five miles in nine hours, much of it uphill, with that first, surprising vertical slope. My father took weeks to reach Teberda, but at this rate we would do so in a few days, which was not my intention, However, I realized that it would be tactless to raise this now. We were burnt raw by the sun and wind, especially on the left forehead and nose. Ali was dark brown anyhow, but I shared my precious Oil of Ulay with the others.

'So refreshing!' Yuri exclaimed as if in a commercial, dabbing the efficacious lotion on his face. I was glad that Ali was outside relieving himself, for I am sure he would have thought this sissified. I am old enough not to mind being a sissy, but he might have been disillusioned in the others.

We slept three in a row and I was disappointed to find that my sleeping-bag had the thickness of tissue paper and could have been comfortable only if there had been a feather bed already underneath. As the floor was hard, stony and uneven, it was difficult to find a position which was bearable to my bones and did not cut them agonizingly. Finally I found a crouching position and tried to sleep, though I was woken constantly by James twisting and turning in his identical bed-roll. Yet, to my astonishment, I woke up suddenly to find it was five thirty and that the others were starting to pack.

We never ate fresh meat again. I was rather glad of that, though I did wonder what became of so much sheep. Instead, Ali opened one of his tins of alleged ham for breakast and this became our diet, including lunch and dinner. Plainly he had acquired a 'job lot'. I quite liked the taste until James convinced me that there was no such thing as ham in Russia, and, even if there were, Ali as a devout Muslim would not consider eating it.

'What do you think it is?' I asked nervously.

'Donkey dick,' said James.

From that moment the 'meat' lost its glamour, though I forced myself to eat it because there was little else. No, there was *nothing* else. Annoyingly, Yuri had used up the entire tube of my Colman's mustard, intoxicated by this unfamiliar taste, smearing it on a slice of bread as if it were jam; otherwise this would have spiced it up considerably. Hadji was waiting faithfully outside the *kosh* in the morning and found the alleged ham so delicious that for one abandoned moment she rolled on her back with delight.

We left Elbrus behind us and I never saw the mountain again. After a few miles we reached a settlement where the Karachaite owner tried to persuade Ali to stay, even offering another sacrificial sheep in our honour. As we had just started out, we refused; also, the place was exceedingly dull, though the man went out of his way to help us, even insisting that I should ride his horse. I meant to have some riding lessons in Devon for such a moment but never got around to it, so I had not ridden since an alarming moment when I was a twelve-year-old evacuee in America. On that occasion my horse bolted through the old colonial town of Williamsburg pursued by police cars and anxious drivers, which prompted the animal to go faster while I clung frantically to its mane, until it came to a sudden stop several miles outside the town. Now I mounted with difficulty and rode a short distance precariously, though even this made me understand how quickly I could learn and how thrilling it would be to cross the Caucasus on horseback like my father.

Pitifully, I was so gratified to find myself on horseback that I shouted to James to record the moment with his camera. It might even make a cover! When I saw it, I realized what an ass I looked, and what an ass I was. Even the kindly Karachaite turned away as I struggled clumsily from the stirrups and fell back to earth.

One of our own overladen horses was now in such a wretched state that she was unable to go much further, and Ali succeeded in exchanging her for another, to be collected from the Karachaite farmer on his way back, such was their trust. I should have thought the nag would have been thankful for the rest, but as we carried on I heard a piteous whinny behind us as the abandoned horse broke free and came racing down the road towards us. I was touched by this unexpected loyalty, but she had to be taken back and tied up again.

My previous day's doubts over Ali's sense of distance were soon confirmed. His smiling assurance that every destination was two kilometres away was as meaningless as pretending that the donkey dick was caviare. I did not mind, for the day was radiant, but as I strode ahead mile after mile I accepted that it would have been madness to have attempted it the night before. A passing army lorry was the only vehicle I saw for several hours and though the smiling young driver stopped to offer me a lift I refused because I had no wish to alert the militia to our journey, for which we had no permits whatsoever. Also, it would have been cheating on the others who had encouraged me to walk ahead but were left to lead the horses.

Instead of Ali's usual 'two kilometres', it had taken me four hours to reach a point where I could at last see the river below. I watched the army truck winding its zig-zag descent, revealing how far I still had to go, and basked in the solitude, for it was blissful to walk on foot and absorb the change in the scenery, the rustling pine trees bordered by exotic dark blue gentian and viper's bugloss, matched by mundane daisies, thistles, dandelion and clover. We had not left the wild flowers behind us after all. A miniature honeysuckle was new to me and numerous other plants as well – there must have been fifty varieties. Approaching the river I cut across the lushest pasture I could remember since my childhood in Bavaria, while a passing farmer drove a team of unbridled horses using his whip which cracked like pistol shots. The long-awaited river did not disappoint: it was a cheerful torrent beyond a clearing, with a wooden bridge on one side, the perfect place for an overnight stop, or two. I stripped to my underpants, scrambled awkwardly down the bank to a small patch of sand and waded barefoot into the surging water, stumbling over the stones, holding my head underneath to emerge purged and tingling. After rinsing my favourite heavy black shirt, I left it on one of the rocks to dry and started collecting fir cones and wood for a fire in the unlikely event that we might have something to cook – not that we had anything to cook it in.

The others limped into the clearing nearly two hours later and I must have looked odiously self-satisfied and rested as I greeted them. Altogether it had taken them six hours from the *kosh* and James looked so exhausted that I cheered him up with the assurance that if we were lucky we might be able to pause for a good half hour before we were off again. This was meant to be sarcastic, because it was unthinkable that we should do anything but stay overnight.

The horses were thankful with so much to graze on and I could have stayed for days in such an enchanted spot, watching Ali fish the stream as my father had done, *if* he had brought his rod. Our meal was 'ham' but the fire boiled the kettle, our only cooking utensil. Plainly, the importance of food played no part in Ali's mountaineering.

My shirt had blown away and I searched for it in the rapids further down in case it was snagged on a rock or one of the fallen branches, but Ali sensed instinctively what had happened and dived below the rock to find the shirt trapped, pressed down by the current.

Lazing on the riverbank afterwards, like one of the characters from *The Wind in the Willows*, I started to doze in the gentle warmth. I was startled to wake up when I heard a cry and saw the horses sagging once more as they were loaded with our equipment. ment.

'What in God's name is happening?' I asked James breathlessly. 'I thought we were stopping here.'

James looked at me coldly: 'But you said you wanted to leave after half an hour.'

'What?' I exclaimed, genuinely astonished.

'Yes,' said Yuri joining us, 'and we've been here now for nearly two and a half hours.'

It took me several moments before I remembered my fatal sarcasm. 'You must have realized I was joking?'

'I wasn't sure,' James admitted. 'I was so tired all I could think of was to lie down.'

'But *you* want to stay here, don't you?'

'We were going to, but you're so contrary we thought you might want to move on.'

'This is madness!'

'You wanted to last night,' he pointed out.

'But that was in order to get *here*! *This* is everything I've wanted all along, it's perfect, and now we're here we're moving on.'

'You complain about everything and change your mind.'

My mind crackled like a computer, trying to sort out the truth, for I was convinced that I had been consistent all along. How was I to know last night that Ali's 'two kilometres', which meant that the river was near by, was, in reality, closer to thirty kilometres or eighteen miles? Trying to salvage my mistaken remark, I explained that I would like nothing better than to idle away an entire day in such surroundings rather than clock up more kilometres as if we were breaking some record. 'Surely we can unsaddle the horses?' I concluded lamely.

'Too late. They're packed,' said Yuri firmly.

And so we moved on, with me cursing my abominable sarcasm which had hoist me with my own petard yet again. I am still not certain whose fault it was, but muttered to myself, 'How could they have taken my sarcasm literally?' Even if James was tired and Yuri did not understand my warped sense of humour. It was so unfair!

I walked ahead less jauntily towards our next stop. This was the junction of the river beside us and the great River Kuban which runs five hundred miles through the northern Caucasus to the Sea of Azov. According to Ali this was less than half an hour away and it occurred to me that it might prove just as attractive as the place we had left behind. With renewed optimism, I strode on with the sturdy stick cut by Ali from a sapling.

After an hour I found a clearing where I sat on a stump to make notes. When Ali saw me there, he whistled to the others to join us and stop for the night because Tricky Nicky was by now so lame that he could hardly put his feet forward. It seemed unfortunate that both our horses should collapse, and that they were shoeless to start with was, I felt, an error in the first place, in view of the terrain they were covering. As we waited for Yuri and James to arrive, I wondered if there was any point in trying to explain to Ali in sign language that it was all a misunderstanding earlier, but felt this would only compli- cate. I was not sure if he was using Tricky Nicky as an excuse to stop, or if even he had to accept that the Kuban was nowhere near. As it turned out, it would have taken us *two days* to have reached the junction, allegedly a mere 'half-hour' away.

Hadji was the only one talking to me now and greeted me rapturously as she started to explore. Unfortunately the new site was dank compared to the haven we had discarded, all ferns and dense damp undergrowth, as if no sunlight ever reached it. Yet it had an endearing melancholy with a cliff face across the river which reminded me of Ruskin's beautiful *Study of Gneiss Rock* in the Ashmolean at Oxford.

By now it was drizzling and everything was so wet that we were unable to start a fire, though we used up several of the precious lighter-tablets reserved for the Klukhor Pass, under my collapsible burner. Even then we could only persuade the kettle to simmer rather than boil the water fetched from the river, though at least this allowed our nightly treat of tea, with condensed milk for the others and a spoonful of Kislovodsk honey for me. With the last of the half bottle of Cognac, we were fortified. I was not hungry. Probably for the first time in my life I had lost all interest in food, though I had an insatiable thirst, and drank constantly from the river. I felt unusually fit.

The two tents were erected by Ali, who knew the ropes literally and draped the impressive, exotic silver material reserved for Soviet gymnasts, which he had bought on the black market. How quickly one adapts. I could not remember when I had last slept in a tent, yet it proved cosy and comfortable.

'Mountaineers sleep with heads near the flap,' Yuri informed me brusquely, breaking his vow of silence.

'Not this mountaineer,' I replied, for it was snugger the other way round.

The ground felt softer through the sleeping-bag than the hard floor of the night before, and I found positions which were almost sensual in their relaxation. At nine o'clock I shut my book, turned off my flashlight, said goodnight to James who made no reply, and went straight to sleep. Seldom have I slept so well. It rained heavily in the night but no water came through and the noise was not too distracting despite sudden fusillades of drops from the trees above. The roar of the river was constantly reassuring.

At one moment I was disturbed by Hadji barking furiously, a reminder that she was guarding us. I woke up and looked at my travelling clock, scarcely able to credit that I had slept for nine hours. Struggling into my trousers and shoes in my half of the tent, I crawled outside to find it was drizzling and misty. Hadji was wagging her stump of a tail and Ali sat there swathed in the silver material looking like something from outer space, having covered our baggage with the same sheeting to keep it dry. He was trying to rekindle the fire, though this proved hopeless. He gave me a cheerful grin and pointed to Hadji indicating that she had barked in the night to frighten off a bear which was threatening the horses. A *bear*! Apparently there are two things a bear detests: a dog and a fire, and though the latter had gone out Hadji remained on the embers trying to keep warm in her vigil. She was shivering now. She looked so game yet so bedraggled that I crept back into the tent for a towel and gave her a fierce rub-down leaving her fluffier than she had ever been in her life, almost debonair with the scrap of broken rope around her neck and highly pleased with her new self.

As I crept back into the tent, I realized it was James's towel.

CHAPTER SEVENTEEN

The Story of a Lake

THERE was now no doubt that Ali's sense of distance was optimistic guesswork. Instead of the proverbial 'half hour', we walked for a further three hours the next morning. As soon as I saw a waiting lorry beside a farm and a modern *kosh* I knew instinctively that Ali would commandeer the driver to take us to the junction of the Khudes and Kuban Rivers which still lay far ahead.

In his broken English and with a fair amount of mime, Ali had warned me that the horses were now so lame that we might have to leave them behind. I was stunned by his suggestion, wondering if I had understood him correctly, that James and Yuri might even continue by bus the following day, taking our equipment to the resort of Dombay, which lay at the foot of the mountains. Ali and I, he said, could continue on foot and join up with the others in Dombay a day or two later. I did not like the sound of this at all, fearing the utter confusion of missed appointments.

My instinct was correct: as soon as he saw the lorry Ali spoke to some Karachaite shepherds near by, who introduced him to the lorry driver who worked for the Caucasian equivalent of British Telecom and was merrily drunk. It was an idyllic scene, with hills behind the farm which were so steep that black sheep and goats poured down them like lava while the shepherds led their horses on foot, whistling to the animals until they reached the fields and were herded into agitated order as they prepared to cross the bridge over the river. Three of the Karachaites posed as if they had stepped from the bogs of Ireland: one short and comic in a peaked cap; the eldest in tattered hat and jacket, smiling broadly; the third plainly simple-minded, red-faced and vacant-mouthed, though determined to be alert. It was a romantic setting, apart from that modern *kosh* built in white lavatorial brick. By contrast an ancient chalet fitted more appropriately into the landscape, though it was derelict with broken windows.

Ali completed his arrangements to leave the horses behind and collect them on his return to Khassaut. Also, it was time to part from little Hadji. This saddened me though she seemed happy enough, having flown at an Alsatian as if this was her territory. She was admired by another dog which looked surprisingly similar though his tail was longer. Plainly they were two of a distinct, Caucasian breed and not mongrels as I had assumed. I tried to impress Ali that it was vital that Hadji should be returned safely to her home in Khassaut and he gave me his word. After the episode in the night-time when she scared off the bear, I believed he meant it. I realized that it would have been selfish to encourage her to continue with us and climb in the Caucasus, though I suspected that she would have coped better than I would; yet I felt a pang of remorse as we drove away in the lorry as she was tied to a rope, especially when I heard a piercing yelp behind me. Looking back anxiously, I saw she had nipped the Alsatian who had dared to come too close, and was wagging her stump of a tail in triumph. Hadji was a born survivor.

While the others sat on our luggage in the back of the lorry, I squeezed in beside the drunken driver and his mute, decrepit father who smelt of roast lamb.

'Would you believe,' cried the driver, 'he is sixty-five!'

'No, I wouldn't,' I assured him, for the old man looked ninety at least and clutched my knee, presumably to show that he was still alive.

Desperate to talk, the driver stopped every few yards to harangue me face to face and finally forced Yuri to perch on his father's lap and translate one of his obscure arguments concerning British horses or football. It was nearly an hour before we reached the promised junction where we were dumped abruptly on the side of the main road opposite a bridge which led to a hunting lodge, marked by signs of an eagle and a bear, where we were due to spend the night. Cautiously, I asked Yuri to find out more about the lodge from a local man who was waiting for a bus. There was no need for a translation; Ali's startled expression told me all. The lodge had no light, no water, and it was derelict, kaput. The set-back seemed so inevitable that I wondered briefly if it had been planned, though I realized that this was paranoic, for Ali could hardly be blamed for the collapse of our horses. After further discussion, Yuri turned to me and explained that I could continue on foot across the Dombay Pass, a new name to me, though this would be difficult to climb with no horses to carry our equipment, nor an interpreter. It could take two days and, with a shrug, the decision was entirely up to me.

I took James aside and explained the situation: 'Ali says we should be able to join you in Dombay tomorrow night.' Even as I said this I began to laugh, realizing the absurdity.

'But that's fantastical!' he exclaimed.

'You mean it might take several days?'

'A week at least and we would be hanging around wondering what had happened to you. Dan, you really do amaze me at times,' he continued as he saw my disappointment. 'What did you expect? Nothing goes smoothly in this country. It's a miracle we found any horses in the first place and have got as far as this. Few other people could have managed it.'

There was some truth in this, and by now the unpredictable was becoming so predictable that I was fatalistic. When a mini-bus crossed the bridge, Ali seized this rare bit of luck to bribe the driver to take us all the way to Dombay and I agreed to abandon any thought of continuing on foot until the start of our ascent.

As we sped along the highway, the driver shook his head at clusters of bewildered passengers waiting wistfully at the bus stops, slowing down for herds of sheep and traffic in the town of Karachayevsk.

Alongside the River Kuban, where my father caught thirty-five trout in a single day, I compared my journey to his and experienced the bitter sense of failure that he must have felt when he had to turn back at the top of the Klukhor Pass. As we continued for mile after mile I realized that James was correct in thinking it would have taken me a week at least to continue on foot, so the change of plan might have been a blessing after all, but this did not lessen my anger at seeing my carefully laid plans come to grief. We had been in the Caucasus for over a week but our actual walk from Khassaut had taken a mere three days. I wondered if anything could be retrieved. If Ali's judgement continued to be so erratic, we stood no chance of crossing the Klukhor Pass from Dombay.

Teberda, which lay in a valley with the snow mountains rising just beyond, had not fulfilled its early promise as a Caucasian Davos, even though it had been spared by Stalin because of its imposing sanatorium for senior army officers. It is now a boring village with no apparent centre and little inducement to linger. We were stopped at the militia post which guarded the entrance to the National Park where our driver bribed the policeman, and were duly waved on into the park which was lined by woods refreshingly green and alpine. At last we arrived at Dombay at dusk and while Ali went in search of rooms, Yuri led us to a subterranean bar with the surprising revelation that this was where he had celebrated the previous New Year's Eve, for this is a favourite resort of young Russians if they are lucky enough to find the transport.

Decorated in simulated elephant skin, the bar was startling: 'Alpeenic', as James described it, with a video screen showing a relay of pop groups, all of whom looked to me identical. They were greeted with cries of recognition from Yuri and James, who seemed more at home here than they had on any river bank, though I could not deny that the two coffees with Cognac did wonders for my own jaded spirits.

'It is like wild western bar, no?' asked Yuri.

'No,' I replied.

Just as it was filling up, the bar closed and after leaving messages for Ali we moved to a disco, which had a certain charm as a solitary girl danced with her child who gurgled merrily. The relentless din of pop is part of the 'soft invasion' beloved by young Russians, a wretched noise to my ears compared to the joyful Caucasian music which followed the cabaret in Kislovodsk. I noticed that groups of young men talked to each other, fidgeting to the sound, though there were few women.

'I wonder what they do for sex?' I asked James.

'Seventy per cent are impotent,' he stated.

'How can you possibly know?'

'I read it somewhere.'

'That doesn't mean a thing.'

'Don't you understand?' he explained patiently. 'Most Russians live in two-room apartments. They haven't the chance to have much sex. That's why most of them are impotent.'

Sensing a flaw in this argument, I pointed out that sex might be difficult in such circumstances but not impossible. Turning to Yuri I asked if there were any homosexuals in Russia.

Flinching from such frankness, he replied gravely, 'I believe a few in the big cities, Moscow and Leningrad. And in the Bolshoi ballet. But I tell you, until recently homosexuals are killed or sent to prison camps.'

'I can see that would be discouraging,' I replied. 'So not many?'

'No, indeed.'

'But better now though still illegal?' (The law was changed in 1993.)

'Better? I do not understand. Please?'

'Well, if it's illegal and sex is virtually impossible in the two-roomed flats, what do young men like these' – I waved around us – 'do when they want sex?'

'Wank ... and how do you say, with animals?'

'*Bestiality!*' I exclaimed with astonishment. 'I can't believe it!'

'Yes, that is right, with sheep and dogs.'

'Good lord!' That helped to explain the number of dogs everywhere. For an alarmed moment, I thought of Hadji – until I realized that she would not stand for any of that nonsense but would bite where it hurt. In fact the answer to my question was provided over the next day or two as scores of young, heavily made-up women arrived at Dombay on their own in search of men, where the hotels gave them the rare chance to enjoy themselves without their families listening to every gasp and moan of pleasure.

Ali found us, having contacted his Karachaite friends in a different hotel where we were signed in illegally as we paid in roubles – five hundred for the four of us for three nights.

'It is a terrible lot of money,' sighed Yuri apologetically, 'but you see, you are foreigners, so ...' He shrugged hopelessly.

'Yes, it does seem a lot,' I agreed, until I reckoned that it came to only ten pounds.

Ali and I piled my luggage into the tiny lift and we carried it to my room, where I had the usual difficulty in opening the door as the handle was broken. Once inside, it was fine and he returned for one more case from the lobby downstairs. To save him further trouble, I waited by the lift and noticed a youngish man sitting at a table near by, writing a postcard. He pointed to his watch to ask me the time – presumably it must have stopped – which led to the inevitable questions about my nationality and 'home town'. I found it simpler to say 'London', rather than a quaint little fishing village in north Devon, and he responded with the news that he came from Stavropol. This seemed harmless enough until the lift doors opened and Ali, scowling, steered me swiftly to my bedroom where he left me tersely.

Yuri explained the scowl when they knocked on my door a few minutes later. 'The man is KGB.'

'You should never speak to *anyone*,' James confirmed, scoldingly.

'Wouldn't it look suspicious if I said nothing?' I pointed out.

'Not here,' said James. 'No one speaks when spoken to. Just shake your head and move on.'

I found their attitude irritating, as if I had done something wrong – yet again.

The restaurant was closed because it was Monday though the remnants of a set meal had been left for us. 'It is in the price for the room,' Yuri explained, which augured ill. The dish was now tepid, an inedible lump passing for meat surrounded by porridge. This was depressing enough, but then I recognized an unwelcome whinny which I thought I had escaped. Looking up I saw a group of English travellers hoping for some food as well. Otherwise the canteen had been abandoned by the Russians who were probably and understandably in pursuit of sex.

Later, in one of the four hotel discos, I turned to Ali with my fatal sarcasm: 'No food; British tourists; Western pop music; bestiality – and the KGB. So *this* is the Caucasus.' I said this brightly, almost hysterically, and he beamed back in the darkened din. The discos shut at ten, and as the others were sharing a bedroom and Ali announced that he wished to go to sleep, I returned to my own room in that state which is worse than drunkenness – half-pissed – from the copious cups of ersatz coffee which I had ordered with my too few glasses of Cognac. Mineral water had proved unobtainable yet again.

After I turned out the light I lay awake as I became alarmingly sober, disturbed by curious sounds from the room directly above me which were hard to identify because they seemed so unlikely: like dancing lessons or moving furniture, in a puzzling erratic rhythm which lasted for a few seconds before relapsing into blessed silence, and then starting up again. A machine, perhaps? Possibly a Russian was weaving a carpet. By the time the noise stopped at three I was wide awake, trying to assess the last few days, alarmed for the climb ahead.

Though James was confused by my bitter sense of failure, for me it was overwhelming. Not only did I suffer in the knowledge of my father's inability to cross the Klukhor Pass;

now I was beginning to doubt if we would reach high enough to learn the reason why he turned back. But it went deeper, with the sense that I had given up too easily, abandoning the journey along the rivers, cooking our meals over open fires, sleeping under the stars. I had been looking forward to this more than the climb itself, but our record so far had been a travesty, as if Ali had planned our dash by lorry from the outset.

I resolved to persuade James to help me find a reliable guide in the morning to arrange the mules for our luggage.

I fell asleep at six, waking sharply half an hour later as I dreamt that a plane was trying to fly through my bedroom window, explained by the noisy hovering of a helicopter outside. Shaken, I took a tepid shower and went down to the dining-room, where the KGB man sidled up to me, forgetting our brief conversation the night before.

'Speak English?' he asked with a smile.

'*Niet!*' I said firmly, remembering that I was not supposed to talk to him.

Three Russian girls, heavily made-up, mute and mirthless, sat down at my table and stared with understandable gloom at the black slice of some animal's tongue and sauerkraut, and went out again without tasting it. Not even the Russians could face that tongue which remained untouched on every table. A pleasant grey-haired lady came over to ask if I would like to join the British group I had seen the night before, and though I detest the concept of groups in principle, they are often delightful when you know them as individuals, and these, the only British to come to Dombay that year, proved to be nice, straightforward people of different ages brought together by their love of walking. The woman was Russian by birth, which explained her fluency when she asked the lady in charge of the dining-room if I could have tea without sugar – 'She may even bring you a boiled egg,' she smiled. This was a nice surprise though I was not particularly hungry; I had not eaten properly for the last three days apart from the donkey-dick, which may have been the reason why I had lost my appetite.

I introduced myself and a young Englishman said he had just finished *Caucasian Journey* and believed that it would be possible to cross the Pass even though snow had fallen early this year. Sokhum, he said, was a further eighty miles away on the other side, which came as a shock, as I thought it was nearer. As they left to continue by Intourist bus to the lodge at the base of Mount Elbrus, the elderly woman was stopped by the KGB man, now wearing a leather jacket. All he did was to wish her '*bon voyage*', but I whispered the warning that he might be KGB.

'I have no doubt of it!' she whispered back, smiling at my naivety.

Still no sign of the others, so I walked outside and sat on a bench. Every detail of the mountains was visible in the clarity of the sunlight which would have been perfect for our ascent, and in other circumstances I would have been elated instead of suffering from the *malaise* which can suddenly descend on travellers, and my particular dread of further delay. What can go wrong today? I wondered.

I was back in my bedroom when the others knocked and entered, wreathed in smiles after their perfect night's rest.

'Sleep well?' asked James, looking at me closely.

I explained about the noise above which had made sleep impossible.

'Oh, that was us,' he explained airily. 'We're right above you.'

'Doing *what*?' I asked incredulously. 'Dancing?'

'Playing cards. Yuri drums his fingers on the table, which is rather rickety.'

When Yuri added that we were off to spend the day by a lake, I had a tiny nervous breakdown, imagining the lake in terms of Seurat or Renoir with ladies carrying parasols, boys in pedalboats, a man fishing and another painting near a café on the water's edge. That I could contemplate such a civilized scene in Russia shows that I was close to hallucination. I had been interrogated by the KGB on the *Pipkin*, my film seized in Baku, arrested in Tbilisi, and all for what? It appeared that we had abandoned any thought of finding guides to help us cross the Klukhor Pass and were heading for a day's outing by a lake instead. I flipped.

The others watched with alarm as I appealed to James for help: 'I knew this would happen,' I stammered. 'Now they've got us to this hellish, snobbish resort – which is what they wanted all along – they're damned if they're going to take a step further. Before we drive to some hunting lodge or kill some unfortunate sheep, or go fishing or take a ski-lift, for God's sake make Ali find us some guides.' Building up steam, I exaggerated deliberately: 'Otherwise, our lives could be at stake. We must have guides.'

James broke the silence that descended. 'Ali left the hotel at dawn to arrange with three of his Karachaite friends to act as porters, as the Pass is too difficult for mules or horses. Everything is fixed for two days' time. We climb on 12 September, exactly as you planned all along,' he announced coolly.

'Oh God,' I murmured, 'you might have told me.'

'I'm telling you now.'

Yuri joined in: 'You must remember,' he added disapprovingly, 'that Ali is our guide. We have no need for other guides, only porters.'

'And he organized that first thing this morning,' James reaffirmed.

I left for the lake totally abashed.

After the others had had some gristle soup for their breakfast at a nearby café, accompanied by the unremitting blare of pop music which pursued us for a hundred yards after we left, I started to relax. Dombay looks pretty in photographs, almost too pretty with 'Alpeenic' peaks which resemble a well-designed stage backdrop, though the foreground had all the detritus of ski resorts with nasty kiosks selling tawdry souvenirs, a Disney-like plastic statue of a bear, and the most appalling outside lavatory I had ever seen. Yet it is one of the truisms of travel that you may hate a place on your arrival but grow to love it when it is time to leave, and so it proved with Dombay.

We began to walk through pine trees with an undergrowth of ferns and wild raspberries, overtaking a group of Russian tourists whose leader was allowing them to pause and take photographs. There was no denying the radiance of that view of the snow mountains nor the exhilaration of the warm September weather, like that of an English mid-summer. We left the pine trees behind and walked across fields of wild white crocus which became pinker and larger higher up, like small tulips. Presumably the lake was near; perhaps this was not such a bad idea after all.

'Will there be a place where we can have a cool drink or an ice-cream?' I asked with a smile, trying to appear friendly after my earlier outburst.

'*Niet,*' said Ali and Yuri in unison.

The road became a path between the alpine fields of crocus and then a track, which was barely distinguishable as I crept under the branches of a low, petrified wood and crawled over rocks. The Russian tourists were left far behind and at first it was fun, though energetic, as I made my way, helped by a fine new stick of beech cut for me by Ali, which was generous considering my tantrum. Even Yuri spoke to me, telling me that the lake was only five hundred yards away. Distances, distances, I thought, promises, promises. By Ali's measurements this meant we still had kilometres to climb.

Then they disappeared. By now the woodland was so dense that I had to guess the direction they had taken, for Ali left no trace. James caught up with me, gasping, 'Do you realize we're above the ice line?' and I was relieved that he was not leaping ahead like something out of *The Sound of Music*. Instead he fell back, out of sight, while I took a possible turning. I suspected that I was being punished, which made me determined to carry on without a cry for help.

It is the treachery of mountains that there is always another peak beyond the one you have climbed, but there is also the unexpected moment when you turn a corner and there at last is your destination. In this case it was the lake and it was vile, a celadon green pond filled by streams from the melting snows above. I guessed that there were underground tunnels too, for there was no visible outlet. Black mud oozed around the rocky edges, which made it difficult to climb down, though Ali was already poised, naked, about to dive, as I trod gingerly to a boulder, slipped on the mud and grazed my hand. Yuri and Ali took no notice of me and there was still no sign of James. *Splash!* Ali emerged, smiling.

Damn you, I thought, I'll show you. With some difficulty I stripped down to my boxer shorts, a jolly image belied by the horrific torso and white hair which confirmed my age. Remembering the advice from an American woman to splash cold water over one's body to prepare it for the shock in case it stopped the heart, I did this now and threw myself in. Plainly the advice was valid for the icy water was not as violent a shock as I feared, though I was protected also by my layers of fat. Even so, it took my breath away.

By now James had appeared, making his way down tentatively like a soldier through a minefield. He stopped and stared at me bemused as I struggled out of the celadon water.

Afterwards, Yuri confessed that Ali had confided that he was amazed. 'When I come out my balls are square. When I see Daniel, I think "Golly!"' I learnt also that Ali had swum across Lake Turie, as it was called, when he was nineteen and remembered this as the stupidest act of his life, for he was alone and if he had suffered from cramp he could have been sucked into one of the invisible tunnels below.

When I joined them, James handed me the last of my big tin of tuna; Yuri gave me a pear; and Ali spooned some honey into a mug of water. I was forgiven.

'We go back different way,' Yuri told us. 'I think it is shorter.' This was a relief, until we started the descent over stones which were far from secure below the glacier, across crevasses which we had to jump, while Ali raced ahead, leaping over boulders, disappearing behind another ridge of rock.

'Keep to the big stones,' Yuri shouted.

'There aren't any big stones where I am,' I shouted back.

Soon I approached the woods and clutched on to the branches of an overhanging tree to break my fall down a slippery face of sheer stone which was wet from the spray of a waterfall. At this crucial moment, Ali scrambled back to give me a helping hand and I gained a second wind, no longer afraid of twisting an ankle or breaking a foot which had seemed likely earlier, threatening the climb in two days' time.

A few precarious logs straddled a torrent and, determined not to lose face, I crossed them, balancing my stick from side to side like Blondin walking his tightrope across Niagara, though I had a mere few feet to fall. Looking back, I saw James crawling across it more sensibly on his hands and knees and, for a fleeting moment, thought I noticed an anxious expression cross Ali's swarthy face.

Down we went, the descent more alarming than the way up, until we reached a point I recognized and soon rejoined the old track across the crocus fields, whereupon all the delays and disappointments of our journey were forgotten as James and I laughed with the conspiratorial glee of young conscripts who had passed an endurance test.

Ali had known exactly what he was doing in putting us through this initiation to prepare us for the Klukhor Pass. His organization might have seemed fraught as one horse collapsed after another but he had brought us here to start the climb on the very day intended. It was obvious that he did not play games.

As Yuri and Ali sped out of sight below, James and I walked at our own pace, slowly. James admitted that he had shared my fear of a twisted ankle and was indignant that they had gone ahead with my anorak for it was suddenly cold by now and almost dark. Though we had only covered ten miles, it had taken us seven hours.

'I wonder,' I said, 'if Ali believes that I want to become a real mountaineer. He acts like an instructor on an Outward Bound survival course, but I'm far too old for all of that nonsense.'

'I have to admit,' said James, 'that after drinking so little I do feel incredibly well, never having done anything like this before. Perhaps it's true that a healthy body means a healthy mind.'

'Oh, I've never believed that. Mind you, I haven't felt so well in years.'

'Wouldn't you love a glass of Evian water in the Groucho?'

'I've been thinking of Perrier. In fact, when we get back I'm not going to drink at all.' I sighed at such absurdity. 'I give that resolution a couple of hours. Thinking of food, do you realize there'll be an R in the month? We'll be able to have oysters!'

As we indulged in these food and drink fantasies, James startled me with a sudden exclamation: 'I can hardly wait.'

'For what?'

'To leave this godforsaken country.'

'James!' I was as shocked as my father had been when Wicksteed spoke ill of his beloved Bolsheviks. 'A whiff of mutiny at last. I never thought I'd live to hear it. Hurrah!'

In total camaraderie we reached the outskirts of Dombay.

The next day we were allowed to recover from our outing to the lake. Ali fussed over us like a benevolent coach whose one concern was our well-being. Miraculously he had found a restaurant in the woods which opened at midday and arranged for trout to be brought from a local fish farm. It was the first time I had eaten fresh fish in Russia – perfectly cooked, too. How I had misjudged him! Like most truly strong men, there was a sentimental side to Ali that was close to chivalry.

He smiled as he saw my delight. 'So long as you are pleased.'

There was no doubt that this was our reward for persevering yesterday.

'They will manage,' he told Yuri.

In the afternoon we swung up a series of four separate ski lifts to a summit surrounded by the Caucasus, less cosy now that we were on their level, with formidable views over the valleys and twisting rivers with the distant Lake Turie which we had reached the day before apparently nestling among glaciers. Pointing to a slope opposite, I asked Ali if that was the start to the Klukhor Pass. He laughed and swung round in the opposite direction to indicate that it was 'somewhere over there!' – hidden in a range which glowered darkly in the far distance.

'What happens if the weather turns bad with rain or snow? Will you call it off?'

'We will make it if Allah wishes,' he shrugged.

Ali went in search of our porters in Dombay to confirm the morning's rendezvous, while we drank coffee in one of the hotel bars. James fantasized over the 'tarts' who paraded in and out in their heavy purple make-up, dolled up in bizarre costumes as if in a parody of a fashion show.

James asked Yuri, 'If the young come here simply to fuck, can the man cancel his room if he teams up with a girl?'

'What a ridiculous question,' I protested. 'You can hardly do that in England.'

Provoked by the prowling around of the young Russians who regarded Dombay as a sexual paradise, James asked Yuri how much a tart would cost. Apparently eight or ten roubles, which seemed very little – just a few pennies by our money. Yuri was covered in confusion, blushing archly as he tried to keep pace with James's scabrous behaviour as he pointed to various women of his choice like a customer at the hors-d'oeuvre trolley in a restaurant. When Ali returned, James asked him if a girl was available and he shrugged with an attempt at a smile – 'Mebbe later.' It occurred to me that James might have fallen into my own fatal trap of sarcasm in which the nuance was misunderstood. Ali might have thought that James assumed that supplying him with girls was part of the service. I suspected that James was joking, but if presented with an attractive girl would he have the willpower to refuse? A night of sex could finish him off for the climb. As for myself, my fear over yesterday's ordeal was confirmed, for I was now so stiff I could hardly move. I prayed for a good night's sleep, a fine day, and that Allah would be well disposed.

CHAPTER EIGHTEEN

Allah Decides

AS I went out on my balcony I was relieved to see that the early morning sky was blue, which meant that Allah was on our side. I had slept soundly and felt fine after our day's rest, prepared for anything. We were due to leave at seven and Ali and Yuri came down to pack my possessions, which I had laid out carefully in order of urgency, with crucial items left to the last. Amazingly, everything was squeezed into Ali's torpedo-like rucksacks, though I noticed he looked tense. Later I understood why.

At eight there was no sign of the Karachaite porters. I expected this to happen. Tomorrow would be the 13th, an irrelevance but symbolic as I told James it was vital to make the descent that day. He looked annoyingly fey and said nothing. Ali had gone in search of his Karachaite friends, so there was nothing I could do but wait, marching up and down. Normally, a couple of hours' delay would hardly matter but every minute is precious in the mountains and we needed to reach the other side of the Pass before dark, a hope that receded as I saw the clouds closing down – Allah was frowning.

Again, I should have trusted Ali. He returned at nine thirty with a mini-bus driven by a friend and we piled inside with our luggage as he explained that the three porters had deserted us. Rather than postpone the ascent, he had seized the initiative to go ahead without them.

Now it had begun, in earnest. We drove halfway to Teberda and took a turning up a rougher road that started to climb through low woodland, saving us an hour's unnecessary walking. Then, as if Allah had tired of us altogether, we faced our next disaster: a boulder which blocked our way with more fallen boulders on either side so that there was no way round. We got out and shoved but the giant rock remained as immovable as the Caucasus themselves. The driver had simply given us a lift and was not continuing with us, so without the assistance of the porter, Ali and Yuri had to carry the equipment on their own, redistributing the load, discarding anything which was not indispensable and could be taken back by the friend to Dombay. Of course it would have made sense to have forwarded our personal luggage in advance but this had not been possible for there was no easy way around the Caucasus.

Those torpedo-shaped bed-rolls proved invaluable. They were an experimental type created especially by the Soviets for their finest mountaineers to take part in international events. There was an inner skin like a foam-rubber groundsheet and our possessions were pushed back inside this as if the roll was as bottomless as a conjurer's top hat. Ali was now going to carry two of the rolls and Yuri the third. I know of no other man who could have done it so effortlessly. Yuri was young and fit but even he found his bed-roll appallingly heavy and complained at one point that his job was originally that of interpreter rather than porter.

My token offer of help was rejected and I did not persist. I had to cope with my camera case as well as a woolly anorak which Ali handed me, though it proved so cumbersome that I wanted to leave it under a rock for him to retrieve on the way back. I grew to hate that garment which apparently had been brought for my benefit, even though it did not fit. My light windproof jacket from London was packed inside one of the rolls and there was no time to exchange them.

James was luckier. With nothing to carry whatsoever he was able to stride along like a Noddy-Head-in-Air, apparently oblivious to the situation around him. I grew to hate him that day. Only later did I understand how hard he was finding it.

And what of the three Karachaite porters – why had they betrayed us?

'Ali is angry,' Yuri confided when we had a moment to ourselves. 'They tell him "Ali, we respect you but this is madness. It is too difficult. Why should we risk our lives?"'

This was hardly encouraging for us, especially when I remembered that Freshfield's Teberdine guides had deserted him too on the grounds that if the Pass was impassable for beasts of burden it was impassable for them too. His own Swiss guides were equally reluctant to attempt any climb in the Caucasus because they could not get there and back on the same day but would have been forced to sleep out in the snow.

Freshfield had to turn back on 27 June 1886, which made it all the odder that my father, knowing this, made his attempt on 27 June 1929.

Ali told me to go ahead to save time so I left the road and found the track which started to climb. Though steep, the going was easy after Lake Turie. Ali and Yuri caught up with me at the first summit, which was marked by a simple memorial to the Soviet soldiers who were killed in the last war as they fought back the Germans, with the advantage of their higher ground. To my surprise, Ali told me that the hardest part was over.

'You *mean* that!' I was so surprised that I was almost disappointed, unaware that this was a clumsy psychological bluff to keep me going, and I did continue up the old military road with a lighter heart. The zig-zag approach was clearly visible. It had been used for centuries by tribes trying to cross to the Black Sea, going as far back as the Alans before the birth of Christ. Later the construction of the Pass had a military purpose, exploited by the Tsarist army in their attack against the Circassians. Even then, the climb was too steep, too difficult and the Sokhum Military Road became obsolete. Eroded by ice and wind it had not been repaired for sixteen years when my father followed it in 1929. Then it was used by the Germans until they too were forced back by the Russian soldiers in the last war. Now it was obsolete again and soon petered out altogether.

True to the beckoning lies of mountains, the next ridge revealed another and beyond that there was still another until suddenly I turned a corner and found I was looking down on Lake Klukhor, sickly green with a smaller, blacker lake with ice-floes dripping into it beyond. If Lake Turie was vile, this was evil.

I had reached the point where my father endured his night of freezing hell. He and his Karachaite guide Yusuf had taken their horses up the same route – 'one of the most picturesque and wildest spots in the Caucasus' – except that they had to forge their way through heavy snow which was firm in the shadow of the immense walls of black rock but starting to turn to slush in the sun. Their gallant horses began to founder, sinking up to their bellies:

The only thing to do was pull them over on their sides, flat as we could get them with their loads, then try to help them to their clever little feet again. Sometimes we only made a few yards. And the pack-horse, which was a weak little creature, soon tired; and we once or twice had to take her load off before we could get her upright again. This took most of the afternoon. The horses did not like where they were being taken; that was obvious. And we were tired.

Even so, they struggled to reach the lake

and there it was – frozen ... A few pools on its mottled surface were beginning to turn slushy green. Water poured through a broken gap in the snow shelf at its mouth and fell over the ledge in a sheer drop of a thousand feet or so. Over this mouth, with a gap between them of only some twenty feet, projected two shelves of snow and ice. They looked strong enough to bear the weight of a man, and the water at the mouth was shallow enough to wade; but it was too tricky a spot to risk horses. We were stymied – 400 feet below the Klukhor Pass.

My father sent Yusuf back with the horses and the instruction to find another Karachaite and bring him back to help carry the kit over the worst of the Pass. He was left alone, and as he settled down for the night he doubted if Yusuf would return. In his notes, which he managed to write at sunset, my father made the facetious comment,

> I am silent on a peak in the Caucasus ... but if I am speechless, the mountains certainly are not. Waterfalls, fine as spun silk, were falling from this sullen monster. And a small piece fell from it, thudding into the slush of the lake as I was looking at it. I sat there listening to the mountains cracking as they cooled; and I no longer wondered why large sections of the old Sukhum Military Road had broken off the cliffs.

He described it as the weirdest night he had even spent on a mountain:

> ... wondering whether it would be really worthwhile to spread out my bed-roll on snow that was a foot deep; while my ears buzzed with the sounds of falling water, and every now and then I heard ominous rumbles and the report of falling rocks. As mountain climbing this was of course sheer child's play; and as for exposure, it was no great hardship. Still – cold is cold; especially when you cannot move about very much. And I had an area of only a few feet of steep snow, the frozen lake, and then the drop of the waterfall. I spent the night there.

Always resourceful, he managed to clear a patch of snow which miraculously revealed a piece of wood. Using pages from his notebook and the last of his fuel tablets, he cut slivers from the wood and succeeded in making a fire strong enough to heat the kettle left by Yusuf, and he made a pot of tea. 'Now I was happy; I had plenty of cigarettes, and I leaned back with some equanimity to watch the night come on.' He was always a heavy smoker, which did for him in the end, but the cigarettes helped his survival that night. Even more astonishing, Yusuf returned with another Muslim and even apologized for being so long, though my father was astounded that he had even thought of climbing back in the dark: 'they must have had the eyes of cats!' Shades of Ali who could also see in the dark and move with the speed of a cat, prepared to carry our kit as Yusuf had – proof of the exceptional nature of the true Karachaite.

In the morning, my father and the two guides climbed the sixty yards of snow-face which makes this the trickiest part of all.

There is a narrow footpath around this spur in August, when it is free from snow; here I slipped, and the stick, heavily jammed in the snow, just saved me from going off it. There is a big drop. After we had got around that, step by cautious step, we thought there was nothing to it; just the long climb up the amazing big dome of snow which makes the very top of the Klukhor Pass. We, or at any rate I, felt that now the worst was over; and all that was left was the long trek on the other side until we found some shepherds and horses, perhaps a walk of two days.

So, what had gone wrong? As I faced Lake Klukhor, I tried to put my father's impressions into my own perspective. In the first place it came as a shock to realize that he *had* crossed the Pass on that 'narrow footpath', yet he must somehow have come to grief on the other side. That footpath was clearly visible as it skirted round the lake, deceptively so for it looked straightforward. As for the 'Dru-like needle' referred to by Freshfield as remarkable, and described by my father as 'weird ... the highest in the Caucasus,' I could see nothing that resembled it, though I have to admit I had little idea what a 'Dru-like needle' looks like.

Ali arrived and pointed to the track which reached the far side of the lake. 'Pass!' he pointed. 'Then ...' He made a downward gesture with his hand to indicate our descent. It looked easy, but as Freshfield and my father had discovered before me, manoeuvring around the lake was the worst of it, with overhanging rocks dripping down on one, falls of rock, and landslides of smaller stones, almost shale, which were the hardest to navigate. All these were invisible from a distance but blocked the track every few yards. Each time I thought I had crossed over the last treacherous landslide, there came another. No horse or mule could have managed it even on the sunniest of days, and at times the ledge – for that is all it was – grew so narrow that I had to place my steps exactly, using my staff, and at one moment I nearly slipped as my father had done, and would have gone over except for the grip of my mountain boots. Recent falls of snow presented a new problem: would I go straight through or would there be rock underneath? The only solution was to try it and see. Fortunately the snow proved firm enough to support me.

There was something sinister about that lake. Even in the early photograph taken by Douglas Freshfield it looked hostile. I learnt later that James and Yuri made a bet: how much money would they need to swim in it? James said he would not do it for a million pounds and I could understand why. A million seemed pointless in such a place, where material possessions were hostages to fortune.

There was one aspect mentioned by my father which I recognized instantly: the noise. It was alarming. The basin of the lake served as an echo-chamber and the hundreds of dripping streams joined together in a single, complaining clash which reverberated round the walls of rock.

At 9,100 feet I crossed beyond the lake to the top of the Klukhor Pass which was marked by more memorials to dead Soviet soldiers. And true to Ali's sexual analogy, I experienced a sense of anti-climax which was almost melancholy compared to the consummation I expected. I recovered by the time the others arrived and congratulated James, suggesting that we took photographs of ourselves on the peak like proper mountaineers.

'For God's sake,' he growled, 'can't you ever keep quiet? After what we've just been through.' Then we sat on the ground exhausted.

We had done it. Why had my father failed? As I have

implied, the simple answer was the snow. He had reached the peak before me – 'But the other side of the Pass held disillusionment. There was no trail and the snows went to the cliff edge and then dropped sheer into a valley that was as white as a bowl.'

They reached a foothold of rock and started to test their luck: if they slipped and slid into the bowl-like valley, that would not be so bad in spite of my father's wounded leg. But if they went over the ledge directly below, that could be fatal.

We selected two boulders of about equal size and shape and sent them careering down the snow-face. The first, gaining momentum every instant, thundered down the snow slope, splashed the snow like spray ... rolled the entire way across the valley at the bottom and part way up the opposite slope. Impressive – but comforting. The next started on precisely the same course, shot down from us and over the cliff – an experiment which, as far as were concerned, settled the argument.

'It is better to live,' said Yusuf in a low voice.

And so they turned back. Somehow my father had mistimed the crossing, which was most unlike him. The end of June must have sounded ideal, but it was too early and Yusuf told him that the snow was the worst he had seen in fifteen years. As they returned to Teberda, they passed three men who laughed when Yusuf told them that the crossing was impossible.

'Do you think they will do it?' he asked my father anxiously. 'It will be very bad for me if they do ... in my village, you know.' But the three men had to turn back too.

With my greater ignorance, I had stumbled accidentally on the right date, fortified by the prediction of Patric Walker, the astrologer, that Capricorns could achieve anything they wished, that 12 September.

However, I had given no thought to the descent. Only three days earlier I had been in despair, convinced that I would fail;

now, I stood on the peak. Looking below, I realized how different and how deceptive this must have been for my father in heavy snow. However, there was no cause for euphoria as I helped to finish off the last tin of donkey dick and we turned the corner to see the whole, terrible terrain stretching far below us with the mountains retreating now that the clouds were closing in. Even after Lake Turie, I had not learnt the lesson that descents are worse, especially now that we were tired.

Lulled by the mountains, I had envisaged a short walk down a path which would lead us gently to the nearest village just a mile or two away. Instead, we struggled over more rock falls and a sheer face of snow which we crossed by stepping in Ali's footmarks. Eventually we entered a wilder version of Richard Hannay's Scotland, with scurrying brooks over which we leapt or crossed, balancing on stepping-stones. After several hours with no sign of life, it came as a shock when several cows materialized out of the mist, belonging to some invisible *kosh* beyond. On and on we walked, in the knowledge that if we were forced to stop we had no protection in the rain and no wood to make a fire. Our tents had been left behind with our sleeping-bags after the treachery of the three Karachaite porters, along with the rest of our tins of donkey dick. We did not even have a kettle. Even if we had been able to make a fire in the rain, there would have been nothing to eat or drink apart from the water from the streams.

Our erratic course took us from side to side of the steep valley which reminded my father of a white bowl, though it was far less smooth and open now; and we crossed three angry rivers, probably tributaries of the 'foaming' River Kodor. Ali carried James and Yuri piggy-back – what an absurdly inappropriate phrase! – while I preferred to wade across with my staff to help me against the currents. By now I was so wet anyhow that it made little difference, and though Ali was powerful he might have jack-knifed under my weight, which was still considerable though lessening by the day. But Yuri confided afterwards that Ali was displeased, for if I had been swept away he would have been held responsible. I had not thought of that.

At dusk we reached a recognizable track, though it was impassable for any wheeled transport because of the constant landslides of stones and the fallen branches of wild rhododendron. Finally we reached civilization in the form of a hut on a tiny plateau. This really was a plateau; the scene was so idyllic that it might have come from Pirosmani or Chagall and was not to be caught by a camera, though it lingers in the memory. A stream ran down from the steep, high hillside behind, through a long ravine, and plunged through a glacier where it left a black hole so perfectly rounded it might have been drawn by a compass. The *kosh* was a simple wooden shack with a wisp of smoke rising straight upwards in the stillness of dusk in which the sounds echoed. A child in clogs beamed with excitement, as did his scrawny father when we paid him five roubles for a pail of milk just taken from the cows, the taste of which was blissful. An old hag threw grain to ducks and hens outside their home while a younger woman performed the interminable see-saw motion as she rocked a slat of wood from hand to hand, making butter or *smetana*.

Idyllic, yet an existence depending on the weather and one of daily repetition. The boredom could have been stupefying and the solitary, tethered horse epitomized the mournfulness of the dying light.

The shepherd dismayed our expectations by refusing to let us stay the night – there was no room. Then another shepherd came down the road and told Ali that there was a smarter *kosh* further down, just the usual two kilometres, so we set off again. Smarter! I yearned to stay in that primitive hut for it was growing dark, and if there was no space I could have lain outside by a fire in my sleeping-bag – but then I remembered we had left these behind. Darkness fell at once and I struggled behind shouting to Yuri that I needed my Scargill flashlight, but this had been packed in Ali's rucksack and he had vanished ahead of us searching for the next *kosh*. Our plaintive cries for help, like those of puppies left abandoned, echoed unanswered. I was exhausted. No longer was it romantic fun.

Then there was a glimmer of light and all was well again as Ali came running back with the speed of a wild animal, my Scargill strapped to his forehead, and took my camera case and the heavy, sodden duffle coat with the good news that he had found the *kosh* mentioned by the stranger. Ali showing me the way, we approached two huts. The first had a wood stove and an oil lamp; no place could have been simpler with its mud floor nor more welcome. The second was reserved for the animals. Though they looked ancient, the *kosh*es had been built only three years earlier; hence their 'smarter' reputation. The first hut had two bedsteads on each side and rough blankets laid over wooden boards instead of mattresses. This was where the shepherd and his gnarled, bent-over wife slept. They came here in the summer and would leave at the end of the month before it was cut off by snow.

Ali was splendid on such an occasion, punctilious in entertaining the shepherd with news from the outside world, for conversation is the obligatory courtesy of the guest. Helping with the fire, he brought a pail to the boil and a handful of tea was thrown in by the shepherd and stirred. We drank it with the last of our condensed milk and our small bottle of Cognac, which Ali had had the foresight to include in the re-packing. After the gallons of ice-water I had drunk from the streams, this was the most satisfying hot drink of my adult life.

Afterwards, the woman went to sleep in the hut with the animals. Her husband slept in his own bed while I, in deference to my age, was given his wife's – an offer I did not refuse, especially as James was given a shelf no wider than a bookshelf without a rail to stop him from falling off. Ali and Yuri slept on the mud floor wrapped in blankets.

After the day's effort I slept the sleep of the would-be just, waking refreshed at six after eight hours sleep to find the shepherd milking his cows while his wife tried to separate two frolicsome, fighting calves. The horse and dog looked at me suspiciously, unused to strangers. When James struggled down from his shelf he looked as if he had been stretched on the rack.

After more tea we set off and after three-quarters of an hour passed the camping site on the far side of the river where we would have stayed had the porters not delayed us. I was delighted that we had not been able to reach it, for this was a swish affair with silver roofs gleaming over modern chalets like a group of superior hunting lodges, though they looked deserted. Soon the track became a road, on which three Russians rattled upwards on a motorbike and sidecar, though they had to return after they were blocked by a landslide. Half-wild pigs and piglets grunted and rooted as they dug at the earth. By ten thirty we strolled into the village of Sumi and had crossed the Caucasus.

It was time to say goodbye to Ali. After unpacking every-thing on a slope beside the single store, which was pitifully bereft of goods apart from some hideous ties and two jars of beetroot, we restored our possessions to our own cases (which had been folded up), in the hope that we might stop a passing truck. This was a forlorn chance, for we were at the end of the road apart from that camp site which turned out to be closed for the impending winter. Yet our hopes rose again when Ali found a man who told him the good news – yes, a bus did leave here once a fortnight, and it was now parked around the corner and might well be leaving in three or four days' time. Ali went off to speak to the driver, but returned dejectedly to say that he had been unable to persuade the driver to take us earlier. We waited disconsolately on the slope until I thought it was time to try again, suspecting that Ali had failed to bribe the man with sufficient money. It was a simple, agreeable village with a few scattered chalets and fruit trees, but there was no telephone and no evidence of life, and I was anxious to be on the way to Sokhum.

Yuri went off to bribe the driver with 250 roubles. Ali looked embarrassed. 'They do not like Karachaites here,' he explained, and this was not surprising if one remembered that they had sided with the Germans in the last war. Also there was the difference of religion. The Karachaites had been Muslim since the sixteenth century, but the Georgians were

Christian and we were now in Georgia. There was a clash of attitudes, too: the Karachaites regarded the Caucasus as holy, while the Georgians in this area were preoccupied with the Black Sea.

One reason why the Karachaites survive is that they have not dispersed. Even a Mongolian Genghis Khan took a thousand Karachaite boys after he attacked the Caucasus, one of these grew up to be a leader, seized a boat to sail from the Crimea to Sokhum and from there crossed the Klukhor Pass to reclaim their fathers' land. Fiercely nationalistic on their side, the Georgians resented both the breakaway Ossetians and the disreputable Karachaites. To them, Ali seemed like a wild gypsy, which explained his failure with the driver and why he was now crestfallen.

Yuri returned glowing with the news that the driver had accepted 350 roubles, which included the price of petrol. For this, little more than seven pounds, we could commandeer the bus to take us on the four-hour journey to the Black Sea.

I have no idea if Ali was glad to see the last of us. I suspect he had never crossed the Klukhor Pass before, in spite of having led me to believe otherwise. But he had seen us through successfully and I believe he was pleased with the presents I left him: the Scargill light to help his mountaineering at night; the snow-gaiters never used; the tiny burner; my sleeping-bag left in Dombay; the excellent map, though I was not sure he could read it; and the First Aid kit with hypodermic needles which commanded huge prices in Russia. He kept also his mountain boots and the colourful Scottish sweater I had brought him from London. Simple people hide their feelings on such occasions, and Ali was undemonstrative. He grinned but he did not thank me, though he indicated that there was one object he really wanted: my cheap, khaki hat which I had bought in a surplus store in North Devon. But of course! While I embraced him in the Muslim way and Yuri translated that I would never forget him and thanked him warmly, he smiled without comment.

As we drove off, Ali returned to the mountains with his

single rucksack and I knew I was unlikely to meet such a decent man again. He made the Caucasus for me. I had been prepared to place my life in his hands and though his sense of distance was crazy at times, I had underestimated him. He had never let us down, and I thought with pleasure of his return to Kara to collect the horses and brave little Hadji, restoring her to her home in Khassaut.

We were in a different land. Literally so because we were back in Georgia in the district of Abkhazskaya. It looked different too, attractively so, with well-tended orchards, compact fields of ripe corn and pleasant gardens in front of the scattered chalets along the way, some of which were painted in gentian blue with decorations carved out of wood and long balustrades. Many had stairs leading to the first floor, because of the forthcoming snow, but now it was hot and the vegetation lush, almost Mediterranean.

The drive was fun as we picked up breathless passengers who ran waving to us, as they heard the bus which would not normally be running until days ahead and was now passing earlier than expected. We made one stop at a cluster of wooden huts on a slope above where the family knew the driver and delayed us deliberately – not that time was of any consequence. With instinctive hospitality, which was also a delaying tactic, they welcomed us with plates of cheese and sliced apple which seemed like ambrosia after the days of donkey dick. Also a homemade schnapps with a delicious flavour of fresh fruit, which I enjoyed so much that one of the women ran inside and returned with two bottles of the magical stuff as a present, plus a large bag of apples. It would have been discourteous to refuse and I did not even think of doing so. An old crone hobbled about with a stick lashing out at a charming black puppy which yelped every time it was silly enough to go near, whereupon she shot me a toothless grin as I protested '*Ne nada!*' – 'That's not necessary!' – and lashed out again.

Eventually we rejoined our requisitioned bus and set off

with the young people from the farm, plainly newlyweds now dressed in their best clothes and fully packed. Joined by more grateful passengers, for they did not have to pay, we swirled along until the scenery became duller and our high spirits subsided as we turned into a main road with traffic. After four hours we reached Sokhum on the Black Sea, the end of our journey.

CHAPTER NINETEEN

Thoughts in the Black Sea

YURI found us an old-fashioned hotel, where my bedroom was worthy of an emperor, being a suite of several immaculate rooms, with writing desks and a balcony overlooking an artificial lake with hugely inappropriate black swans; and it was ridiculously cheap. Yuri befriended the lady in charge after they discovered that she had studied French and German at the same language school in Pyatigorsk. Though she gave us parrot information she proved invaluable in showing us around and arranging our tickets back to Moscow. James and I had abandoned our plans to continue to Trabzon on the Turkish coast, and from there to Istanbul and London; we felt we had gone far enough.

'Madame' drove us past the largest statue of Lenin I had seen, dominating the front of a lifeless government building, and then drove us up the hill to Stalin's former dacha. Communism might have been pronounced dead but the ghosts lingered on.

This was his favourite villa, and that of Beria, his sadistic head of the KGB, was near by. I had to admire their taste. Guarded as a fortress on Stalin's visits, the glistening white building had large windows but was unpretentious. The views over the Black Sea were reminiscent of Portofino, a shimmering fantasy enhanced by the gardens which, still in blossom in late September, had a sub-tropical lushness, sporting tangerine trees with green fruit which proved orange and juicy though bitter inside. It was satisfying to realize that we would have been shot for picking them if Stalin had been alive.

In the evening she drove us to dinner at the best Georgian restaurant in Sokhum beside the road which ran along the coast. It was called the Merkhevly, and all the men there wore ties and suits and were drunk. Yuri and 'Madame' wanted to eat in one of the private alcoves higher up until I persuaded them to join the main floor, open on all sides, where people were dancing, which looked more fun, though I was unaware at this point just how drunk everyone was. We were a polite party by comparison, almost refined. Yuri was already shocked that Georgian men started drinking at ten in the morning: 'They drink vodka,' he complained, 'but no Pepsi!' This seemed about right to me until a rough-looking customer swayed on the dance floor and after some menaces to his friends fell against our table, dropping a long-bladed knife as he did so, while a fight broke out at the table he had left. One after another the customers were hurled out while the band played on, smiling all the way. After all, it was Saturday night, and though the new Federation of Russian states might be in turmoil the people were united in two respects: disillusionment and vodka.

It seemed correct to finish our journey the next day by swimming in the Black Sea from the stony beach that lay across the railway tracks. The water was cleaner than I expected and soothed the muscles which had been strained over the last few days.

'I lose the pain from my shoulders,' said Yuri happily. 'I have not been to seaside for five years, except for the filthy water at Scarborough.'

Earlier I had studied the Georgians enjoying themselves in the grounds of the hotel, where there were also Russians on holiday though no foreign tourists. They concentrated with severity on chess marked out on gigantic boards, or played with their children. Young girls wore their best clothes and a few looked elegant. There seemed to be a swift transition from girlhood, after which they became women, gross and masculine.

On the beach, everyone looked as unattractive as the British do on holiday. Sunbathers enjoyed the small vanities of the seaside; a naked little boy ran wild with excitement, scolded by a doting father. They retained the foibles and wistful longings of us all, even though they had been suppressed for seventy years. Perhaps there was real hope now that the coup had failed; resilience is everything. I remembered Tolstoy's description of a plant that had been crushed by a cartwheel yet inspired Hadji Murad. One stalk was broken and stuck out like a mutilated arm, another hung down with a soiled flower at its tip, the other though soiled with black mud stood erect though twisted to one side as if a piece of its body had been torn off;

> and yet it stood firm and did not surrender to man, who had destroyed all its brothers around it ... 'What energy!' I thought. 'Man has conquered everything and destroyed millions of plants, yet this one won't submit.'

I felt certain then that the Russians would regain their incentive now that the coup had failed, and would end the century in control of their lives as they had never been before. How little I estimated their innate subservience, their apathy yet addiction to chaos, for that was at the end of 1991 and events have overtaken optimism. To write about 'Russia' of a week ago is out of date. To do so a year later is to step back into history.

In the autumn of 1993, Sokhum was partly destroyed, falling to the troops of nearby Abkhaskaya which claims independence from Georgia. Hundreds of the town's inhabitants have been killed; thousands have fled, including President Shevardnadze who accused the Russians of supporting the rebels. The holiday resort below me when I picked tangerines in Stalin's garden no longer exists. The beach where I swam has no swimmers, empty apart from litter and the scars of tank tracks.

No doubt Georgia will reclaim Sokhum in the see-saw of Civil War; probably Shevardnadze will return, with the irony that he was instrumental in disbanding Soviet Russia only to see his own country of Georgia gain independence and fall apart. A sort of peace may descend, but I wonder if the pieces of the Federation, like Humpty Dumpty, can ever be put together again.

I wondered to start with if there was a single word to parallel the great 'sarcasm' which Denis Finch-Hatton found in Africa. Cynicism is too easy; ennui is everywhere; paradox is always relevant. Perhaps there is no single word, just as there is no single truth about Russia but a thousand lies. But there is a terrible *irony* that in finding their freedom the Russians have torn themselves apart like sharks in bloodstained water.

There was a final, more reassuring incident on the evening flight to Moscow. First the plane was delayed, and though there was nothing unusual in that, the rumour spread that not only was the pilot drunk but the second pilot too. Then we had an emergency stop at Mineralnyye Vody because we had run out of petrol, and at the landing and take-off the antediluvian jumbo jet creaked and cracked as if the poor thing was going to fall apart, as it must have done since.

Privileged by being put in the front, we were penalized by the bright emergency lights which kept James and me awake while the other passengers dozed and snored behind us in semi-darkness. Yuri had left us at the airport to make his own way back to Kislovodsk.

I had made an initial plea for vodka, showing some dollars shamelessly, for it was obvious that we would not reach Moscow until four in the morning and I needed it as an anaesthetic. The steward had appraised me with a shocked expression and now reappeared with a small mug of mineral water and gestured with a smile that I should drink it.

Mineral water! I knew my Narzan by now and spluttered as I knocked back the lethal mix of vodka mixed with Cognac. With a further conspiratorial smile, the young steward beckoned me to follow him and led me to a tiny lift like an upright coffin which I hesitated to enter until he pushed me inside.

There was barely room for the two of us as we descended. The plane had lost its identity; we might have been in an aircraft carrier or the kitchens of a grand hotel. The lift stopped a few seconds later and I found myself in the crew's galley, where six or seven young men and one stewardess were having a party. Why they should have welcomed me so charmingly I cannot imagine. There was the usual mime and list of names – 'Me Georgian, Georgia very good. Georgia! Glasgow Rangers. Liver-pool.' A nice-looking steward was presented as an interpreter who knew English and I kept up this pretence, though it was plain he could hardly speak a word. He looked at me gratefully when I exclaimed *'Horosho!'* the old standby for 'Very good', though he would persist in telling me that Lenin was a footballer.

Then it clicked. 'Ah! *Lineker.*'

Cries of happy recognition: 'Gary *Leninker.*'

More toasts. The lethal drink was shared around yet kept everyone surprisingly sober. Toasts were drunk to Georgia and to Britain. In such rare privacy the young can relax without any fear of being overheard. The young are still young in Russia; that is the only hope.

The gigantic plane grunted, rattled and roared as we started to descend.

'Moscow?' I asked fatuously.

'Da! Da!' they told me eagerly. How nice they were.

Was the journey worth it?

The elation had not hit me until I relaxed in the Black Sea and even then my feelings were not what I had expected. If I had learnt anything it was my own inadequacy, and I had had a pretty shrewd idea of that before. I had crossed the Klukhor Pass but could not have done so without Ali. There was no mountaineering skill involved. My father's endurance on that freezing night made my accomplishment seem puny.

Yet there is a greater vanity in denigrating one's achieve-ments too far. I *had* crossed the Pass! For me it was a triumph, if for no one else. And as we had waited on the slope in the

Georgian village I asked Ali if he knew how many Englishmen had crossed the Klukhor Pass in recent years. He thought hard for a whole minute before he shook his head and answered 'None'. Possibly he was telling me what he thought I wanted to hear. Conceivably it was true, for why should anyone else bother without a personal motive like mine? I attempted it because of my father, not to make any comparison – which would have been the depth of arrogance – but as a form of filial salute – something the Karachaites understood at once.

My father's sense of failure had been painful as he returned to Teberda and his gloom was absolute as he flung himself down on a cot and listened to Yusuf's father telling him what he *should* have done, with alpine stocks and so on.

It was old Wicksteed who stirred him from his lethargy: 'Bless my soul, what are you so surly about? Man proposes and God disposes – and don't you know that you just can't "buy a railroad ticket" over the Caucasus?'

That did the trick. 'Listen, Wicker,' said my father, 'I am now going to arise and buy as many bottles of that strong Caucasian purple wine as I can get hold of – and get thoroughly plastered.'

'Wait a minute,' said Wicksteed, hastily putting on his sandals, 'I'll come with you.'

As they were drinking comfortably in the 'local' situated among shimmering trees, Wicksteed announced, 'I have come to the conclusion that the happiness or the oblivion that one gets from alcohol is not altogether illegitimate.'

Little wonder that my father dedicated *Caucasian Journey* to his memory. When he gave his farewell party in Moscow in September 1929 he asked Wicksteed to be guest of honour and the old boy rose nobly to the occasion.

'Must I put on a tie?' he asked.

'Lord no,' said my father. 'Just wear your stinking old Russian knee-boots, and if you have one, a clean *rubashka*. You are to be the toastmaster.'

'The more I have travelled the stupendous Caucasus with Farson,' Wicksteed began, wearing the cobalt-blue corduroy *rubashka* he had bought for the occasion, 'the more I have trudged behind him up some of those breathless precipices, those Olympian peaks above which only the eagle soars, Farson magnificent on his horse; the more I have seen him amid savage, unknown tribes . . .'

My father sat there trying hard to look modest as the younger members of the Diplomatic Corps gazed at him admiringly, and his own colleagues looked less delighted.

'. . . the more I picture him dealing with our porters,' Wicksteed continued, 'bargaining for our food, cooking our meals over those rose-red Caucasian campfires – and *what* cooking: I have never known anything like it! – the more do I begin to realize what a wonderful woman his wife must be.'

That was the last my father saw of him: the most congenial, witty and unexpected man he had ever travelled with. 'To me, Wicksteed was the Caucasus.'

My mother incidentally, the 'wonderful woman', was looking after me in London, where I had just been born. Otherwise, with her shared wanderlust, I am sure she would have been with him on his *Caucasian Journey*. My father's last line explained that the book was for Wicksteed. I need hardly add that in my turn, this book was written for my father, and, come to think of it, for Wicksteed too.

And for James, it shows his forbearance that we are still on speaking terms, able to laugh about the *Pipkin*, bonded by the experiences of our small adventure. One morning after a night out in Soho on our return, I woke up to find a white paper napkin stuffed in my pocket with a message. I do not know who put it there or where the quotation comes from, but it sums up everything for me: '*Life is an adventure always to be gained.*'

Index

Underlined references indicate illustrations (plate numbers).
Family relationships to the author are given in brackets.